Black Public History in Chicago

THE NEW BLACK STUDIES SERIES

Edited by Darlene Clark Hine and Dwight A. McBride

A list of books in the series appears at the end of this book.

Black Public History in Chicago

Civil Rights Activism from World War II into the Cold War

IAN ROCKSBOROUGH-SMITH

UNIVERSITY OF
ILLINOIS PRESS
Urbana, Chicago, and Springfield

Cataloging data available from the Library of Congress
Library of Congress Control Number: 2018933961
ISBN 978-0-252-04166-2 (cloth : alk.)
ISBN 978-0-252-08330-3 (paper : alk.)
ISBN 978-0-252-05033-6 (ebook)

Part of chapter 2 is based on the article by Ian Rocksborough-
Smith: "Margaret T. G. Burroughs and Black Public History
in Cold War Chicago," *The Black Scholar: Journal of Black Studies
and Research* 41:3 (Fall 2011): 26–42. It is reproduced here with
permission.

*This book is dedicated to
my parents, Brian and Jennifer,
and my brother, Michael.*

Contents

List of Illustrations

Editorial Note

In this book, "radical left" refers to the Communist left and its fellow travelers and allies. "Black left" is a synonym for African American engagements with the Communist left unless otherwise noted.

Acknowledgments

I have more people to thank than are listed here. Those who are listed deserve more praise than simply their names on these pages. This book would not have been completed without the generous time and knowledge offered to me in my ten months of living in Chicago some years ago by Margaret Taylor Goss Burroughs, Timuel Black, Bennett Johnson, Sterling Stuckey, Leslie O'Rear, Beatrice Young, and Clarice Durham.

I would also not have finished this book if not for the tremendous support, patience, resources, and direction offered by my supervisors at the University of Toronto. I owe a great debt to my senior supervisor, Rick Halpern, for his unwavering backing throughout my PhD studies—studies that helped form the bulk of research for this book. I also credit Rick for directing me toward Chicago as a fruitful and enriching site for study. I feel honored, humbled, and privileged to be a small voice among the many distinguished scholars who have chosen to study aspects of black Chicago in their academic pursuits. I also owe a debt to Dan Bender for his helpful comments on my earliest writing on this project and for pushing me when I needed it and to Michael Wayne for his sage advice and helping me burn off steam while we were on the ice at Moss Park. Thanks also to Alisa Webb, Sylvie Murray, and Chris Leach at the University of the Fraser Valley as well as Donna Trembinski, Chris Frazer, Ron Charles, and Robert Zecker at St. Francis Xavier University. And to Davarian Baldwin at Trinity College, whose incisive comments from my PhD defense helped kick-start the revision of this project into a book. I also thank the faculty and graduate students at Dalhousie University for their astute comments on aspects of this research as it was revised into its current form.

I have deep respect and admiration for my Toronto friends Nathan Cardon, Laura Butler, Lowell Heppner, Megan Hope, and Will Riddell. Thanks to Camille Bégin, Paul Lawrie, Jeremy Milloy, Jared Toney, Holly Karibo, Brandon King, Rowena Alphonso (RIP), John Dirks, Stuart Parker, and David Stiles for comments on chapters, advice, and camaraderie.

I made many good friends in Chicago who helped me navigate the archives and who directed me in ways that have had an unmistakable imprint and influence on my scholarship. Foremost, I thank Martha Biondi, my Fulbright doctoral award supervisor at Northwestern University, for her generous advice and support at many stages of this project, especially near its inception. I especially thank Erik Gellman, who generously shared countless conversations and sources with me about Chicago and African American history. I will always be grateful for his advice and friendship. I also thank Antonio Lopez for his companionship in the archives, for help with retrieving vital images for this project, and for being an even better friend. Many thanks also to William Adams, Keeanga Yahmatta-Taylor, Rhone Fraser, and Lionel Kimble.

The staffs at many archives, libraries, and institutions that impact midwestern and Illinois historical communities were extremely helpful throughout the making of this book. In particular, I thank Beverly Cook, Michael Flug, Cynthia Fife-Townsel, and Robert Miller at the Vivian G. Harsh Research Collection, Carter G. Woodson Public Library, on Chicago's South Side. Your patience with my questions and for enduring my presence in your research room for so many hours demonstrate how your archive is one of the best (with some of the richest materials to work with) in the country. Also, thanks to Bea Julian at the DuSable Museum for answering my questions as the museum underwent renovations. The Chicago History Museum staff were incredibly helpful, especially Lesley Martin, to whom I owe a great debt for her help in gaining permissions to use the Chicago Red Squad files.

I also thank the administrators of important funding bodies, notably, the Canada-U.S. Fulbright Program and the Black Metropolis Research Consortium in Chicago.

Final revisions to this manuscript would not have been possible without the erudite and scrupulous input of the University of Illinois's editorial staff and peer reviewers, notably Dawn Durante and Jennifer Comeau, and copyeditor Mary Lou Kowaleski.

My debts to close family and friends are too many to count. I would not be here today if not for their love and support. In particular, I thank my parents, Brian and Jennifer, and my brother, Michael. I will never be able to express how you've helped me through some trying and turbulent personal times. The same goes for Chris Miki, Brenda Ostonal, Owen James, Kevin Tilley, Shannon Tulley, Matt Lum, Erin Lee, David Baird, Margot Leichti, Phillip Gander, Willow Fuchs, Charles Demers, Cara Ng, Jacqueline Maloney, Lisa Pasolli, James MacGregor, Laurie Stanley-Blackwell, John Blackwell, Margo Boyd, Shannon Ezzat, and Rose Keurdian.

I owe a special thanks to Jack O'Dell, Jane Power, Karen Ferguson, and John Munro for encouraging me for many, many years on my journey toward fulfilling knowledge in African American history. The truest form of American history.

Any errors are mine and mine alone.

Abbreviations

AAHA	Afro-American Heritage Association
AMSAC	American Society of African Culture
ASNLH	Association for the Study of Negro Life and History
BAM	black arts movement
BPP	Black Panther Party
CHM	Chicago History Museum
CIO	Congress of Industrial Organizations
CORE	Congress of Racial Equality
CPUSA	Communist Party of the United States
CTU	Chicago Teachers Union
FEPC	Fair Employment Practices Committee
HUAC	House Un-American Activities Committee
NAACP	National Association for the Advancement of Colored People
NACW	National Association of Colored Women
NCNW	National Council of Negro Women
NNC	National Negro Congress
NNMHF	National Negro Museum and Historical Foundation
NOI	Nation of Islam
OBAC	Organization of Black American Culture
SCLC	Southern Christian Leadership Conference
SSCAC	South Side Community Art Center
UPWA	United Packinghouse Workers of America

Black Public History in Chicago

Introduction

A 1942 banquet honored Chicago's public school superintendent William Johnson for his attention to a proposed reform of local social studies curricula concerning African American history. On this occasion, Johnson met with South Side schoolteacher Madeline Morgan, an advocate of local black public history. Morgan had devised these curriculum reforms as units for grades 1 through 8. Morgan (later Stratton Morris) taught at Emerson Primary School. In the nearly two years prior to the banquet and at the behest of the district, Morgan and a small team of colleagues had devised history units that would underscore the crucial role African Americans played in the nation's history from slavery through emancipation and into the twentieth century. From the perspective of those who honored Johnson, his presence at the banquet was more than just a trivial photo opportunity. The banquet was attended by more than three hundred people and sponsored by local middle-class black women's clubs and civic organizations. Beyond the adulation afforded Johnson, the banquet also recognized the labors of public schoolteachers like Morgan and those of other African American public-history activists and educators who through the 1940s and 1950s sought to revise local curricula to include significant modules on black American history.

The range of support these curriculum reforms received signaled that change was imminent—not just in Chicago but elsewhere in the country. "Cordial" telegrams were sent from Eleanor and Franklin D. Roosevelt, which, in the *Chicago*

Defender's optimistic estimation, helped validate a "revolutionary trend" in public education. Notwithstanding this optimism, the sorts of curriculum reforms envisioned by the likes of Morgan as early as 1940 were not fully implemented in Chicago until the mid- to late 1960s. The curriculum measures she devised were only used experimentally by the city from 1942 to 1945, but the 1942 banquet demonstrated that civic officials had at the very least conceded that the inclusion of black history in curricula was possible.[1] Such observances marked the beginning of changes on these educational and cultural fronts.

Given the earnestness of this curriculum-reform endeavor, *Black Public History in Chicago: Civil Rights Activism from World War II into the Cold War* suggests that locally observed black public-history events, celebrations, and initiatives received more than merely symbolic civic recognitions. Indeed, today it is easy to suggest that Negro History Week (as it was called until the 1970s, when it became Black History Month) was devoid of political impact and importance and that it was simply a collection of platitudes expressed by celebrities and politicians at a certain time of the year. But the quest for relevant affirmations of usable pasts remains as valid in today's public sphere as it was in the politically repressive decades of the mid-twentieth century, especially given the endurance of racial segregation and inequalities in urban America—starkly apparent now in light of recent public school closures, police brutality incidents in poverty-stricken communities of color, and the ongoing criminalization of black and brown life.

This book shows how some Chicagoans used events like the celebration and commemoration of black history in February for explicitly political ends. The related public-history endeavors of curriculum reforms and museum projects were employed to wage real political struggles for civil rights and social change throughout the post–World War II era. Numerous efforts to promote and teach this history demonstrated how dissident left-wing political currents from previous decades remained relevant to a vibrant and ideologically diffuse African American public sphere despite widespread Cold War aspersions, white-supremacist reactions, and anti-Communist repressions. Such activism coalesced around a series of connected public-history endeavors, from attempts to place curricula on African American history in public schools, to the promotion of Negro History Week celebrations through vital African American print engines like the *Chicago Defender* newspaper, to the imagining and establishment of a pioneering and autonomously run black-history museum (later the DuSable Museum of African American History).[2] These endeavors were carried out in a period when America's movements for civil rights reached their zenith, through the mid-twentieth century and at the height of the most repressive years of the

Cold War. Black American public-history activism was a small but significant part of this larger story and demonstrated especially how an older generation of local activists stayed engaged in social-change labors over decades.

These public-history projects were mainly but not exclusively undertaken by teachers, writers, librarians, and archivists on Chicago's South Side. They tried to advance curriculum reforms and provide alternative programs, venues, and modules for black history from World War II through the late 1960s. Some of the figures previously involved in left-wing popular fronts who went on to make black public-history activism a key manifestation of their continued cultural labors were also initially Communists. Others were at times fellow travelers with the Communist Party left or radical leftists in their own right but with at least some association with the Party (whether the historical record can indicate a clear and definite Party affiliation). Writings by black Communists involved in policy decisions of the Communist Party of the United States (CPUSA) in the late 1940s and 1950s certainly suggest the likelihood of these claims. The CPUSA had abandoned popular front–style liberalism in the 1940s but maintained a sectarian Stalinist political program strategically focused on notions of "culture" as a weapon in the freedom struggles of African Americans.[3]

Margaret T. G. Burroughs and Charles Burroughs were influenced by figures of the old black left, such as Paul Robeson and W. E. B. Du Bois, who maintained sympathies with segments of the broader U.S. left for its sustained attention to black discrimination, the grievances of organized labor, and working-class social movements, as well as anti-imperialist and anticolonial politics. This coalition of left-wing and African American activists has been described as the "black popular front" in the 1930s and 1940s and the "anticolonial front" of the post–World War II era. This book borrows the term "cultural front" from Michael Denning to work synonymously with these categorizations for radical left "fronts." The term underscores the roles of African American cultural workers whose labors on black-history projects bridged the radical political cultures of the 1930s and 1940s with the resurgent nationalisms of the 1950s and 1960s.[4]

Collectively, these workers' continued strivings through the 1950s certainly complicate declensions for left-inflected activisms over the long mid-twentieth century. Scholars, such as Penny Von Eschen, Gerald Horne, and others, whose writings on race and the Cold War are indispensable to the historical record, chart largely tragic narratives, especially for left-wing black politics and their related trajectories.[5] While fully appreciative of the contributions of this scholarship, this book challenges such denouements for the radical black left in early Cold War America and lends itself to the cultural front conversation associated with Denning's scholarship because it also helps characterize the efforts of black public-history activists whose lifeworks bridged the radical political cultures of the 1930s and 1940s with the more acclaimed nationalisms and civil rights activities of the 1950s and 1960s.[6] Chicago's black public-history activists engaged closely with the rapidly shifting terrains of U.S. civil rights, international anti-colonialisms, Black Power and black arts movements, and urban politics to arguably continue the cultural legacies of the Communist Party–influenced black popular front that had nominally ended with the onset of the Cold War.

Another useful question this book addresses is, how did black public history in Chicago challenge and/or adhere to the ideological limits of mid-twentieth-century U.S. politics? In other words, how did the Cold War's prevalent racial liberalism effect expressions of black history and activism in the public sphere? How did such cultural projects connect to African American strivings, which affirmed their "Americanness" in a country that from its inception continually elided such aspirations? As many scholars now argue, mid-twentieth-century racial liberalism exported America's democratic image abroad to oppose Communism at home and to influence global anticolonial movements in Asia and Africa, especially. The degree to which African American struggles for civil rights and racial reform were confined by the restrictive parameters of Cold War politics is now well documented. As such, many civil rights struggles were framed in terms of how American democratic ideals could be affirmed against the backdrop of these world-historical moments of racial change and democratic transformation.[7] Such mid-twentieth-century forms of racial liberalism, however, typically separated civil rights, black nationalist, and nominally "left-wing" working-class movement activities into analytically separate spheres—especially during the 1950s, at the height of the Cold War. This knowledge paradigm has resulted in static historiographical compartmentalization of mid-twentieth-century, black freedom-movement categories. As Nikhil Pal Singh suggests, historians need not "yield" to this "narrative of declension."[8]

Such a historiographical impasse reflects the very real ambiguities black Americans experienced when they engaged historically with the political left through the mid-twentieth century. Black Chicago's relationship to the radical left was a case in point and is worth reviewing briefly. During the early 1930s, nearly four hundred black Chicagoans were CPUSA members—when the party successfully organized unemployment councils to fight the poverty of the Great Depression. In Chicago, these members made up nearly 24 percent of the local chapter and six times the numbers of blacks in the "famed Harlem branch."[9] Even at this juncture, Party leaders faced the ambivalences of black membership in the Party in Chicago. As political scientist Michael C. Dawson indicates, "Southside blacks were too independent, too religious, and most of all too nationalist—in short, too embedded in black culture and politics. . . . Blacks both in and out of the party . . . [were] more concerned about how communism and communists could make conditions better for blacks than about how blacks could aid communism."[10] Literary scholar Mary Helen Washington suggests that by the end of the 1950s, tensions arose "between civil rights, black nationalism, and the radical left, tensions all too evident in Chicago black politics."[11] Cultural historian Bill Mullen indicates that by the 1950s and 1960s, tensions between the old labor left and blacks had grown: "[White] big labor, the Communist Party, and the old left were challenged and in many ways superseded by civil rights coalitionism, insurgent black nationalism, and interracial alliances under black political leadership."[12] *Black Public History in Chicago* largely agrees with these trajectories for African American radical left politics and their conflicted engagement with black politics and culture through the late 1950s and 1960s. However, the current volume also suggests that a closer examination of black public history as an activist repertoire in a city like Chicago is useful because the city has been a site of both the ambivalences and highest levels of engagement by black Americans across the nation with the radical left. A study of black leftists involved in public-history activism is helpful for demonstrating one of the key areas through which the radical left generally continued to engage with African American community politics and culture during the early Cold War.

Recent works on black Chicago have taken exciting new directions: from examinations of migrant consumer and religious cultures to local studies of business and print enterprises, housing struggles, neighborhood politics, labor, educational, and black women's activisms. Many of these newer studies uncover complex histories of community formation, civic politics, and civil rights activism focused on housing, education, and employment struggles from the early twentieth century through World War II and the immediate postwar era when the Great Migrations of African American southerners shaped much of urban America.[13] Between 1940 and 1960, the area's black population grew from 277,731 to 812,637. By 1970 over 1.2 million African Americans lived in the city, marking a decades-long period of exponential metropolitan growth that "created a Black Metropolis" highly diverse and variegated in class and neighborhood composition.[14] Historian William Grimshaw notes how "a sizable middle class black political community began to emerge in the 1950s. By the 1970s, it made up about a third of the black population. . . . By 1971 there were five middle-class wards: Sixth, Eighth, Seventeenth, Twenty-first, and Thirty-fourth." These wards contrasted sharply with the "plantation wards" of the West Side, notably the Twenty-Fourth, Twenty-Seventh, Twenty-Eighth, and Twenty-Ninth. Grimshaw further indicates that the South Side had the most black middle-class wards, and the West Side the least. For him, this also reflected the levels of independence from the city's historically corrupt machine politics—with the middle-class wards demonstrating the greater independence of initiative and the plantation wards the least.[15] These distinctions between South and West Sides, especially in terms of relative propensities toward political activism historically, can be overstated. Historian Jeffrey Helgeson perhaps best captures the complexities of these historic and shifting social dynamics among black Chicago's rapidly changing and growing population over the mid-twentieth century. After World War II, "Chicago turned out to be a place where great suffering mixed with increasing access to economic and political opportunities—at least for some of the city's black residents." Helgeson remarks that "out of struggles to counter racism and economic exclusion day after day," average black Chicagoans "constructed a political culture in which pragmatic nationalism and a commitment to opening the city for individual opportunity overlapped with the long history of more radical labor and civil rights activism."[16]

Black Public History in Chicago is cognizant of these community life and neighborhood studies but fits more explicitly alongside those that treat aspects of art and intellectual life as foci. As such, this book engages more with a new scholarly consensus surrounding the emergence of a black Chicago renaissance that rivaled earlier cultural movements of New York City's from the 1920s, in both scale and scope. The works that tread into this area include the scholarship of Davarian Baldwin, Adam Green, Anne Meis Knupfer, Bill Mullen, Robert Bone, Richard Courage, Stacy I. Morgan, James Smethurst, Elizabeth Schlabach, Darlene Clark Hine, and others who have each examined aspects of related cultural, literary, and aesthetic movements that flourished in black Chicago from the 1930s through the early 1950s.[17] The Chicago black renaissance emerged through public lectures, plays, literary readings, discussions, and educational programs in what Schlabach calls the artistic and literary landscapes of Bronzeville. The name Bronzeville was adopted by South Side activists and leaders during the 1930s and 1940s as a way to denote the vitality and cultural sensibilities of the community over and against pejorative names like the Black Belt, which had been used by early sociologists and activists to describe the formation of racial ghettos throughout the city but especially on the South Side.[18]

Sites for these events included institutions, such as libraries, schools, and community centers, some of them funded initially by the New Deal Works Progress Administration, while others were institutions of the radical left, institutions on the South Side public, private, and leftist that gave shape to the black renaissance in Chicago, such as the George Cleveland Hall Branch

Library, DuSable and Dunbar High Schools, the Abraham Lincoln Center, the John Reed Club, the Parkway Community House (also known as the outreach ministry of the Congregational Church of the Good Shepherd), the South Side Writers Group, the Skyloft Players Theater Group, and, most notably, the South Side Community Arts Center on Chicago's South Side (which exists today). These institutions and organizations gave institutional backing to the early cultural labors of important African American writers, artists, performers, and thinkers, such as Richard Wright, Gwendolyn Brooks, Charles White, Margaret Walker, Fern Gayden, Charlamae Rollins, Vivian Harsh, Frank Marshall Davis, Sterling Brown, Langston Hughes, Richard Durham, Margaret Burroughs, and Katherine Dunham, among many others.[19]

Public-history labors in Chicago were an integral part of this milieu. But they can also be examined beyond the purview of the periodization that scholars have assigned the black renaissance in Chicago—which usually hits a wall at the height of repressive McCarthyism in the early and mid-1950s. Rather, black public-history activism bridged generations of left-wing radicalism, racial liberalism, and various forms of resurgent and nascent black nationalism and Black Power politics into the 1960s and early 1970s. Squarely situated in the longer trajectories of black movement scholarship, *Black Public History in Chicago* moves beyond studies of struggles for black rights and cultural activism in cities such as Chicago that focus primarily on the 1930s and 1940s (such as the literature on the black Chicago renaissance) or on the late 1950s and 1960s when the labor-left cultures and movements of the Great Depression decades yielded to either the integrationist thrust of civil rights or the militancy of Black Power.[20] Such renderings offer less space for understanding how fascinating moments of both political and generational continuity manifested through sustained tactical alliances, activist practices, and cultural repertoires.

Most scholarship to date on Chicago museums also omits or sidesteps discussions of black public history in the city. Scholars have examined ethnic museums that represent the mosaic of European (Jewish, Italian, Polish, Ukrainian, Swedish, etc.), Chinese, and Mexican communities that underscore the Second City's cosmopolitan history and its role as "promised land" for urban migration over much of the modern era.[21] These were all communities that played significant roles in the making of Chicago's political and cultural modernity—and, indeed, partly inspired the decision of Margaret Burroughs and her cohort to found what became the DuSable Museum of African American History.[22] But to date, no scholars have explicitly addressed how African American public-history efforts might have related to civil rights and racial justice struggles through the politically repressive years of the early Cold War.

It is these questions that animate much of this work and that make it, largely, a problem-solving case study for how scholars might continue to reenvision the expansiveness of mid-twentieth-century black American social movements and politics—especially given the present context of #blacklivesmatter movements for social change in the twenty-first century.

Some excellent book-length studies of black museum makers over the course of the twentieth century include by Mabel O. Wilson, *Negro Building*; Andrea Burns, *From Storefront to Monument*; and Max Van Balgooy, *Interpreting African American History and Culture at Museums and Historical Sites*, but none that situate the work of Chicago museum and public-history activists as lifelong labors connected to the experiences of the U.S. black radical left.[23] Both Wilson and Burns offer useful treatments of many day-to-day workings of the DuSable Museum and the collaborations museum founders Margaret and Charles Burroughs had with Charles H. Wright from Detroit, who founded the International Afro-American Museum (today the Charles H. Wright Museum of African American History), as they established the African American museum movement through the late 1960s and 1970s. Indeed, this book agrees with Burns's suggestion that the few African American–led museums that had emerged by the 1960s, such as the DuSable Museum in 1961, the International Afro-American Museum in Detroit in 1965, and the Anacostia Neighborhood Museum in Washington, D.C., in 1967, were "contesting and reinterpreting traditional depictions of African and African American history and culture" otherwise ignored by mainstream white museums. Mullen and James Smethurst look at the left-wing sensibilities of the founders of the DuSable Museum and place them in the broader context of an emerging black arts cultural movement through the mid-twentieth century.[24] But few studies to date have situated the DuSable Museum fully in the radical left currents of black Chicago history while taking seriously the repertoires of public-history activity the founders of the museum chose to focus on through the 1950s and 1960s. As a cultural historian, Mullen suggests that Margaret and Charles Burroughs founded their museum project in 1961 partly as a response to the "conservatism" that renaissance institutions like the South Side Community Arts Center (which she also helped found) had shifted to by the 1950s.[25] It is this book's contention that the Burroughses and their associates were fully emboldened by the McCarthyist repressions they faced to continue their earnest black public-history labors through this entire period.

With both these local and wider historiographical concerns in mind, *Black Public History in Chicago* offers an extensive close reading of numerous sources that demonstrate a diversity of understudied public-history repertoires in black Chicago. This book looks at a selection of oral-history interviews conducted by the author and others. It also offers extensive treatments of biographical, auto-biographical, personal papers, and archival manuscripts, local newspapers and magazine articles, and children's literature. Some of the sources used in this book also come from Chicago Police Red Squad surveillance files at the Chicago History Museum, with some brief reference to Federal Bureau of Investigation (FBI) files and surveillance. In certain cases these were the only sources of information available in archival form about particular local organizations or individuals. As such, a tertiary methodological dimension of this book is to appreciate the utility of local police and state surveillance archives as sources for black American social-movement history.[26] Black-history labors were clearly viewed by local and federal law-enforcement agencies as a significant part of the African American movement activism of the mid-twentieth century. The level of engagement afforded these activities beyond the polite civic obser-vances that public officials allowed is telling for why these activities mattered—especially during an era of history when the state monitored nearly all forms of black activism (regardless of ideology or outlook) as a potential source of Communist or radical infiltration.[27] Because of this surveillance and the public recognitions they eventually afforded to civic officials at various points over the mid-twentieth century, black-history labors certainly became the focus of what Michael Omi and Howard Winant might call a hegemonic engagement with the racial state. The simultaneous surveillance and recognition these black public-history labors received shows yet another front where wholesale attempts at containing black-movement activities occurred.[28]

This book makes no claim to comprehensive treatment of these activities. Still, the public-history repertoires in Chicago examined throughout are both diverse and highly significant for how particular repertoires of local black radicalism and activism were sustained through the mid-twentieth century. This book first charts important curriculum-reform efforts in South Side public schools that set the stage for curriculum reforms nationally. These initially widely supported efforts were followed by more contested labors of pioneering museum makers and public-history associations (led by black leftist figures, such as Margaret Burroughs and Ishmael Flory). Collectively, they sought to represent African American history in Chicago and the world and to shepherd these endeavors into the insurgent 1960s normally associated with the Black Power movements of younger generations.

This book also employs specific definitions for "public history" and for black identity formation based on recent influential scholarship. The use of the term "public history" reflects ongoing discussions about the practice of history in the public sphere and the degree to which history was deployed by a variety of social actors with some degree of professional and occupational training beyond academic orthodoxies. This book emphasizes settings outside of ivory towers but inevitably connects to discussions about knowledge production and disciplinary boundaries that occurred from within.[29] These repertoires of public-history activism were not government or liberal philanthropic commissioned "race relation" projects, done in the style of a Gunnar Myrdal (*An American Dilemma*) or under the tutelage of Robert Park at the University of Chicago's infamous School of Sociology.[30] Neither were they restricted to the solitary efforts of itinerant community historians or radical orators such as those who preached from soapboxes in Chicago's Washington Park from, at least, the Great Depression era.[31] The National Council of Public Historians defines "public history" as "the many and diverse ways in which history is put to work in the world."[32] Indeed, this book examines a range of public-history repertoires that follow from such insights about the accessibility and utility of historical knowledge to publics. It traces the activism of public schoolteachers around curriculum reforms and examinations of how museum practices worked to transform urban social spaces into places that affirmed local black pasts in the making of twentieth-century Chicago.

Certainly, black-history movements existed in cities across America from the early years of the twentieth century. In mainstream channels of African American thought, the acclaimed and pioneering historian Carter G. Woodson helped found the Association for the Study of Negro Life and History (ASNLH) in 1915 in Chicago and soon relocated it to Washington, D.C., and later renamed the Association for the Study of African American Life and History (ASAALH). Today, the ASAALH is arguably the most influential professional organization devoted exclusively to the study and promotion of African American history both within and outside the academy.[33]

Woodson and his associates felt the promotion of black history could, in the words of a recent biographer, preserve the nineteenth-century credos for social uplift and "serve the dual function of instilling cultural pride and self-esteem in African Americans while combating racial prejudice by exposing white society to Africans' and African Americans' monumental contributions to American and world culture."[34] From at least the 1910s, a variety of intellectual and public-history projects led by middle-class, black social workers, public schoolteachers, librarians, union activists, church clergy and laity, fraternity and sorority members, and clubwomen, such as Mary McLeod Bethune and the National Association of Colored Women (NACW), engaged with the uplift tradition promoted by Woodson and helped build various regional organizations in many American cities from Atlanta to Chicago. They organized exhibits at

World Fairs and helped promote Woodson's idea for a Negro History Week, an event designed initially to reach working-class African American audiences and which evolved into a national Black History Month by 1976.[35] African American women were particularly critical to the development of the early black-history movement across America. As historian Pero Dagbovie demonstrates, "black women supported Bethune's quest to popularize and democratize black history" by supporting the ASNLH's activities and its print engines like the *Negro History Bulletin*, which began publication in 1937. Indeed, as the founder of the ASNLH and arguably the entire black-history movement in America, Woodson frequently praised African American women from around the country, such as in Terre Haute, Indiana, the state of Michigan, and in rural areas nationwide where "field representatives" of the association operated.[36]

Because the ASNLH began in Chicago and because its black metropolis expanded so prolifically through the middle decades of the twentieth century, Chicago is ideal for a study of this nature about the history of black public-history activism in one locality. Though it is beyond the purview of this book to do so, it would behoove scholars of other cities with significant and large black communities historically, such as Washington, D.C., New York, Detroit, Philadelphia, Atlanta, St. Louis, and elsewhere, to specifically explore the dynamics of regional black-history movements in those spaces.

In Chicago, many African American public-history activists initially connected their work to struggles for racial justice at least partly in the tradition of the ASNLH. In an effort to continue the public-history traditions of the ASNLH (like Negro History Week), Chicago black public schoolteachers and some of their white allies took initiatives to promote black-history curriculum reforms in the context of wartime America. Chapter 1 of this book examines the curriculum-reform projects of teachers who continued the pre–Cold War roots of the black-history movement in Chicago, teachers like Madeline Morgan and her husband, Samuel Stratton, on Chicago's South Side. In particular, the chapter considers how curriculum reforms represented important local interventions into revisions about racial and historical knowledge taking place in U.S. society through the mid-twentieth century among pioneering scholars of black American history, such as Woodson, W. E. B. Du Bois, St. Clair Drake, Melville Herskovits, and others, particularly with regards to histories of racial slavery and its lived legacies in urban locales like Chicago. These reforms, which were used experimentally by Chicago Public Schools from 1942 to 1945, highlighted widespread, tightly contested and controlled efforts from across the political spectrum to redress public school curricula so that they were more attentive to the civic virtues of growing African American urban communities and their many contributions to the American nation.[37] While seemingly trivial, these forms of historical knowledge rarely circulated in mainstream U.S. culture during this period and so were themselves viable repertoires of civil rights activism for how they represented African American identities in the public sphere. Indeed, this chapter also demonstrates how these efforts at curriculum reform were situated in the city's local black-history movement, which arguably dates back to the 1920s when the DuSable Memorial Society was established to commemorate the city's first settler, Jean Baptiste Point DuSable (a man of Haitian descent).

The second chapter of this book looks at how a vision for a black-history museum in Chicago persisted despite the stifling conditions of Cold War America. As such, chapter 2 deals explicitly with how this vision for such a museum existed in the context of a highly contested struggle for the control of black-history celebrations in Chicago among public historians, increasingly divided by Cold War–era ideologies. It proceeds to show how the idea for a black-history museum evolved out of these contestations: from the left-wing backgrounds of the museum's founders, whose efforts spanned decades of activity and attracted opposition from some liberal black Chicago civic elites to a sustained vision for a museum first expressed by the National Negro Congress–backed National Negro Museum and Historical Foundation (NNMHF) in the 1940s, through the actual implementation and chartering of museum space at 3806 South Michigan Avenue by the early 1960s. This chapter is particularly animated by the revealing insights of an oral-history interview given by local Roosevelt College professor St. Clair Drake in the late 1960s. In this interview, Drake suggests that African American leftists were encouraged to channel their activism into public-history labors in light of the Cold War's widespread political repressions. Unlike Drake's conclusions, which suggest that black Communists were a "broken breed" as a result of McCarthyist repressions that forced them "in for the study of Negro History," chapter 2 argues that public history was empowering and innovative. From the perspective of the DuSable Museum's founders and their many colleagues and friends, such experiences actually emboldened their commitment to public history as a viable form of cultural activism.[38]

The third chapter of this book shifts to address the question of nationalism and its historically contingent forms in urban America. This chapter specifically looks at how black nationalism in Chicago became a complex phenomenon that drew on older traditions and modalities of black politics through the local organizations and activists that challenged simple dichotomies of integrationalism and separatism, militancy and accommodation. As a primary focus, the chapter examines the establishment of the Afro-American Heritage

Association (AAHA) in 1958 and its subsequent public-history efforts—notably, the promotion of Negro History Week in the city through the early 1960s. Under the leadership of local figures like South Side Communist Party–chapter organizer Ishmael Flory and the Nation of Islam's University of Islam principal Christine C. Johnson, the AAHA bridged local nationalist politics with radical-left anticolonialism from the 1950s, into the Black Power 1960s. Moreover, the AAHA also played a significant role in promoting the late-career, knowledge-producing efforts of the embattled but still eminent scholar of black America W. E. B. Du Bois. The chapter ultimately offers a useful local counterpoint to national institutions active in the same moment, such as the Central Intelligence Agency–funded American Society of African Culture (AMSAC) and continues to demonstrate how radical black leftists used black history to fight for social change.

The fourth chapter of this book examines how important intergenerational discussions revolved around black public-history labors in Chicago into the Black Power era. Many Chicago Black Power and black arts movement (BAM) activists were impacted by the growing influence of the DuSable Museum over the 1960s, whose programs were expanding and continuing to reach younger generations as the museum's founders had intended. BAM leaders in Chicago—such as Haki Madhubuti and pioneering black-studies historian Sterling Stuckey—were mentored by Margaret and Charles Burroughs and some of the cohort who founded the DuSable Museum. Overall, this chapter considers the fascinating intergenerational collaborations, discussions, and engagements among black radical leftists involved in the city's black cultural renaissance during the 1930s and those who promoted resurgent forms of nationalism and racial militancy that highlighted the urban crises of late 1960s and early 1970s. The chapter argues that an important focal point of these interactions was the work and programs of the DuSable Museum in Chicago and ultimately the repertoires of black public-history activism it espoused.

Chapter 5 of this book concludes this focused study of local black public-history activism by looking at how the DuSable Museum conducted its expansion and physical development in the context of the Black Power era. The museum's move to a new location reimagined a historically African American social space and neighborhood in the city's geography and can be considered alongside the highly diverse engagements of Black Power and BAM activists around the country with civic-level politics. The politics this expansion effort brought into play also demonstrated how museum work became a significant part of local movements for urban racial equality through the 1960s and early 1970s—a process that further reflected growing interest in African American heritage, culture, and history over this period. This chapter shows how the museum's push for relocation constituted an example of how Black Power and public-history activism worked together. This chapter also adds to knowledge about the conflicted role that state and foundation power structures played in attempting to shape various forms of cultural activism and knowledge production, setting the stage for the crises and challenges such cultural projects would face in the closing decades of the twentieth century.

Overall, the political stakes for activists involved in these black public-history labors were very real, although the results (such as significant public recognition for Negro/Black History Week/Month) may still seem by present-day standards to be both tokenistic and trivial.[39] The effort to imagine these labors in concrete projects and institutions provides examples for how significant figures active in black Chicago's left-labor cultural fronts survived and established diverse public-history projects from the early 1940s through the 1960s. These labors were emboldened by Cold War and white-supremacist repressions faced by U.S. blacks universally (regardless of their politics) and the global issues of racial inequality that energized and underscored many aspects of African American politics and culture throughout the mid-twentieth century. This book ultimately seeks to emphasize the earnest spirit of these labors and humbly suggests that, perhaps, present activities of this nature could be reinvigorated by the stories contained within.

CHAPTER ONE

Curriculum Reforms in World War II Chicago

It is not a huge revelation to point out that black American history was not always part of U.S. public school curricula. It is more provocative to say African American teachers once independently and at great personal and professional risk provided alternative curricula to their classrooms and communities. In oral histories, some local black schoolteachers and public historians, such as Margaret Taylor Goss Burroughs and Timuel Black of Chicago, mention how their and other black classrooms in the city from the late 1940s through the 1950s were closely monitored by white colleagues. Sometimes, these colleagues expressed concern to administrators over how Burroughs and Black approached their lesson planning—especially if these colleagues suspected that students were being taught seditious forms of African American or U.S. history.[1] Burroughs quite explicitly relates her experiences with such surveillance:

> I, of course, was a strong advocate of black history, which was considered subversive in itself at that time. God forbid that you would teach Harriet Tubman or Sojourner Truth in class, and if you had anything to say about Nat Turner or Denmark Vesey, well, you had better just keep it to yourself. While my students were painting, I would be in the middle of a discussion about the Scottsboro boys, and I'd look over and see the white principal appear at the classroom door. Turning back to the class, I'd say, "And that's how Betsy Ross came to sew the flag. Now, boys and girls, let's talk about Patrick Henry. . . ." My students knew

enough to hold in their chuckles until the principal had passed the door. As soon as he was gone, we'd go back to Clarence Darrow's Scottsboro defense or Ida B. Wells's upbringing or Mary McLeod Bethune's activism.[2]

Timuel Black describes a similar experience from the early 1950s when he started teaching the sons and daughters of mostly white steelworkers in Gary, Indiana—just beyond the borders of Chicago's South Side:

> My challenge was to prove to them that they weren't dumb. I won that. My attitude was there was a whole school there . . . almost all white. Their mission was to prove to this "dumb nigger," that he shouldn't be there. . . . My mission was to say it don't make any difference. And I had an inner feeling in myself to say, to myself, "You don't know who you're fucking with." White and black students were trying to get into my class. And the principal came and said white teachers [were complaining] about me. I have all this demand for my class . . . 'cause I give them good grades. And so the principal came and he sat in, and said, "What is that you're teaching? . . ." I said, "American history." But he said, "That's not in the curriculum." I said, "Corrected American history. Go check it out." . . . I was just inserting it where it belongs.[3]

These recollections reveal the contested terrain of school curriculum and racial knowledge production that public educators (African Americans, in particular) encountered in the conservative climate of early Cold War America. Though far from being the only or worst period of duress in U.S. history for black Americans, many scholars have shown how any sort of advocacy for antidiscrimination became easily equated with Communist or, at least, unwanted dissident activity.[4] The attempt to teach black history in classrooms, especially outside of mainstream civics curricula, was no exception. Looking back just a decade before the repressive climate of the 1950s had fully set in, however, shows that teachers like Burroughs and Black were not pioneers in their thinking about the need for curriculum reforms on matters of race in U.S. history. Burroughs's and Black's reflections show that such surreptitious pedagogy in the classroom was arguably emboldened by an earlier period of very public, contested, and significant black public-history activism on Chicago's South Side. Much of it focused on getting African American history, in particular, into local school curricula and to the wider community. This chapter demonstrates how curriculum efforts originated in the early 1940s and extended through the mid-twentieth century.

Well before Burroughs and Black supplemented their individual classes, a February 7, 1942, article, "Development of Negro History in Chicago," appeared in Chicago's influential black newspaper the *Chicago Defender*, which was celebrating Negro History Week.[5] This article also underscores the influence that Carter G. Woodson, founder of the Association for the Study of Negro Life and History (ASNLH) and Negro History Week, had on black-history observances for African American communities nationwide. According to the *Defender* article, Chicago teachers sought to emulate Woodson and the ASNLH's efforts and so became the chief practitioners of black public-history activism in 1940s Chicago. South Side teachers spearheaded curriculum-reform efforts as well as extracurricular events and clubs they helped organize in schools and in the community to promote the teaching of black history. The author of the *Defender* article, Mavis Mixon, a teacher at Stephen A. Douglas Elementary on the South Side, was also a poet who sometimes worked alongside Margaret Burroughs and acclaimed writer Gwendolyn Brooks in writing groups that met at the South Side Community Arts Center—an important locale for Chicago's black cultural renaissance from the late 1930s through the 1950s (not to be confused with the more famous Harlem Renaissance). Mixon was a lesser-known figure but, nonetheless, a part of the larger community of South Siders who comprised this mid-twentieth-century black Chicago literary and cultural renaissance.[6]

Mixon's assessment of black-history labors in Chicago focuses on the efforts of African American teachers and a few white allies in public schools who promoted alternative curricula and programs. Mixon explains that a number of South Side schools had many teachers and a few supportive principals who helped establish extracurricular Negro History Clubs during the 1930s and 1940s. As Black recalls, progressive white teachers were among the first to actually begin teaching supplemental African American history to their civics students.[7] Ultimately led by black Americans, the local movement for curriculum reform certainly had interracial dimensions at its outset.

Public schoolteachers (black and white) on Chicago's South Side regularly took part in public-history efforts geared toward reforming the city's underfunded public schools through the 1940s. Among these influential teachers were Walter H. Dyett, music and drama; white English teacher Mary L. Herrick; Samuel Stratton, social studies at DuSable High School (formerly New Wendell Phillips); and Madeline Stratton Morris, Dunbar Public High Schools (figures 1 and 2).[8]

Stratton Morris, however, was the most pivotal for initiating curriculum reforms in Chicago during the early 1940s. Born Madeline Robinson in 1906 to John and Estella Robinson, she was the eldest of six children. She attended Chicago public schools, received training at the Chicago Teachers College to teach first through eighth grades, over the course of the 1930s and early 1940s

Figure 1. Madeline Stratton Morris, 1964. Madeline Stratton Morris Papers, Vivian G. Harsh Research Collection, Chicago Public Library.

received a bachelor of science in education and a master's in education from Northwestern University, and pursued postgraduate work in various fields at the University of Chicago and the Illinois Institute of Technology. After a successful career as a South Side civics teacher, she became an important mentor to Chicago teachers through the 1960s and 1970s. She was active in educational leadership, civil rights, and black-history movement activity throughout her career as president of the ASNLH from 1970 through 1977. She also served on the board of the National Association for the Advancement of Colored People

Figure 2. William Stratton, ca. late 1960s. Madeline Stratton Morris Papers, Vivian G. Harsh Research Collection, Chicago Public Library.

(NAACP) and service organizations like the National Council of Negro Women's Chicago chapter as well as the Church of the Good Shepherd.

Dyett, Herrick, and the Strattons were part of a significant cohort of South Side public schoolteachers who became instrumental in actively supporting local black public history.[9] As Anne M. Knupfer writes, "[m]ost black teachers were keenly aware of the discrimination and other problems faced by black students." Among the many solutions that these teachers sought, which included the initiation of private elementary schools and the development of "human relations curriculum" through the 1950s was one "to create meaningful curricula in black history, literature, and the arts."[10] These black-history units were never fully or permanently implemented during this period. Still, as Knupfer indicates, Chicago was the "only city to use such a citywide plan" for curriculum reforms for which the teachers received acclaim from around the country and the world.[11]

This chapter focuses especially on these African American–led curriculum-reform efforts and, in particular, the ones for which Stratton Morris was recognized. Her efforts were connected to ongoing public-history programs and initiatives in the community in the early 1940s and later impacted not only local but also national efforts to redress curriculum deficiencies for black American history. Curriculum-reform measures and related public-history activities were near the center of efforts to generate popular interest about black history in the country and were connected to struggles for civil rights. The high stakes of the efforts concerned with expressions of black history and public identity certainly produced concerns about who had the authority to communicate such knowledge to the community: school officials, teachers, representatives of the ASNLH who were disciples of Woodson, professional or community scholar activists of various political affiliations, or "race" experts (whether local club-women and African American civic elites or white academics and politicians). These contestations revolved for a time over proposed reforms to the civics curricula of Chicago's public schools and revealed how these endeavors became significant repertoires for black public history in the city. Moreover, such reform measures were proposed well before the better-known civil rights struggles of the 1950s and 1960s engaged most famously with issues of educational justice and racial reform, marked especially by the *Brown v. Board of Education* decision in 1954, which struck down de jure racial segregation.[12]

The Curriculum

Arguably, still no historical consensus exists on matters of educational-reform initiatives through mid-twentieth-century Chicago. Historian Michael W. Homel contends that the city's African American community held concerns "relating to vocational training, Negro history and increased numbers of Negro teachers" during the 1920s through the early 1940s, but such issues "held relatively minor priority throughout these years."[13] An appraisal of teacher Stratton Morris's proposed reforms, which consisted of supplementary social studies units geared toward elementary education from first through eighth grades, indicates that influential African American teachers definitely felt otherwise. Rather, for some, curriculum reform about black history was a priority. The impact of these endeavors is illustrated in how Stratton Morris's curriculum reforms were part of a larger, often contested, field of black public-history activism. For a time, this field seemed to be nominally united around desires to express black identities as vital and virtuous forms of American identity from the World War II years through the 1950s.

Part of how Stratton Morris achieved civic authority to conduct the necessary research for her curriculum reforms was because the project involved extensive consultations with professional and/or scholarly experts of "race." These consultations with educational elites suggest that Stratton Morris negotiated the development of her project within the parameters of racial liberalism that arose especially during World War II and the 1950s. She framed her project as decidedly American in orientation and scope; it became a universalizing curriculum designed to enhance student understandings of how black Americans were central to the "U.S. family." She infused her units with insights from revisionist scholarship on the cutting edge of radical approaches to U.S. history from scholars such as W. E. B. Du Bois, Woodson, Melville Herskovitz, Herbert Aptheker, and others. That these civics units were never permanently implemented in Chicago suggests that the efforts of curriculum reformers like Stratton Morris to redress omissions of black history in key areas of the public sphere had a long way to go. Still, the story of how they got off the ground at all remains highly significant.

Stratton Morris's development of black-history units received approval of the school district and other civic and state-level public officials. In her own reflections, she comments that Chicago Public Schools superintendent William Johnson "readily accepted" the proposals for the black-history units that she and her school principal, Elinor McCollum, first brought to the district's attention. Based on her successes as a South Side public schoolteacher, in 1940, Stratton Morris was released from her teaching duties to work for a year and a half with an assistant of her choosing to develop the units. Stratton Morris chose Bessie S. King, a Chicago elementary schoolteacher. An overseeing committee, chaired by McCollum, included one of the city's few African American school principals, Ruth Jackson, of Colman Elementary.[14] Stratton Morris and King were then assigned to the district's Bureau of Curriculum and "given all of the freedom" they deemed necessary to complete their project.[15]

Much of the research for her units was carried out late into evenings and over weekends at the George Cleveland Hall Branch Library, a key cultural institution then of the black South Side. Stratton Morris's research was also conducted in the stacks of the University of Chicago, the Field Museum, and the Art Institute of Chicago. She submitted drafts of her units for review and approval to a distinguished and interracial list of academics and "race" experts whose interests extended to combating American racism and supported the black community in its efforts to combat racial discrimination. These scholars included Woodson, ASNLH head; Charles Wesley, then president of Wilberforce University and Woodson's eventual successor as ASNLH leader; Herskovitz, founder of African studies at Northwestern University; Avery O. Craven, a professor of southern U.S. history at the University of Chicago, who wrote sympathetically during the 1940s of civil rights and worked to complicate mythologies about the "Solid South"; Fay Cooper Cole, an English professor at the University of Chicago, known for his role with Clarence Darrow's defense team at the Scopes trial in Tennessee during the mid-1920s; Walter Johnson, an English professor from the University of Illinois; and numerous South Side public schoolteachers and administrators, including African American school principals Maudelle Bousfield and Ruth Jackson and three outstanding teachers of history, Ciara Anderson (DuSable High), Samuel Stratton (DuSable High), and Thelma Powell (Wendell Phillips High).[16]

The cumulative advice of these educators and "race" experts helped Stratton Morris produce curriculum units that reflected the global and transnational sensibilities of what was then cutting-edge revisionist history. Her third-grade unit on the West African nation of Dahomey (which became Benin in 1960) describes how African farmers in the diaspora were viewed by Europeans as backward—surely, also a reference to how southern U.S. black sharecroppers were often perceived. An excerpt from the unit mentions, "The African Negroes have to work very hard for a living. . . . Farming [was] not easy." This validation of agrarian life was likely intended for the many working-class sons and daughters of southern black farmers Stratton Morris anticipated in Chicago classrooms through the 1940s. Fifth- and sixth-grade units feature various black explorers and pioneers. The students learned that Chicago's first pioneer, Jean Baptiste Point DuSable, was a "Negro" and that he "lived and traded with the Indians," that he sold his cabin in the area to Le Mai, "a Frenchman," who in turn sold the cabin to an Englishman, John Kinzie. While setting out the central historical actors in the struggle for the Ohio frontier and the founding of Chicago, Stratton Morris does not emphasize how DuSable possibly sympathized with the French side in these conflicts—given his Haitian background. However, the purpose of establishing the notion of a black "first" in Chicago as well as the basic constellation of populations involved in the ongoing process of colonization was surely useful. Sixth graders learned of Estevanico, credited with "discovering both Arizona and New Mexico," and of Matthew Henson, the only "American" chosen by Admiral Robert Edwin Peary to go on his North Pole expedition in the early twentieth century.[17] Stratton Morris expressed a desire to imbue prospective pupils of her civic units with a global and transatlantic sensibility for black subjectivities and to promote youth self-esteem. These sensibilities definitely expressed an American exceptionalism, notably their suggestion of heroic "firsts" for U.S. history. But these units also mapped alternative coordinates for histories of Africa and the Americas that challenged the prevalent centrality of white-settler colonial myths in U.S. history.

Despite their focus on younger age groups, Stratton Morris's curriculum reforms were at the cutting edge through the mid-twentieth century of pedagogy and intellectual thought related to the improvement of race relations. In many ways, her work both reflects and anticipates trends in intercultural education that emerged during the 1930s and 1940s and the later cultural pluralism that helped expand American liberal thought into the post–World War II era to ultimately become multiculturalism. In this sense, curriculum-reform efforts such as Stratton Morris's fit squarely with the brevity of government-supported intercultural education movements nationally over these decades, for the most part, loosely supported by top officials and lasting roughly from the mid- to late years of World War II. These movements paralleled the local message of various liberal-aligned Chicago mayor's conferences on race relations during the 1940s, which "verbally committed to the ideal of equality of opportunity for Negroes" and were held in the spirit of human "brotherhood."[18] As historian Daryl Michael Scott has shown, however, such experiments in race relations evolved into postwar pluralism. Although much of this thought could be characterized as "culturally shallow and intellectually bland," it also "developed an institutional foundation that would make it an enduring and influential feature of American life . . . [and help to develop] a model for American race relations." Indeed, for Scott, while such forms of pluralism were perhaps bland and shallow, they anticipated later twentieth-century multiculturalism and were part of innovations in American racial liberalism through the post–World War II era.[19]

Stratton Morris's curriculum reforms reflected exactly this sort of liberal pluralism. In a reflection of her work, she felt that the educational methods adopted by Superintendent Johnson and the Chicago schools would "bring about a change in the kind and quality of attitude in our American family and gradually bring about a change in interracial as well as racial behavior" among young people. A questionnaire completed by South Side schoolteachers reported that students were generally "surprised to learn that Negroes had made so many contributions to American life." Another teacher who tried the units reported that her students' interest in independent research was so great that she was prompted to organize a "Negro history club."[20] The teacher added that she hoped the monthly "tolerance" pamphlets sent to local schools might encourage "white children" to change for the better upon learning about black achievements.

Stratton Morris's work also became relevant to state-level officials during this period and reflected the increasing popularity of racial liberalism in the public sphere. Indeed, she eventually appeared at the behest of Illinois (and South Side) state representative Corneal Davis in 1945 before the state's Education Committee at the Sixty-Fourth General Assembly to enact a bill that stated how the "[h]istory of the Negro race may be taught in all public schools and in all other educational institutions in this state supported or maintained, in whole or in part, by public funds."[21] Historian Knupfer contends that Stratton Morris's reforms were "some of the most innovative black curricula in urban schools."[22]

Stratton Morris's curriculum units envisioned a comprehensive treatment of the African American past distilled to an elementary level. They also reflected the revisionist scholarship of radical historians from this period. For example, her seventh-grade unit advanced new studies and approaches to American slavery histories (now classic ones) Aptheker and Du Bois pioneered. These scholars' collective works on slavery and Reconstruction emphasize the agency of African American slaves in the making of their own freedoms during both the Revolutionary and Civil War eras. The work of Du Bois on Reconstruction as well as Aptheker's document-rich though embellished account of American slave rebellions were far from the mainstream of American academe in their time. Historian Robin Kelley relates that he had trouble getting his academic supervisors to consider figures like Aptheker and Du Bois in graduate studies he took during the 1980s when African American studies had supposedly "made it" as a major subfield of American history.[23]

Presented in heroic and teleological terms, Stratton Morris's units offered biographical treatments of freedmen who became republican soldiers during the Revolutionary War. Historical figures examined by the units include Boston's Crispus Attucks and leaders of early nineteenth-century slave insurrections and conspiracies, such as Gabriel Prosser and Nat Turner in Virginia and Denmark Vesey in South Carolina, and abolitionist leaders of the mid- to late nineteenth century, such as Frederick Douglass and Sojourner Truth. Stratton Morris's first-grade unit focuses on a story about the civic virtues of a distinguished "colored" policeman named Billy Glide and provides tales of African American Pullman porters, who were central to black Chicago's early urban history and African American migrations to the north. These figures were depicted as dignified rail-road workers who held positions of respect in black communities nationwide (which, indeed, many did). Second graders looked at the accomplishments of scientist George Washington Carver; third graders looked at Dahomey and the West African ancestry of most U.S. blacks. Fourth graders examined the careers of world-traveling artists Marian Anderson and Paul Robeson; fifth graders read about the life of Chicago's first settler, DuSable; sixth, seventh, and eighth graders learned about a "Negro captain" named Alonzo Pietro on Christopher Columbus's *Niña*, alongside a brief overview of American slavery and its abolition. The units end with discussions of black military "heroes" from the War of 1812 through World War II and by examining the cultural products of the local black cultural renaissance. For example, eighth graders focused on black Chicago institutions founded in the first half of the twentieth century, such as the South Side Community Arts Center, the Parkway Community House, the Hall Branch Library, the Good Shepherd Community Center, Providence Hospital, and "black insurance companies and newspapers."[24]

These individual and institutional biographies were presented in narrative forms as "thrilling and stirring stories" to engage younger audiences. The imperative of presenting usable pasts to younger audiences through civics curricula surely informed Stratton Morris's treatment of U.S. Reconstruction and its aftermath as well as what was then recent early twentieth-century history. Her units focused on important forms of race leadership under southern Jim Crow racial segregation, exemplified by figures like Booker T. Washington. She followed this with appraisals of civic and intellectual leaders from mid-twentieth century African American public life, such as Mary McLeod Bethune of the National Association of Colored Women, Mordecai Johnson and Alain Locke of Howard University, and other pioneering scholars and cultural luminaries of black studies, such as Du Bois, Woodson, and Henry Ossawa Tanner.[25] In an autobiographical statement from 1943, Stratton Morris extols her own work in ways that demonstrated how it fit alongside the cooperative models of liberal and pluralist race relations from the period. For her, the curriculum units were a "masterpiece in organization, technique and presentation . . . skillfully designed to fit in with the existing topics in the social studies curriculum." Moreover, she notes how "all sugestion (*sic*) of bitterness and resentment have been supplanted by absorbing and inspiring facts" and that her units exemplify "the first time any public school system in the United States" had "officially accepted and sponsored a teaching program giving due accord to the whole contributions of the Negro Race." To her, these initiatives helped build "momentum for similar movements in various parts of the country."[26]

The units were not the most objective of scholarly approaches to the construction of historical narrative; indeed, they certainly glorified and lionized their subjects as inspiring heroes whose life accomplishments were irrefutable "facts." However, these units were completed in an era when the racist Plantation School of U.S. and southern history still dominated conventional understandings of U.S. racial slavery and Reconstruction (not to mention American history, generally). Through the early to mid-twentieth century, the Plantation School of southern history viewed slavery as a benign institution and suggested black Americans would be better off in bonded servitude than in freedom. Stories during the Civil War and Reconstruction depict the actions of freed peoples as corrupt and savage, northern armies and the federal government as treacherous, and suggested the "lost cause" of the South was redeemed when southern white Democrats retook control of the South by the late nineteenth century. C. Vann Woodward is the historian generally credited with overturning these views of U.S. southern history, but Du Bois and other pioneering black American and radical left-wing white scholars, such as Aptheker, a Communist, arguably did it well ahead of the mainstream historical profession usually attributed to Woodward's generation of scholars.[27]

The emergence of Stratton Morris's curriculum reforms are also significant when considered in light of the development of modern sociology, particularly the work done by the University of Chicago School of Sociology's "race relations" scholars as well as early efforts to chart black Chicago's local history. Indeed, Stratton Morris's wartime project was initiated in the intellectual shadow cast by the sociology school's figurehead Robert Park, who worked at the university from 1914 to 1933.[28] As historian Davarian Baldwin has written, "Park's discussions of Black people in this critical period reveal a 'cultural turn' that was infused with equally rigid categories of identity and distinction. The dynamic events of Black migration, urban racial violence and 'New Negro' resistance posed direct threats to his paradigm of cultural cohesion and order." Baldwin indicates that Park sought "scientific certainty" by devising his race relations theories in ways that deployed notions of "race conflict and racial traits into his overarching social system, as natural elements to be overcome by the inevitable force of cultural assimilation."[29] The intellectual legacies of these assimilationist theories of race relations, devised as they were by such prominent white liberal scholars, had implications for how black American pasts were interpreted and represented through the mid-twentieth century.

An example of the influence of another relatively static and rigid racial-conflict approach to understandings of black Chicago history is seen in *Black Chicago: The Making of a Negro Ghetto, 1890–1920* (1969), Allan H. Spear's now classic interpretation of the city's African American community through the early twentieth century. Written during the ostensibly liberal 1960s, Spear's study "angrily" labeled the "making of a ghetto" to denote black Chicago's emergence as a racially proscribed and relatively powerless community in an area of the city that was, in Spear's evaluation, euphemistically viewed as the "Black Belt."[30] Spear's work fits into a generation of scholarship often referred to as the "ghetto" theses, which treat other "major" northern cities, such as New York (Harlem),

Detroit, and Cleveland. This cluster of influential studies charts specific patterns for black community formation in urban areas through the early twentieth century as generally quiescent or defensive responses to white racism and city governance structures and institutions. In these understandings of history, black community enclaves emerged as worse off than equivalent European migrant slums from the same and earlier eras. As the prolific historian of black Chicago Christopher R. Reed writes, the "ghetto" theses were primarily concerned with urban "blight" and "demographic disorganization" and how such issues were linked directly to the Great Migrations of black southerners, whose movement, by and large, catalyzed negative outcomes for urban life. As Reed suggests, these interpretations of the urban "African American experience" were "constructed on the belief that forced racial segregation, but never voluntary clustering, led to a dense concentration of blacks within residential areas" and that such homogeneous neighborhood formations were simply negative and inevitable in outcome.[31]

Thus, approaches to U.S. history, even through the mid-twentieth century, still treated black Americans as at worst subhuman and at best fairly quiescent and static subjects beholden to negative urban forces—if these approaches even included black Americans at all. Thus, simply having positive representations, even if they offer glorified portraits of heroism as Stratton Morris's curricula do, were still exceptional images of black American life in the public sphere. Moreover, such labors could also be seen against an even-wider North American backdrop for racial state formation, wherein the diffusion of white-washed public school history textbooks through the middle of the twentieth century omitted people of color, generally, beyond the conventionally perceived black-and-white binary of U.S. race relations. For example, Canadian public schools generally omitted any discussion of Asian Canadian history in school textbooks through the early to mid-twentieth century.[32]

In the United States, early twentieth-century textbooks, which employed antiquated ideas about racial hierarchy, continued to be used in public schools through the 1950s. According to Robin Lindley, *An American History* (1911) by David Muzzey "became a standard text and dominated teaching into the 1950s." Muzzey "told a compelling story featuring mostly white Protestant males—some flawed—making history, and questioned industrialization and immigration from eastern and southern Europe." Though the book was criticized in the 1920s for "impugning" the nation's Founding Fathers, by the 1960s it was "disparaged" for its "racism and paternalism." A 1930s textbook rivaled Muzzey's in more progressive terms because it focused on "ordinary citizens" and encouraged some critical thought—indeed, the American Legion suggested the book was "Red-financed by Russia." However, by and large, mainstream history textbooks (and likely civics curricula overall) became "decidedly nationalistic" during the early Cold War in the 1940s and 1950s. The same omissions about people of color in most American history textbooks over this period apply to treatments of women and gender, as well. A 1971 study of more than a dozen high school history books "published between 1937 and 1969, found that women were rarely mentioned," and if they were, these depictions were "incomplete and inaccurate."[33] The effort then to simply circulate sympathetic or positive portrayals of freedmen, slaves, and abolitionists—especially in public school curricula—can be seen as a vital task for black public historians from this period.

The process through which Stratton Morris devised these social studies units reveals a strong pedagogical current in black Chicago at the outset of the 1940s. These units were not simply a wartime reform measure devised by elites to paper over widespread racial discrimination in America. Rather, they were part of larger, activist cultural projects. As such, Stratton Morris was partly inspired to devise black history curriculum when she attended the American Negro Exposition of 1940. This event, held in Chicago, took place one year before the infamous attack on the South Pacific island base that provoked overt U.S. involvement in World War II.[34] As historian Adam Green notes, the exposition's organization was impeded by financial mismanagement thanks to missteps taken by the local businesspeople who sponsored it. The exposition also avoided difficult discussions of racial slavery's legacies by not showcasing the innovative scholarship done since the 1930s to rebut the still-dominant Plantation School of southern history—which completely elided black Americans' agency in the making of their freedom. Indeed, the work of Du Bois, Aptheker, and L. D. Reddick, among others, did not feature prominently at the exposition. These omissions resulted in an overall sense of "confusion" among the event's exhibitors and artists about "notions of 'racial nationalism' and the obligations of 'American nationality.'" Green suggests this feeling "endured" for many in their future efforts to engage with representing the meanings of black community. Despite such ambiguities, the event featured the exhibition of a variety of work by mostly local African American artists and writers—notably, by local artist-teacher Margaret Burroughs and dancer-choreographer Katherine Dunham (who each went on to future work in educational fields related to black public history). It also featured contributions from Harlem Renaissance luminaries with Chicago ties, such as Arna Bontemps and Langston Hughes. Indeed, the exposition was, as Green describes, a "rehearsal for more sustained imaginative enterprises within Black Chicago in years to come."[35]

The 1940 Negro Exposition made a significant impression on Stratton Morris. She was "greatly interested and impressed by the contributions that had

been made by Negroes in science, health, art, and literature to American life."
She visited the exposition "several times" and dreamed of a "time when Negro
boys and girls would be given an opportunity to read about the achievements"
of black leaders "and their deeds."[36] Stratton Morris took direct inspiration from
the exposition and applied this to her curriculum-reform labors.

Beyond the 1940 Negro Exposition put on by black businesspeople, black
Chicago's growing knowledge repositories in this period became important
sites for public discussions about histories of racial slavery and discrimination.
Collectively, they shaped the local context for Stratton Morris's work on these
curriculum reforms. Many black Chicagoans worked on similar public-history
projects that reflected Chicago's centrality to intellectual interventions and
revisions of the country's racial history. As such, local black American public-
history activists, like Stratton Morris, were key players in a broader discussion
that helped reassert black American citizenship rights in the twilight years of
Jim Crow. Historian Nikhil Singh remarks how "[o]ne of the most significant
and least remarked upon features of the early 1940s was that [the decade] gave
rise to a profound re-conceptualization of the terms of racialized citizenship
within the United States." Singh further suggests that Chicago's South Side was
"less intellectually isolated than the larger society" and became a "site for a generation of cosmopolitan discourses" that "surpassed conventional American
views of the world."[37]

Despite the rich intellectual life of Chicago's South Side, which supported
such a wide array of projects and ideas, Stratton Morris's black-history units
were never permanently implemented. They were only used "experimentally"
in schools for a few years from 1942 to 1945. In 1945 Chicago public school curriculum director Mary Lusson suggested that the social studies units Stratton
Morris designed had been "sandwiched" into general social studies curricula
but only in "appropriate places . . . naturally, and without undue emphasis."[38]
Moreover, many African Americans felt rightfully concerned about not only the
potential of such reforms being implemented poorly and as token gestures but
also who might author them in the first place. In sum, the field of curriculum
reform over this period was highly contested, and black American voices were
far from being at their center, despite the earnestness of these efforts.

Against "Ill-Designing" Persons

The stakes for such black public-history labors were made explicit by leaders
of national black American history organizations. In a letter to Stratton Morris in 1946, ASNLH leader Woodson warned of "ill-designing persons seeking

every opportunity to use occasions" like the History Week celebration for unethical "political" or financial "exploitation."[39] Woodson entrusted Stratton Morris as an unofficial representative of his association in Chicago, which, at the time, lacked an active ASNLH branch—a situation that continued into the early 1960s. Woodson enlisted Stratton Morris because she had developed the curriculum units on African American history for primary schools in Chicago and promoted the ASNLH's work through her activities as a local clubwoman and schoolteacher. Without giving names, a *Chicago Defender* editorial in 1940 had similar concerns and warned of "bogus literature" being distributed to a "deluded public."[40] Historian Pero G. Dagbovie notes how Woodson "believed that there was a class of people who were exploiting the celebration for their own benefit." Indeed, Woodson implored teachers in 1941 to "not call in some silver-tongued orator to talk to" their school "about the history of the Negro."[41] Woodson was clearly concerned about imposters who would use black history for their own opportunistic purposes, whether political or financial.

Chicago's long history of engagement with black-history activism potentially demonstrates the veracity of Woodson's concerns about imposters, given the diversity of enterprises and organizations engaged in such endeavors. For one thing, Woodson's ASNLH, founded in Chicago in 1915, frequently used the city as a site of its national convention, although the association eventually head-quartered in Washington, D.C. Another enterprise was the *Chicago Defender*, whose coverage of Negro History Week in Chicago through the late 1930s and 1940s demonstrates how staff on the paper engaged closely with the politics of local public school curricula and the representation of black history. For instance, a 1939 editorial promotes the ASNLH's Negro History Week celebra-tions and underscores the role of "blacks in the evolution of world culture" as a "fact" and "not a fiction." This editorial and numerous others emphasize a civilizational and modernist rhetoric, worldly in scope, with emphasis on the timeless race heroes of the modern era, such as abolitionist Douglass, Tuskegee College founder Booker T. Washington, journalist and antilynching crusader Ida B. Wells, and the midwestern cosmetics magnate Madame C. J. Walker (Sarah Breedlove). These editorials stress an imperative to change national civics cur-ricula, with the goal of changing perceptions in the public sphere about the positive virtues and achievements of black Americans, with one column sup-porting the need to work "persistently toward the goal of offering the American children of both races the same opportunity to study the Negro that they have to study all other peoples of the earth."[42]

Leading these efforts at the paper was Morris Lewis, the circulation manager in the late 1930s and a former secretary for U.S. Representative Oscar Stanton

De Priest (Republican, 1929–35), of Illinois's First District (Chicago's black South Side) during the Great Depression. Lewis was instrumental for promoting ASNLH national conventions in the 1930s and 1940s. These conventions attracted thousands in 1935 and again in 1940—the latter event alone drew a crowd of nearly two thousand to Ebenezer Baptist Church to hear Woodson speak. As the ASNLH's Illinois state chairman and secretary, Lewis helped organize an annual ad-hoc city-level committee to organize Negro History Week events in churches, schools, YMCAs, and other community centers from the late 1930s through the mid-1940s; he also helped promote the association's membership drives there. While there was interest in sustaining local ASNLH branch activities during this period, an official local chapter was never regularly active in the city from the late 1930s through the 1950s because of attempts "by some to use it as a partisan tool."[43]

Fears over partisanship in these endeavors were founded given the diversity of groups involved in representations of African American cultural politics. Through the late 1930s, Chicago featured a number of left-wing and cultural nationalist groups engaged in radical and anticolonial politics related especially to African liberation. These groups generally received little coverage in the *Chicago Defender* but, nonetheless, sought involvement in citywide Negro History Week observances. Though never large in numbers, groups ranging from nationalist Garveyites to Marxist labor organizers gathered regularly in Washington Park. One of the black South Side's most important public spaces through the mid-twentieth century, the park featured popular soapbox speakers, lectures, and outdoor meetings led by such groups. Shortly after Communist leader William L. Patterson and his wife, Louise Thompson, moved to Chicago in 1939 to work with the local party chapter, they relocated close to Washington Park and became witnesses to important weekly events there. Patterson recalls how "Southsiders crowded into the park and formed a circle around the speakers. There were often well over a thousand listeners in the audience."[44] In his classic study of black nationalism, E. U. Essien-Udom lists a range of organizations active in Chicago during the 1930s and 1940s from the Garveyite-inspired Peace Movement of Ethiopia, the Ethiopian World Federation Council, an Islamic sect called the Moorish Science Temple, and the Joint Council of Repatriation to the Washington Park Forum led by figures like Otis Hyde. Essien-Udom notes that "membership in some of these organizations" was "too small to justify extensive comment."[45]

Still, it was clear that in addition to the popularity of Washington Park speaking forums, some of these groups operated within the mainstream of black Chicago urban life. For example, the World Wide Friends of Africa, headed by "world-traveler" and *Chicago Defender* history columnist F. H. Hammurabi Robb, was invited in 1940 to lecture on the history of black women to the Chicago and Northern District Association of Colored Women.[46] In 1944 the ASNLH hosted a mass meeting at the Metropolitan Community Church for Negro History Week in collaboration with the DuSable Memorial Society, and a joint committee hosted a citywide banquet in Woodson's honor. Other events included African art at the South Side Community Arts Center; a banquet the Frederick Douglass Afro-American Association hosted; a panel discussion Hall Branch head librarian Vivian G. Harsh organized; and numerous programs held in elementary and high schools.[47] Despite the best efforts of the ASNLH to have its imprimatur on these related activities, the proliferation of different groups carrying out Negro History Week celebrations demonstrates the difficult prospect of addressing such a task.

To be sure, by the early 1940s, wartime civil rights issues overshadowed many local-level observances for black history. This was exemplified by a demonstration in February 1941 attended by over a thousand people who marched down South Parkway Avenue. Held at the outset of Negro History Week, the Demonstration for Democracy echoed national civil rights and union leader A. Phillip Randolph's demands for a march on Washington movement, which protested discrimination in defense industries and related vocational training. The event promised to bring out a significant cross-section of black Chicago and included representatives from over 125 organizations, including the Chicago Baptist Institute, Chicago Urban League, NAACP, Chicago Council of Negro Organizations, Chicago and Northern District Federation of Colored Women, National Negro Congress, and numerous labor and church leaders. The co-chairmen were Enoch P. Waters, a *Chicago Defender* editor, and St. Clair Drake, who, in the *Chicago Defender*, has described his experiences. Prior to his prolific work as a professor of African studies at Roosevelt College, Drake was secretary of the Conscientious Objectors to Jim Crow, a secretary of the demonstration's organizing committee, and a graduate student at the University of Chicago. The overwhelming focus of slogans and messages at this demonstration focused on job discrimination and underscored themes of Christian brotherhood and race relations in wartime America. Slogans at the march were, for example, "Separate units aren't right if you want Negroes to fight" and "Christianity means justice to humanity."[48]

In the same time frame, the *Defender* also gave space to fairly left-wing antiwar perspectives. Margaret Burroughs, in one of her first pieces of writing in the paper as a "Negro mother," asked provocatively, "Why . . . war?"[49] Her strategically gendered article outlines a basic chronology for U.S. history that charts

African American roles in the country's wars from King William's War during the seventeenth century through the Revolutionary period when colonists took up arms against the British and through to the Mexican annexation in the nineteenth century. The Civil War period was cast heroically through well-known episodes and figures who sought both the union's preservation and slavery's abolition. After this, a "new form of slavery began" with the onset of Jim Crow segregation despite the best efforts of black soldiers, John Brown, and Abraham Lincoln's warnings in his first inaugural address about preserving the union. Despite the brevity of these historical treatments, Burroughs's editorial underscores a vital opposition to World War II on the basis of American "DEMOC-RACY that promised for the Negro masses economic and social equality." She characterized both Allied and German war efforts as imperial in nature and drew parallels with more recent histories of militarization in Europe and its persistent reaches in racial colonies worldwide.[50]

Beyond the nation's preoccupation with World War II, the *Defender*'s coverage of the ASNLH and Negro History Week events focuses on Woodson's efforts to promote school textbook reform and influence public school education. A 1936 article by Woodson suggests that specific units with accompanying textbooks devoted to black history were needed in public school curricula. He points to experiments in Georgia, Texas, and Delaware where full-credit courses were first developed for high schools and that such approaches were needed elsewhere in the country. He singles out influential postsecondary institutions for criticism, such as Columbia, Yale, and Harvard Universities and the University of Chicago, for not "teaching the Negro except as a problem." The ASNLH clearly viewed competing practitioners of black public history in a suspicious light. Without giving names, a *Defender* editorial in 1940 promotes this view and warns of "bogus literature" being distributed to a "deluded public." These warnings are much like the tone and message of the letters Woodson wrote to Stratton Morris in 1946 about competing interests who sought to profit (both politically and financially) from Negro History Week celebrations.[51]

Woodson and Stratton Morris's dialogue about bogus literature also demonstrates how her curriculum efforts did not occur in a vacuum. Other groups involved in activities that promoted black history were the local affiliates of the Communist Party of the United States, which founded the Abraham Lincoln School over this period, and groups from within local Catholic, Unitarian, and Methodist Church denominations who experimented with similar educational initiatives.[52] But the local context in which Stratton Morris and her Chicago public schools colleagues operated through the 1940s while devising these curriculum reforms and supplementary black-history units meant that they were part of conversations that led their activism on these issues into the purview of Communist and Catholic pedagogues alike. Indeed, Stratton Morris herself consulted with radical leftists like Aptheker and worked with Catholic educational institutions in ways that might not have sat well with Woodson given his concerns for the ASNLH's programmatic integrity over black-history matters.

The ASNLH favored those who agreed to distribute ASNLH materials and to agree with their perspectives on African American history. Woodson had advocated for many years about the control over distribution of ideas about public school curricula related to African American history. Part of the effort to redress the serious omissions of black history in the public sphere came down to questions of intellectual authority as much as the need for historical revision. In a move that anticipates the school boycott and education segregation issues of many civil rights struggles of the 1950s and 1960s, Woodson urges Stratton Morris to enlist the support of local churches, schools, clubs, and community organizations in Chicago for her ongoing work. This support was intended to assist appeals to the city's board of education to purchase history books about African Americans for its school and city libraries and to raise funds for the ASNLH by selling these public institutions the black history resources the association produced. Woodson outlines the ASNLH's program as one that promoted what "we have learned about the history of the Negro and to extend the effort into places where it has not yet become widely known" throughout the United States and the world. One of Woodson's chief concerns, however, was sustaining the programmatic integrity of the association over and even against potentially competitive curriculum developers. The prospect of having others impersonate (or emulate) what he saw as the rightful domain of the ASNLH, whether for political or acquisitive purposes, clearly worried Woodson, who sought to oversee the nation's Negro history observances as closely as he could.[53]

The stakes for creating such knowledge for curricula were clearly not lost on practitioners of black public history. From local schoolteachers to academic black-history scholars and pioneers of the African American history field like Woodson, all were stakeholders in the nascent (yet still vulnerable) field of black history, generally, and felt the need to direct these endeavors as much as they could. Such concerns are understandable given the precariousness of what were still very unrecognized and unvalidated endeavors in the public sphere. Indeed, the very prospect of realizing curriculum reforms demonstrates the degree to which public officials and the teachers who pushed them could use symbolic recognition of cultural and historical achievements by black Americans as indicators of actual progress toward future goals of racial equity. This fact itself marked a significant moment in the circulation and production of important forms of local knowledge about black history and helped encourage black public-history activism as a significant repertoire for civil rights activism in later decades.

Stratton Morris's curriculum work was critical to this moment. Indeed, her proposals had a much-further reach than the staged approval they received from public officials during World War II. The curriculum units eventually became blueprints for the development of educational resources and projects elsewhere and received widespread consideration among progressive educators and intellectuals throughout the country and around the world. Within the United States alone, her curriculum ideas were appraised sympathetically in *Time* magazine, *American Unity*, *PM New York* newspaper, and *Common Sense*, as well as in the black press and journals, such as the *Chicago Defender*, *Negro Digest*, and *Journal of Negro Education*. The decidedly mainstream *Time* article on her units characterized them as "unusual" and fixated on her "handsome" youthful appearance (she was thirty-six). Still, the article also offered praise for these intellectual and pedagogical pursuits. *Time* highlighted Stratton Morris's optimism about the curricula and the fact that New York school officials as well as U.S. Catholic "pedagogues" demonstrated "interest" in her work.[54]

From a more internationalist view than *Time* offered, the antifascist, liberal magazine *Common Sense* notes how requests for Stratton Morris's study units came from Italy, Africa, and South America, not only from the United States. Her work was praised for being part of a broader movement of pluralist educators during the 1940s who had taken their "gloves" off against racial "intolerance." Hilda Taba, listed as director on the letterhead of the National Council for Social Studies Departments in New York, also part of the National Education Association, approached Stratton Morris about her work and the "problem of inter-racial cooperation." Certainly, beyond Chicago, other cities attempted to initiate plans for curriculum reform. Raymond Nathan presented the Springfield, Massachusetts, public school plan as one that offered a pluralist and antiracist curriculum and that demonstrated a measure of success in that region during the 1940s when anti-Semitic and antiblack race riots were occurring in nearby cities, such as Bridgeport and Hartford, Connecticut.[55] Knupfer writes Stratton Morris's units were part of this intercultural education movement as it emerged "in Chicago and nationally" because the units fundamentally "challenged traditional concepts of race and promoted ideas of cultural pluralism."[56]

Stratton Morris's social and personal life from this period reflects these more worldly sensibilities. Her curriculum work was recognized at a luncheon of the Chicago Metropolitan Council of the National Council of Negro Women

(NCNW), a group that honored her nationally four years later (figure 3). She was awarded a plaque at a meeting that directly recognized her curriculum units. Bethune, black American educator and former president of the National Association of Colored Women, praised the units as a "splendid piece of work."[57] The meeting also featured Farima P. Sinha as guest speaker, a former secretary of the London bureau of the Indian National Congress Party. Sinha spoke about the Gandhian techniques of India's independence movement and the challenges posed by "quisling" elites as well as British "overlords" in the subcontinent. At the time, Sinha was also an economics professor at the Central YMCA College in Chicago. He later joined the dissident liberal and left-wing faculty members who chartered Roosevelt College downtown (now Roosevelt University). Sinha's contribution to this NCNW meeting of middle-class African American women was meant to inspire their own commitments to social action in the United States. A *Defender* columnist reports that Sinha felt U.S. blacks

Figure 3. Madeline Stratton Morris at a 1942 banquet honoring her curriculum-reform endeavors and Superintendent Johnson of the Chicago Public Schools. Madeline Stratton Morris Papers, Vivian G. Harsh Research Collection, Chicago Public Library.

could "secure their full measure of democracy" and that this might advance the worldwide prospect of enabling "subjected countries to choose their own governments and leaders."[58]

These global perspectives connected universal notions of racial equality with changing educational models for revisionist race relations. These models increasingly focused on psychosocial and affective remedies for racial discrimination through the mid-twentieth century. The best example of this approach in relation to African Americans was the "doll" tests devised and utilized by NAACP legal activists in school desegregation cases during the 1950s.[59] Stratton Morris underscored such views in her reflections on the need for curriculum reforms through the 1940s and 1950s. In her view, "wholesome attitudes" could be directed from early childhood. She hoped the country's "post-war history" would "reflect the change in attitude by new thinkers who will accord the Negro his rightful place in American history."[60] The educational and cultural projects undertaken by Stratton Morris also echoed an early Cold War orientalism similar to the one scholar Christina Klein examines. This orientalism forged transnational and intercultural relationships, just as it reinforced exotic notions of Asian mysticism and clairvoyance. For example, a *Defender* columnist describes the audience's reaction to Sinha's speech at the NCNW luncheon as "deeply moved" because of his "soft-spoken, fluent and convincing though somewhat plaintive voice." Sinha used no manuscript but spoke from "a heart which seemed at times to overflow with emotional (*sic*) because of the abject misery and futile efforts of his people."[61] On another occasion, in a *Defender* photo with the article "East Meets West," Stratton Morris is with a grade-school classmate, Tsuchen Kuan, at a tea that Stratton Morris and her husband, Samuel Stratton, hosted in Kuan's honor. Like Stratton Morris, Kuan was also involved with "youth education" but had returned to her native China for work.[62] Such middlebrow concerns over "youth education" displayed in East-meets-West scenes of collegiality could easily be mistaken as traditional African American uplift rhetoric for their embrace of respectability. Yet, a closer look at what teachers like Stratton Morris were trying to accomplish through such collaborations reveals a more complex vision for social change and educational method. These visions were clearly conscious of vital changes taking place on the terrain of global race relations.

Stratton Morris's curriculum work was also viewed as a valuable resource by the very leftist scholars whose work she researched to develop the units. The leftist perspectives and affiliations of such scholars may well have worried figures like Woodson, who wanted public-history efforts closely controlled in the context of early Cold War America. Still, she had no hesitation about corresponding with them about her work. Aptheker read about her curriculum units and asked her for information for his ongoing scholarly work. Such correspondence demonstrates fascinating collaborations between African American public schoolteachers and an influential Jewish American pioneer and authority in the growing field of African American history. Aptheker's engagement with black Chicago's cultural milieu during the 1940s was enhanced by the fact that he occasionally traveled from New York to lecture directly to South Side audiences. Much has been written on Aptheker's influence on the development of African American historical studies as a discipline and his influence, especially, on increased interest in black public history. Aptheker's legacy as a Marxist historian has also received extensive treatment and represents an important point of entry into any discussion about the Communist Party's engagement with black history as well as Jewish American engagements with civil rights, black nationalism, and the African American liberation struggle.[63]

Stratton Morris's correspondence with a figure of stature on the radical U.S. left such as Aptheker also reflects the attention leftists gave at midcentury to children's education, particularly children's literature. Julia Mickenberg notes how this shift may have been partly because many on the left were disillusioned with the politics of conventional revolutionary organizations like the CP after World War II. Notwithstanding how Cold War repressions and revelations of Soviet atrocities rendered CP appeals unpalatable, children's literature, as a distinct cultural form, offered left-wing activists a more hopeful, less ideologically driven medium through which to express pedagogical concerns and ideas.[64] Indeed, in 1947 Margaret Burroughs published her first book of children's literature, *Jasper the Drummin' Boy*, about the exploits of a young protagonist, Jasper Anderson, whose infatuation with drumming becomes a trope for engaging youth in a discussion about the contingencies of black identity. His mother first admonishes him for acting out on his "drums" at a piano recital at church after which he is grounded from attending a jazz show at Bronzeville's famous Regal Theater. "You're not an African warrior," she says. "You're an African American." Through a negotiation with his elders, Jasper proves his passion for drumming and connects to a worldly, if essential, notion of wishing he "was an African drummer . . . and [that he could] send messages all over Africa." He aspires to be like Barzillai Lew, a drummer and soldier who fought for the American Revolutionary cause, and to be like his grandfather, who played in the fictional Duke Oliver Windy City Band. Jasper also strives to be a "great drummer" like the fictional Chicago jazz man Stomp King and to be heard in the annual South Side community festival's Bud Billiken parade.[65] As a teacher, Burroughs's mapping of local, national, and worldly imaginaries through the story of *Jasper* stands as an important pedagogical statement from the 1940s. The book portrayed complex African American cultural and political themes in a positive frame at a time when few similarly designed forms of children's literature circulated in such a way. Burroughs's other works in children's literature include her most famous poem, "What Shall I Tell My Children Who Are Black," and books *Did You Feed My Cow* (1955) and *Whip Me, Whop Me Pudding and Other Stories of Riley Rabbit and His Fabulous Friends* (1966). This work made her part of a significant wave of left-wing women in the United States who expressed political dissent through children's literature during the early Cold War era.[66]

The engagement of leftists in pedagogical activities and black public history extended to institutional settings, as well. In the Abraham Lincoln School, Chicago had its equivalent of the Communist Party–founded New York–based Jefferson School of Social Sciences. Lincoln School, founded in 1943 by William Patterson, who taught "Negro History" there, after having worked on the recently disbanded local Communist newspaper, the *Midwest Daily Record*. The school was a collaboration between Patterson and various Chicago-based liberal educators and philanthropists, like Bousfield, and businesspeople who supported New Deal liberalism, such as department store magnate Marshall Field III, stockbroker Si Wexler, and interior decorator Clara Taylor. These well-heeled figures helped secure the school's location at the top of an office building in the Loop (Chicago's downtown business district). An afterthought of the popular-front coalition from earlier years and very short-lived, given the repressions of Cold War America, the school was only fully active for three years, from 1943 to 1946. It nonetheless brought together a significant cohort of Chicago cultural workers and progressive educators with broad social-justice agendas for their pedagogy—styled after the Whiggish legacies of the school's namesake. Patterson was inspired to form the school after "listening" to the discussions of itinerant preachers, workers, and political radicals in Washington Park. As such, he wanted to establish "a broad, nonpartisan school for workers, writers and their sympathizers." In the style of many contemporary left-wing labor and political organizers from his generation, Patterson felt that African American migrants fleeing oppression in the rural south and Europeans who fled religious and economic persecution could find common interracial ground in schools geared toward "worker education."[67] At the same time, Patterson emphasized that "[a]bove all . . . the many and varied contributions of black Americans to the economic, political, artistic and social life" of the United States "had to be uncovered."[68]

Lincoln School stands as a significant legacy of Chicago's radical left and popular front—with its open collaboration of leftists, liberals, and business leaders. This educational effort, in particular, illustrates how a significant current of black Chicago's cultural politics during the 1940s represented an uneasy merger between a popular front–style leftism rooted in Chicago's radical and working-class political traditions with new, highly differentiated entrepreneurial and professional classes who emerged from changing African American religious, business, and community networks.[69] Located at 30 West Washington Street, the school offered "low-tuition night courses, extension courses in factories and lectures." Associated Negro Press editor, poet, and left nationalist Frank Marshall Davis taught histories of jazz for the school. Other teachers included midwestern, white novelist Jack Conroy, who taught courses on creative writing. Chicago writers and bohemian literati, such as Bontemps, Willard Motley, Nelson Algren, and Richard Wright, at some point gave guest lectures at the school. The school's first director was British-born A. D. Winspear, an Oxford-educated scholar of Greek history. The board of directors came from the "ranks of labor, the middle class, the black nationalists, and somehow they found in one or another . . . a common interest." Patterson describes classes he taught on "Hitler racism," European imperialism, white supremacy, and anti-Semitism in the United States and emphasizes "the fact that these [racism and imperialism] were twin evils." In 1943 Langston Hughes opined that if he "had a kid," he would send them "neither to Howard nor Harvard" but, rather, to a "workers' school like the School for Democracy in New York [the Jefferson School] or the Abraham Lincoln School in Chicago." With the onset of the early Cold War in the late 1940s, many of Lincoln's erstwhile liberal supporters backed away from its upkeep, given the growing fears about international communism in the post–World War II era, so the school ceased operating regularly after 1948. Nonetheless, Patterson notes in his autobiography, he "never enjoyed any experience more than the building of the Abraham Lincoln School."[70]

Even more significant for the history of Chicago's South Side and left cultural politics, Patterson's wife, Louise Thompson, undertook the organization of DuSable Lodge 751 of the International Workers Order (IWO), which had nearly eighty-five thousand members nationwide through 1947 "at its height." Later known as the DuSable Community Center through the late 1940s and the packinghouse workers union hall in Chicago after 1949, the IWO became a significant cultural front organization during the World War II years. Like the South Side Community Art Center, the DuSable center was a site where numerous left-wing figures (notably, black artists like Elizabeth Catlett and Margaret Burroughs) organized art and writing workshops for South Side youth and where important progressive white artists with national reputations, such as Rockwell Kent, spoke. The community center occupied the old Bacon's Casino building at Forty-Ninth and South Wabash—just a block north of DuSable High School. When it was a casino, the building had also been a dance hall and thus already a prolific cultural site. Historian Erik McDuffie notes how the DuSable Lodge thrived under Thompson's directorship "as a bustling black political and cultural community center." The lodge reached over a thousand members by the end of the war years and also ran membership drives through other local community centers like the Ida B. Wells. [71]

Not unlike the Communists, U.S. Catholics were interested in worker education but from a differing ideological perspective that was more in line with the country's Cold War prerogatives. A school was opened in Chicago called the Sheil School of Social Studies, named after one of the city's liberal bishops, Bernard Sheil. During World War II, Sheil House had an enrollment of nearly 75 percent female students. It also focused on recognizing U.S. civil rights for the wartime services of African Americans. Teachers at Sheil House included black Catholic labor-organizer John Yancey and Harlem Renaissance luminary Claude McKay. Because she was a prominent, local curriculum reformer, Stratton Morris was asked to teach African American history courses through a lecture series that carried titles such as "The Negro in America," "History of the Negro People," "American Negro Literature," and "The History of Race Prejudice in America." The school continued into the early 1950s, but Sheil's brand of Catholic New Deal liberalism increasingly isolated the progressive bishop and his educational efforts from the mainstream of the mainly conservative Catholic Church throughout the Cold War era.[72]

Beyond Catholics, a small group of University of Chicago students (white and black) became pacifists during this period through a Methodist religious grouping established in the early 1940s called the Fellowship of Reconciliation (FOR). This group evolved more famously into the major mid-twentieth century U.S. civil rights organization known as the Congress of Racial Equality (CORE). FOR's activities consisted of small, nonviolent civil disobedience against Hyde Park gentrification and the segregation of local roller rinks and recreation areas. While its nucleus would grow into the nationally significant organization of the late 1950s and 1960s, its initial small membership and the fact that some members were ambivalent about independent black political and cultural initiatives limited its early impact. For instance, one of its founding members, Bernice Fisher, a white divinity student at the University of Chicago, opposed African American "bloc voting" and felt that Negro History Week was "mere chauvinism." On the other hand, she defended Randolph's March on Washington movement, which called for the desegregation of America's wartime industries. Such perspectives from this interracial educational and activist-oriented organization were certainly nuanced. They also reflected ambiguous (if limited) understandings of black politics by well-meaning white liberals.[73]

Other significant pedagogical institutions developed independently of public schools during this period, as well. Many of these institutions focused on early childhood education and elementary school–aged children. For example, the Howalton Summer School was established in 1946 at the Michigan Boulevard Garden Apartments by a group of African American teachers who had complained but received no response from Mayor Edward Joseph Kelly about the conditions of many South Side grammar schools. The school, which served "graduates" of a nursery school on the boulevard, went from kindergarten to eighth grade.[74] Moreover, the Abraham Lincoln Center in Kenwood (which continues to function, not be confused with the CP-founded school) was founded in 1905 and run by Unitarian ministers and teachers. Today, the building houses the Jacob H. Carruthers Center for Inner City Studies and is a campus of Northeastern Illinois University. The center became a significant South Side hub for extracurricular activities, such as dance classes, drama classes, and art education—especially after the neighborhood became predominantly African American through the 1910s and 1920s. In the early 1940s, the center hosted numerous receptions for figures such as Hughes in 1940 and Du Bois in 1941. While a professor of sociology at Atlanta University, Du Bois gave a lecture there on the history of slavery's abolition in the United States and abolition's failure to usher in an "era of economic opportunity" for blacks. Du Bois prophetically emphasized that any wartime peace arrangements had to "take into consideration the economic as well as political rights of the darker races" or else risk future wars.[75] Clearly, the center was also a significant site for the circulation of knowledge about black history on the South Side.

Outstanding Authorities

As the diverse engagement of religious progressives and leftist radicals with local black public history demonstrates, Stratton Morris was not alone in the curriculum and public-history work she did. Many became involved in black public activism of some form, and it is not difficult to see why, from the formative and authoritative perch of Woodson and the ASNLH, it might have been worrying that there was so much activity around black history outside of their purview. Foremost among those engaged in such activities, however, remained black teachers on the South Side—and these teachers, for the most part, seemed to recognize the importance of the ASNLH to their work.

Many Chicago public schoolteachers who were Stratton Morris's contemporaries and colleagues pioneered and promoted black curriculum supplements and extracurricular history activities. One such teacher was Florida Sanford, who organized a Negro History Club for "teaching boys and girls their own history" at Mixon's school, Douglas Elementary. After Sanford transferred to Burke Elementary, she established a similar club; her colleague Julma B. Crawford continued the one at Douglas. The Douglas club grew quickly and attracted other teachers, namely, Mary Williamson, Charlotte Stratton, and a "Mrs. McFarland." In her *Defender* article, Mixon recognized these teachers as "outstanding authorities on Negro history." The school's vice principals, Grace Mason and Howard B. Smith, contributed materials and guidance to the club. Though Mixon likely emphasized Douglas's teachers because she worked there, she also felt the school was unique because "the entire faculty furthered the study of Negro history throughout the school year." Also, the school had "an annual Negro History exhibit during Negro History week" to which it invited the entire South Side community and other schools. Nearly 50 percent of Douglas faculty had a subscription to the *Negro History Bulletin*—the ASNLH's chief organ for promoting public history.[76] Other schools in the district achieved similar levels of engagement with extracurricular forms of black public history that connected with civil rights work in the community. Even better than Douglas, Keith Elementary School claimed to have subscriptions in 1942 that reached 100 percent of its faculty. A teacher at Forestville Elementary, Ethel Hilliard, organized a club that achieved a 75 percent subscription rate among teachers at the school.[77]

The most important South Side high school for promoting black public history in the community was DuSable. The school at 4934 South Wabash opened in 1935 to accommodate the growing population at Wendell Phillips High School. The school was first called the New Wendell Phillips and renamed DuSable after the city's first settler.[78] One of the school's history teachers then was Samuel Stratton. His involvement in organizing black public history–related events on the South Side also made him a respected community figure. "More than any single individual," describes Mixon, "[Stratton] has made Negro history a living force in Chicago." Born in Asheboro, North Carolina, in 1897, Stratton first came to the city like many African American migrants seeking opportunity through education during the Great Migrations of the early twentieth century. He eventually received teachers training at the Chicago Teachers College (now Chicago State University) and pursued graduate studies in education at the University of Chicago. After teaching for several years in Baton Rouge, Louisiana, and St.

Louis, Missouri, Stratton came back to Chicago and taught in South Side public schools for the next thirty-two years, mostly at DuSable High School and Dunbar Vocational High School, from which he retired in 1962 as head of the social studies department. Stratton became closely involved with South Side social and civic life as a chief organizer of numerous public history–related clubs. He also helped to further the agendas of community institutions and organizations, such as the Parkway Community House and the local NAACP chapter, and of the radical left-wing cohort who founded the National Negro Museum and Historical Foundation (NNMHF).[79] The influence that prolific teachers from DuSable High School like Herrick, Walter Dyett, and others had on several generations of African American South Siders is recalled in Black's *Bridges of Memory* oral-history collection. Black, himself a DuSable High School alumnus, went on to a successful teaching career in public schools and city colleges. In Black's rich oral-history volume, former Chicago mayor Harold Washington (1983–87) talked about his history teachers at DuSable with fondness from the late 1930s and 1940s, notably Anna Sublette, who "made history come alive" through her infectious personality.[80]

These positive reflections of former students from South Side schools about teachers who promoted black history were paralleled by the civic-level liberalism of some school officials who, at least through the 1940s, were relatively open to addressing racial inequities in education. For instance, Mixon notes how school superintendent Johnson was liberal on racial issues for his time. If Johnson is compared to subsequent and notorious superintendents who oversaw the more famous school boycotts in the city during the late 1950s and 1960s— notably Benjamin Willis—Mixon's perception of a liberal moment in the early 1940s seems to ring true. Willis became a nation-wide symbol for northern white reactions and slow response to desegregation and school-funding issues. He was especially notorious for backing stopgap measures to create temporary school buildings in Chicago that became notoriously overcrowded and frequently dysfunctional. These temporary classrooms were derisively called Willis Wagons.[81] Superintendent Johnson never faced such controversies and actually acted on initiatives progressive educational reformers proposed, such as Stratton Morris's black-history units. He sent bulletins that compelled recognition and observance of Negro History Week and made some effort to cancel high school transfers of white students to the suburbs—a process white parents vociferously opposed and largely ignored.[82]

Notwithstanding Johnson's racial liberalism, historians of Chicago's public schools and its teaching profession feel his record was less than stellar. They note that he was squarely in the camp of the city's corrupt Democratic political machine through the 1940s and that he did little to advance public education overall. He also made patronage appointments for school-board members, fixed tests for principalships, offered school infrastructure contracts as political favors, and sometimes assigned textbooks written by him at a profit (which a National Education Association report states were in fields in which he was not a "recognized" authority).[83] Johnson ignored teachers' interests as unionists, was a nemesis of the Chicago Teachers Union (CTU), and opposed efforts by the union to influence school policy. Still, the union itself remained relatively uninterested in pushing for racial reform during the 1940s. When it came to supporting Stratton Morris's black history curriculum, the teachers union had little to say on the issue.[84] Black South Side teachers and their white allies were virtually alone (especially, among the wider profession of teachers in the city) in this period as the main proponents for antiracist curriculum reform in public schools.

Black public schoolteachers on the South Side were also at the forefront of supporting public history in the community and as extracurricular activities. The Strattons, in particular, were involved in efforts that extended well beyond the classroom, including his work to organize and publicize Negro History Week celebrations from the 1930s through the 1960s and hers to develop the city's first black-history curriculum.[85] South Side schools with Negro History Club programs included Copernicus, McCosh, Coleman, Douglas, and Doolittle Elementary Schools and Dunbar, Wendell Phillips, and DuSable High Schools. Mixon singled out Henry Mendellsohn, a Jewish American principal, for his work in promoting clubs at Doolittle. She explained how he was a "pioneer of Negro history in the public schools." Mendellsohn joined Samuel Stratton to sponsor a program on black history at Doolittle in 1937 before Stratton became a prominent civics teacher at DuSable High School and later at Dunbar Vocational High School. Knupfer has shown that Stratton Morris was also closely involved in the local DuSable History Club, started by her husband and which promoted black history in the community. He was also a key figure in the establishment of the NNMHF later in the 1940s.[86]

Many of these same teachers also became closely involved with the DuSable Memorial Society, another local public-history club, founded in 1928. Beyond the activities of local adherents of the Association for the Study of Negro Life and History, local public-history groups that paid tribute to the city's first settlers, such as the DuSable Memorial Society and the DuSable History Club, represented the pre–Cold War black-history movements of Chicago. The founder of the DuSable Memorial Society was Annie E. Oliver, a black migrant and teacher from Tennessee, an active clubwoman in the 1930s and 1940s, and a successful local beautician and entrepreneur.[87] While the DuSable Memorial Society's full relationship with the ASNLH remains unclear, the society certainly "aided" the national black public-history organization through the promotion of local Negro History Week efforts in the spirit Woodson set out at local churches and Washington Park, one of the South Side's historic gathering and outdoor public spaces.[88] These connections were underscored by the early use of the name DuSable in the society's name. Four decades before Margaret Burroughs's museum group members sought to rename their museum project this way,[89] the DuSable Memorial Society was, arguably, the first significant group to memorialize and celebrate the city's first settler. DuSable, a figure whose mixed "French-Negro" Haitian heritage and imagined involvement in the Revolutionary War with the British on the Ohio frontier, over time came to symbolize black Chicago's stake at midcentury in the founding of a modern city built on the southwestern mudflats of Lake Michigan.[90] The DuSable Memorial Society certainly represented an important aspect of the pre–Cold War black history movement in Chicago.

A key institution outside of local public schools that became a central site for the proliferation of black public history was the George Cleveland Hall Branch Library.[91] The library is only a few blocks from the famous intersection of Forty-Seventh and South Parkway, the symbolic cultural epicenter of black Chicago through midcentury. Horace Cayton and St. Clair Drake comment that if someone was "trying to find a certain Negro in Chicago" during this period, one stood "on the corner of 47th and Park long enough," and one was "bound to see him."[92] Stratton Morris would spend many nights and weekends at Hall Branch Library over the year and a half she devoted to her early curriculum-reform projects. Several scholars have demonstrated how the library became a major midwestern repository for African American history and culture—much like the Schomburg Center for Research in Black Culture is for New York City.[93]

Vivian G. Harsh, Hall's head librarian, and Charlamae Rollins, its children's librarian, spent years building branch holdings through travels mostly in the U.S. south from the 1930s onward. Together, Harsh and Rollins organized local study, storytelling, and drama groups and programs for a range of age groups. Harsh was also on the ASNLH's local Negro History Week committees; Rollins became a member of the Progressive Librarians Council (PLC) and under its auspices began a letter-writing campaign in 1941 to book publishers to raise awareness about the lack of available literature that spoke to "the experiences of African American children"—a campaign that resulted in an annotated book project, *We Build Together*. American studies scholar Julia Mickenberg notes how *We Build Together* was "one of the earliest guides to books about African American children." The Progressive Librarians Council, formed in 1939 through Librarians on the Left, fought segregation in public libraries throughout the United States, cooperated with organized labor, and promoted the acquisition of materials about labor issues and civil rights.[94] Together, Rollins and Harsh fostered a supportive and flourishing research environment for a teacher like Stratton Morris to carry out her curriculum-reform project. These black public-history spaces and projects were clearly simpatico.

Numerous other Chicagoans utilized the Hall Branch Library as an important site for developing innovative knowledge projects related to black public history. *Chicago Defender* writer and one-time Communist Richard Durham researched and wrote much of the content for his historical radio dramas at the library, namely, *Democracy U.S.A.* and *Destination Freedom*. These radio plays feature vignettes of African American figures in history and underscore histories of racial discrimination. They aired on a local NBC affiliate and a University of Chicago radio station during the late 1940s. One successful local African American bookseller Durham interviewed in the mid-1940s said how he and his wife had donated a collection of books on African Americans to the Hall Branch Library and envisioned the library's holdings as a rival of the "famous" Schomburg Library.[95] In an autobiography of his career in black journalism, *Chicago Defender* beat writer Enoch Waters relates how the library was an "invaluable resource" for his research while he worked for the paper during the 1930s and 1940s.[96] Overall, the Hall Branch Library played a crucial role as knowledge repository for African Americans involved in Chicago's cultural renaissance for the entire mid-twentieth-century period.

Through these vital and diverse Bronzeville institutional settings, the influence that schoolteachers and librarians, such as Stratton, Stratton Morris, Mixon, Harsh, Herrick, and many others, had on their students and on future efforts to reform curricula and promote black public history was profound and far-reaching. When asked about the effect such pioneering South Side schoolteachers had on education struggles, Timuel Black replied, "You see, we had the models." His view underscores the commitment that many South Side teachers had for working toward quality education—a point that surely reflects the ongoing frustrations many public educators have expressed in recent years about structural racial inequalities in the education system.[97] Black's use of the term "models" reflects the important role that teachers had (and continue to have) as conduits for state power and as conveyors of behavioral mores. Yet, in his telling, Black's terms are clearly used to underline a teacher's strategic role as a cultural activist, an interlocutor capable of transmitting values for a more democratic society to an informed citizenry and to young people, especially.

Despite the consistent funding shortfalls that plagued public educators, particularly in African American neighborhoods, the diverse models and resources for understanding social relations accessed by a significant number of public schoolteachers in Chicago during the 1930s and 1940s further reveal the complexities and richness of African American cultural politics and activism from this era. This was especially true as African American struggles for civil rights, jobs, and freedom accelerated through the 1950s. A useful terrain to further explore these important questions about connections between black public history and civil rights is to look at the work of those who envisioned building an African American–led museum project out of this same period.

CHAPTER TWO

Imagining a Black Museum
in Cold War Chicago

In its founding year of 1961, the home-based Ebony Museum of Negro History and Art, which a few years later was renamed the DuSable Museum of African American History, attracted 2,664 visitors (figures 4 and 5). By 1966 the museum's popularity had increased, since it attracted over 7,000 people annually to see exhibits of African, African American, and Mexican art. It also had a growing collection of cultural artifacts from poetry and folk-song manuscripts to recordings, writings on history, sculptures, and crafts that Charles and Margaret T. G. Burroughs had been collecting from their well-traveled friends through advertisements in the *Chicago Defender*, from the early 1950s to the museum's opening.[1] In his history of the museum, cofounder Eugene P. Feldman recalls his first experience at one of the Burroughses' popular salon parties that became the intellectual and physical settings from which the institution was ultimately envisioned and built:

> Here I found a most unusual cultural scene. There was a fellow there giving guitar lessons. Then Charles Burroughs, Margaret's husband, who had since boyhood gone to school in the USSR, began giving lessons in Russian. After the "hellos" they had all made me welcome. I waited in a butterfly chair . . . in an apartment that served as a gallery also. It had beautiful paintings, black and white sketches and sculpture. It had a large wooden picnic table around which we were, in many weeks, months, and years, to drink coffee and give birth to projects including the building of a Museum. I was thrilled to be in such a wonderful atmosphere.[2]

Feldman's recollection of the rich salon milieu from which the museum project was born was not unlike descriptions of other South Side cultural events. One reflection by the acclaimed African American poet and writer Gwendolyn Brooks of a party hosted a decade earlier by sculptor Marion Perkins, one of the Burroughses' closest fellow travelers, is strikingly similar in tone. Brooks notes how the salon she attended was not a "typical" Bronzeville affair but a racially "mixed" event that included black and white writers, artists, and various professionals from social workers to physicists—all enjoying martinis among

Figure 4. The original home of the DuSable Museum of African American History, 3806 South Michigan Avenue, in historic Bronzeville, ca. late 1960s. Eugene P. Feldman, *The Birth and the Building of the DuSable Museum* (Chicago: DuSable Museum, 1981), 48. Courtesy of DuSable Museum of African American History, Chicago, Illinois.

friends. While there was no "over-mastering din," Brooks observes that Margaret Burroughs sang the classic song "Hard Times Blues" from a cross-legged position on the floor, after which a local photographer encouraged others to offer more song and dance.[3]

This chapter examines how similar scenes, based on the reflections of DuSable Museum founders and their attendant public history–related labors,

Figure 5. Charles and Margaret T. G. Burroughs at the original location of the Ebony/DuSable Museum of African American History, ca. 1960s. The 3806 South Michigan Avenue mansion doubled as their home and is in a cultural hub of Bronzeville. The South Side Community Art Center is across and down the street. Eugene P. Feldman, *The Birth and the Building of the DuSable Museum* (Chicago: DuSable Museum, 1981), 47. Courtesy of DuSable Museum of African American History, Chicago, Illinois.

became vital for sustaining repertoires of black-history activism in Chicago from the 1940s through the early 1960s. Institutional histories, oral and written autobiographies, archival manuscripts, and local newspaper and magazine coverage deal, specifically, with the cohort of activists and friends in Chicago (led by the Burroughses) who founded what became known as the Ebony/DuSable Museum in Chicago—the first major, independent, black museum of its kind in the United States. Originally called the Ebony Museum of Negro History and Art, the museum was in 1968 renamed after the city's first non–Native American settler, Jean Baptiste Point DuSable. Today, over three hundred such museums operate throughout the United States and Canada.[4] This chapter considers the people who founded the DuSable Museum and from where they drew their inspiration for public-history activism. For many of the museum's founders, desire to create this cultural project was rooted in the leftist politics many had been involved with in previous decades—particularly, through the work of the National Negro Museum and Historical Foundation (NNMHF), an organization that enabled them a space to operate as leftists well into the 1950s. Such a longer-term vision for museum making explains why they engaged so earnestly in these efforts through the 1950s McCarthyism and contributed to larger discussions about black cultural politics and representations of black American identity in Chicago.

This chapter explains why the stakes of black public history in Chicago were so high—especially, through the early years of the Cold War. Before the vision came together for what ultimately became its first physical site in 1961, Margaret Burroughs and her colleagues attempted to lead a local chapter of the Association for the Study of Negro Life and History (ASNLH) to carry out similar work. As noted in chapter 1, the ASNLH was one of the main clearinghouses for African American academic and public-history materials and programs nationwide through the twentieth century. However, the McCarthyism of the 1950s is highlighted in this instance by the actions of black clubwoman Irene McCoy Gaines and hampered the efforts of Burroughs and her friends to reestablish a local ASNLH chapter. Gaines was suspicious of leftists of any stripe, as many U.S. liberals were during the Cold War years, and aggressively sought to control the establishment of a local ASNLH chapter—ultimately blocking Burroughs's attempts to recharter it. A review of this dispute, along with the important backstory about local black public-history activisms that this episode reveals, helps demonstrate how the vision for what would become the Ebony/DuSable Museum emerged from a highly contested political process as well as a longer local history of black public-history activism in Chicago. This very process of contention over black history was in and of itself a vital intellectual and political intervention into broader discussions concerning larger issues of representing African American identities in the public sphere from the early Cold War years through the early 1960s.

The Founders

The Ebony Museum's first physical locations and the backgrounds of its main founders underscore how public history in Chicago enabled the survival and persistent activity of an interracial group of cultural and labor activists from the 1940s through the 1960s. Burroughs first exhibited materials on African American history in a mansion on South Parkway (formerly Grand Boulevard and now Martin Luther King Jr. Drive) that she and her first husband, artist Bernard Goss, rented and used to display their artwork in the 1940s.[5] In 1959 she and her second husband, Charles Burroughs, bought the mansion at 3806 South Michigan Avenue in Chicago from the Quincy Club, a group of retired, black, railway workers and Pullman porters who had lived in the house since 1937.[6] One of the Quincy Club members was a migrant from Missouri named Ralph Turner, who remained centrally involved as a founder and lecturer for the museum when it became a prominent South Side institution through the mid-1960s and 1970s.[7] The founders of the museum also include librarian Marian Hadley; retired postal worker Gerard N. Lew, the museum's first president; Wilberforce Jones, a United Auto Worker member and later an Oxford University student fellow; Thelma Wheaton Kirkpatrick (who is the aunt of African American studies scholar Abdul Alkalimat/Gerald McWorter); and Feldman, teacher. Feldman was Jewish American and was originally raised in the Midwest, though much of his extended family lived in Montgomery, Alabama. He had been a civil rights and labor organizer in North Carolina during the 1940s and, like many local African American griots and elders, was an autodidact in black history. Feldman sought to continue similar work when he moved to Chicago in the 1950s and became acquainted with Margaret Burroughs through the Lake Meadows and Chatham neighborhood art fairs that she helped initiate.[8]

The Burroughses' biographies also fit earlier paradigms of activism that crossed ideological spectrums and diverse black experiences with human migration and community life through the mid-twentieth century. A descendant of slaves from Virginia, Charles Burroughs was raised by socialist parents in Harlem and Moscow, where he learned fluent Russian. His parents were products of northeastern U.S. public colleges and had been involved in depression-era welfare rights and tenant organizing in Harlem. Along with his siblings,

Burroughs attended school in Moscow during the 1930s. Inspired by Charles Chaplin's *City Lights* (1931), Charles became a circus trapeze artist; he drove a truck in Moscow in a self-described "patriotic activity" during World War II. He returned to New York and in 1950 moved to Chicago and married Margaret. Historian Erik McDuffie writes about Charles's mother, Williana Burroughs, her experiences with the Communist Party of the United States of America (CPUSA), and her conflicted residency in the Soviet Union through the 1930s. A number of other recent scholarly works have also treated African American engagements with the politics and culture of Soviet Russia during the middle decades of the twentieth century—notably, those of Mark Solomon, William J. Maxwell, Glenda Gilmore, and Kate Baldwin.[9]

Margaret Burroughs's self-representation as a leftist was more ambiguous. In autobiographical texts, Burroughs notes how she has been described as a "progressive," a "militant," or a "radical." Still, in these texts, she does not fully self-represent in these terms. Burroughs maintains she was never a member of the Communist Party. Rather, Burroughs underscores her Catholic upbringing (from her mother's side) and, particularly, the influence of an Irish Catholic primary schoolteacher in Chicago, Mary L. Ryan, who encouraged her early interest in visual art. Burroughs could not afford to supplement a scholarship she received to attend Howard University, and Ryan mentored her through teaching degrees at Chicago Normal College (1939) and a master's degree at the Art Institute of Chicago (1948). Burroughs recalls Booker T. Washington's uplift "bucket" metaphor to explain her decision to situate her cultural labors locally in Chicago—which certainly extends the black political traditions she lays claim to. She also represents her family's history as typical for migrants from the U.S. south following World War I. She highlights her father's mixed Native American and African ancestry; the family's proximity in St. Rose, Louisiana, and the linguistic cultural world of the French-Spanish Caribbean, where she was born in 1915; and her family's working-class status (her mother was a domestic, her father a farmer and in Chicago secured temporary work in the stockyards). Moreover, Burroughs highlighted her family's subsequent struggles to establish themselves as part of the first major wave of black southerners from the trans-Mississippi-Louisiana region to the urban north. Burroughs's narrative collapses the political geography of migrant experience into her recollection of the cultural salons she convened on Chicago's South Side as part of the city's black cultural renaissance. To her, these informal and diverse Bronzeville-based gatherings in people's homes fostered both her intellectual and political commitment to public history from the 1930s through the 1960s and became her "family's St. Rose dinner table from memory, displaced-good times transferred across state, class, and cultural lines."[10] Though her experiences reflect the inevitable personal changes wrought by human migration, they also reflect a temporal sense of continuity across both time and space.

The persistence of figures such as the Burroughses and their black-history allies over the 1950s defies conventional understandings of black American experiences during the early Cold War. James Smethurst suggests that for Chicago, in particular, "left-influenced African American institutions of the 1940s largely disappeared during the Cold War" and those that survived this moment, such as the South Side Community Arts Center and the *Chicago Defender* (like in the labor movement of the same period), purged many known leftists from their ranks.[11] There were certainly many Cold War dispersions in the late 1940s and 1950s with Chicago writers and cultural workers, such as Richard Wright, Lorraine Hansberry, and many others, compelled to move far afield to practice their crafts. Still, Smethurst notes, the remainder of the black left in Chicago (chiefly, Margaret Burroughs and her museum cohort) focused "on art and education even more intensely as a means of maintaining a presence in the African American community within the constraints of McCarthyism."[12] It was through institutions, such as the South Side Community Arts Center and the DuSable Museum of African American History, that such black leftists maintained their presence during an otherwise politically repressive period.

Museum Origins

The vision led by the Burroughses and their friends for a black-history museum in Chicago was a long-standing one. It was sustained from the 1940s through the 1960s by a broad and intergenerational cross-section of activists who associated closely with the Burroughses and worked over decades to realize the vision for a black-led history museum through the NNMHF. Margaret Burroughs became a key member of this group of ten black labor, civic leaders, and teachers. The NNMHF was based in Chicago and initiated the city's first significant attempt to establish an African American history museum in 1945. Its activities immediately preceded the curriculum-reform efforts of the ASNLH and the Chicago Board of Education.[13] As Andrea A. Burns notes, "the networks Margaret and Charles Burroughs established through their prior activism in organizations like the NNMHF and the ASNLH became crucial resources."[14] Thus, the NNMHF's efforts were but one front among many diverse ideologically driven efforts to promote black history in ways that underscored the regional identities and public representations of black Americans in the Midwest and Chicago through the Cold War era.

While it existed, the NNMHF became closely associated with militant civil rights formations in the city and around the country. NNMHF members included Margaret and Charles Burroughs, community activist John Gray, local Communist Party member and union activist Ishmael Flory, Associated Negro Press editor and writer Frank Marshall Davis, and older, well-respected community figures, such as public schoolteacher Samuel Stratton and John Bray of the Colored Episcopal Church. Margaret Burroughs became the NNMHF's financial secretary. Most of these members were also local members of the National Negro Congress (NNC), a broad civil rights organization that became progressively Communist-influenced over its history. The NNC's first convention, in Chicago in 1936, attracted 750 delegates from twenty-eight states. Generally made up of left-leaning, liberal black labor activists with chapters in cities across the United States, the NNC's activities highlighted a wartime and immediate postwar era of significant militant black activism and protest and certainly help support the notion of a "long" civil rights era over the mid-twentieth century. The NNC was more than just an average civil rights organization. In the words of historian Erik Gellman, it worked to confound "class and racial boundaries." Initially, it attracted the support of the acclaimed black American socialist, labor, and civil rights leader A. Phillip Randolph, who felt that the NNC could set "a great precedent on the part of Negro Workers . . . [by] . . . destroying all of the poisonous seeds of jim-crowism." In effect, the NNC hoped to lead a broader movement for economic and racial justice in America. Tragically for the congress, its increasing association with the radical left in the U.S. labor movement enabled "much of its activism" but also "hampered associations with other New Deal and urban African American constituencies."[15] Figures such as Randolph ultimately broke with the NNC and contributed to its demise in 1947. This demise reflected the growing anti-Communism of Cold War America, which would dissolve many other institutions on the radical left (such as the Civil Rights Congress and the National Negro Labor Council) by the early to mid-1950s.

However, just prior to the NNC's decline in the late 1940s, the NNMHF effectively continued the NNC's cultural activities in Chicago through this decade. These activities revolved especially around public celebrations and recognitions of black history.[16] Federal Bureau of Investigation (FBI) files characterize the NNMHF as a Communist-led organization designed to encourage the "research and study, and the collection, compilation, integration and dissemination of information, data, material and objects on and in connection with the history and progress of the Negro peoples."[17] Gray, the last NNC Chicago council executive secretary, also held the same position with the NNMHF—a connection that highlighted how civil rights activism and black public-history labors could be two sides of the same coin. In the late 1940s, Gray made some important reflections and political interventions on the significance of black-led public-history efforts in the city. Gray appealed to U.S. Senator Glenn Taylor of Idaho, who had spoken against the seating of segregationist, white Mississippian Theodore Bilbo in the U.S. Congress. In a letter to Taylor, Gray solicited his participation in a "mass meeting" to celebrate Negro History Week in February 1947. Although "History Week" was certainly celebrated in other American cities with growing populations of southern black migrants, Gray felt that Chicago's celebrations had become one of the more "prominent traditions" for the city. A proclamation from Mayor Ed Kelly indicates that both the NNC and the NNMHF "extended activities during this week," and an NNMHF news release promotes local history events and describes a joint meeting of the two organizations that coordinated the celebrations.[18]

The connection between public-history labors and leftist politics was not lost on important observers of black Chicago from the mid-twentieth century. Local college professor and coauthor of *Black Metropolis* (the classic study of Chicago's African American community) St. Clair Drake recalls the significance of the NNMHF in a revealing unpublished interview from 1969. In this interview, Drake comments extensively on Chicago history and politics—for which he was a living expert, beyond his formidable expertise in what was then the pioneering field of African studies. Reflections by one of Drake's former students at Roosevelt College, John Bracey (who himself became an expert in African American history), indicate Drake's openness to ideological viewpoints inside and outside his classroom. This same respect was shared by community activists, such as Flory and fellow Communist Claude Lightfoot, as well as the local griots who organized the regular Washington Park Forum, who encouraged students from Roosevelt to learn as much as they could from Drake.[19] Such intergenerational and cross-ideological rapport clearly gave Drake's local perspectives additional importance beyond that of *Black Metropolis* to any study of the city's African American community.

In the 1969 interview, Drake notes the uniqueness of Cold War conditions in the city for black Communists who channeled energies into public history–related "cultural" projects and noted how the communists by the 1950s were "a broken breed in Chicago," that "[t]he McCarthy thing had put them down," and that they were "infiltrated with the FBI so heavily that they" did not "know which way to turn." He suggests an entente had been reached between the NNMHF's more left-leaning members (notably, Margaret Burroughs and Flory) and Chicago's black Democratic congressman, William Dawson, whose race-brokerage style of politics as the titular head of Chicago's black Democratic submachine kept him in an ongoing struggle to appease the city's notorious and corrupt Democratic civic leadership. Drake suggests that from that point, Chicago's black Communists "never raised an issue of an international nature. They stayed off of issues about war and peace and revolution and that sort of thing. They never got into a real local fight but they went in for the study of Negro history." In exchange, Dawson helped the NNMHF and history groups that emerged later with the civic machine. For example, the Afro-American Heritage Association (AAHA), founded in 1958 by Flory and Christine C. Johnson, encouraged Chicago mayor Richard J. Daley (1955–76) and Illinois governor Otto Kerner Jr. (1961–68) in the late 1950s and 1960s to proclaim Negro History Week, "as long as . . . [the Communists] . . . stayed on that strict cultural nationalist line."[20]

Writings by black Communists involved in the CPUSA leadership and policy decisions in the late 1940s and 1950s certainly suggest the potential for these claims. At this time, the CPUSA advanced a program that strategically focused on notions of "culture" as a weapon in the freedom struggles of African Americans just as it continued to focus on organizing in the labor movement through the late 1930s and 1940s.[21] Indeed, the focus of many black Communists in Chicago was still on interracial trade-union activism through the mid-1950s—hallmarks of the popular front of previous decades. This is well illustrated by the successful role of the United Packinghouse Workers of America (UPWA), affiliated with the Congress of Industrial Organizations (CIO), in promoting antidiscrimination and civil rights on the shop floor and in black community issues—in effect sustaining a black-led cultural front. When the UPWA decided to move its headquarters in 1949 to the old Bacon's Casino/DuSable Community Center building in the heart of the black community, the location had most recently been used by the International Workers Order, where Louise Thompson Patterson (wife of renowned black Communist William Patterson) helped organize CP-sponsored cultural events in the late 1930s and 1940s.[22] While there is much more to be understood about the complex role of Communist race relations and African American political culture in 1950s urban America, generally, it could be that another key focus and front for black Party members, fellow travelers, and their allies were the fostering of diverse cultural sites for public history. These efforts were not explicitly about political protest on the shop floor or in the street but, rather, offered expressive repertoires for creative dissent within and from the black community.

Margaret Burroughs clearly regarded her efforts to promote black history as a different repertoire than civil rights protest. "[W]e had sympathy with [the civil rights movement]," she notes. "I imagine a lot of Chicagoans participated in it. I spent my time working on black history work and didn't have time to work with them because of what I was working on."[23] Regardless of any backroom deals with the civic machine and/or FBI infiltrations, this perceived shift to historical labors could have come down to a question of tactics and strategy for the activists involved, given the political atmosphere of Cold War America. Such endeavors certainly attracted attention from government surveillance networks although risked less in this moment than more overt forms of public protest, such as direct action sit-ins and demonstrations or rallies. This was especially true if these activities were conducted under the auspices of Communist and/ or other leftist peace banners that were sure to attract greater repression and negative attention.[24] Indeed, it was risky enough at the height of the McCarthy period with anti-Communist equations of anything that smacked of civil rights and/or black strivings for self-determination to Communism, often regardless of affiliations on the political spectrum.[25]

Though an entente with Congressman Dawson and the civic Democratic machine may well have taken place, the activities of the historical foundation were not strictly cultural in orientation.[26] In fact, the NNMHF continued to make broad appeals in its promotional materials and activities to radically reform U.S. democracy in an international context. For example, a 1946 poster demonstrates that the foundation was a black-led, broadly based, multigenerational effort.[27] The NNMHF's activities stretched over several decades and reflected cosmopolitan concerns to redress racial discriminations globally, assert universal citizenship rights, and publicly represent distinguished African American pasts in the making of an inclusive American "Present and Future" through the celebration of abolitionist figures, such as Frederick Douglass and Sojourner Truth. The group also highlighted the world historical moment of the late 1940s. This period marked a shift away from the wartime observance of black history that the parent organization, the NNC, conducted. Gellman notes how the NNC actually used black history to "understand the current war."[28] For many African Americans, this shift in perceptions within the black public sphere occurred against the backdrop of fascism in both Europe and the United States and of Jim Crow proscriptions at home. With wars against fascist states ended in Europe, the group criticized American statesmen for ostensibly "democratizing" China while the poll tax was "protected" in the U.S. south, preventing one-tenth of the country's people "the right to participate in the selection" of government.[29]

The NNMHF's promotional materials also reveal more about the foundation's diverse activities. Like the NNC, the NNMHF explicitly connected civil rights and protest activities with black-history celebrations. The 1946 poster describes how the foundation had been "established to stimulate a wider interest in the Negro History Week movement," with the goals of establishing a museum of black "history and culture," to collect records of cultural achievements, and to host classes and seminars on black history.[30] A Negro History Folder the NNMHF produced the following year contains similarly captioned photographs as the 1946 promotional poster but also recalls a downtown demonstration "against lynching" that featured Sam Parks, then a young leader of a Chicago UPWA local. The event also featured prolific black actor and progressive spokesperson Canada Lee as keynote speaker.[31] Indeed, the NNMHF held annual Negro History Week exhibits at the UPWA's district 1 union hall, East Forty-Ninth Street and South Wabash Avenue in Bronzeville.[32] While such figures as writer and poet Frank Marshall Davis would leave Chicago during the McCarthy period, others less overtly left-wing in their politics, such as Sam Stratton, stayed in the city and promoted black history and other related cultural events while keeping the vision for a black-history museum alive. Promotional materials for the NNMHF also feature pictures of a proposed site for a museum in Chicago and mentioned an imagined future to rival the most widely acclaimed U.S. black-history research archive, the Schomburg Center for Research in Black Culture in New York. The NNMHF also announced a mass meeting to discuss opposition to a filibuster against the proposed U.S. Senate bill to make permanent the Fair Employment Practices Committee (FEPC). The announcement highlights southern anti–Jim Crow protests and demands for minimum wages and features captioned photo montages of black pastors and older cultural figures of the 1930s and 1940s, such as Paul Robeson and Langston Hughes, as well as younger figures, such as Lena Horne.[33]

Coverage of the nascent museum foundation in the *Chicago Defender* suggests that its organizers, Stratton and Gray, were at the center of FEPC and anti–Jim Crow campaigns in Chicago. In particular, the paper featured a rally in the Loop after Loop hotels banned attempts to organize Black History Week events on their properties. As black community historian and housing rights activist Dempsey Travis has written, "[t]he Stevens (later the Hilton), the Sherman House, and the Congress Hotels in downtown Chicago refused to accommodate the NNMHF for a planned celebration of 'Negro History Week.'" The boycott garnered support from a broad coalition of liberal and labor groups from the Chicago Civil Liberties Committee to the Federated Hotel Waiters Union (local 356), and local representatives of the UPWA, notably Sam Parks from the Wilson packing plant (local 20) and Armour plant (local 347) organizer Herbert March. Support from the left-leaning UPWA was especially significant. In the late 1940s and 1950s, the UPWA occupied a fairly unique position (even compared with other left-leaning CIO affiliates) as an institutional facilitator of black community activism from the 1940s through to the 1960s.[34] As historian Lionel Kimble has shown, labor and housing "[p]rotest activism was amplified at a time when a brief window of opportunity emerged where African Americans and their allies saw a realistic chance to challenge entrenched employment and housing discrimination in the city in the wake of World War II."[35]

The observance of black-history week reached significant levels of public recognition. It consistently involved prominent city labor activists and South Side civic leaders alike in these activities. As such, the event also linked to broader issues of fair employment and the open use of public facilities (issues that were synonymous with civil rights in the city).[36] Moreover, the attempt to promote spatial recognition within Chicago's historic hotel district as well as a future site for a history museum on the South Side mapped a significant juncture in the making of twentieth-century black Chicago's modern political geographies.

The NNMHF is recalled in oral and written texts produced by DuSable Museum founders and shows how the histories of both organizations are connected across the "long" civil rights era. These texts demonstrate how the cultural activism embodied in black-history projects from the 1940s, such as the NNMHF, relate directly to the labors of black public-history activists during the 1950s and 1960s. An early written history of the DuSable Museum was done by one of its founders, Eugene Feldman. Feldman situates Margaret Burroughs's nationalism "back in the 1930s . . . [when she] was writing and thinking Black," belonged to the youth chapter of the NAACP, and wrote for the Associated Negro Press. Feldman relates how in the 1940s, Margaret Burroughs, Gray, and others formed the NNMHF. He also suggests that the foundation contained "the spirit and premier effort that finally gave birth to the DuSable Museum."[37] Thus, the spirit for a black-history museum extended from the mid-1940s when the NNMHF was first established through the very conversations and discussions that gave "birth" to the museum by 1961.

In many of her autobiographical reflections, Margaret Burroughs echoes Feldman's contention about the museum's vision rooted in previous decades of activism and left ideologies. Burroughs's primary identity as a left-wing cultural activist is exemplified by her retrospective on the politics of art—whether through her actual artwork or even her sense of aesthetic self-representation. Burroughs felt that "[a]rt should make a statement . . . a positive statement." On the question of both subject and audience in art, Burroughs indicates a primary concern for "the little people, the street people." She felt that "every artist or every writer, whatever they say should be a statement for the total, complete liberation of our people." She also realized the danger that "the capitalistic system encourages artists to do all this stuff that says nothing," and so prudence as an artist was always needed.[38]

Burroughs's commitment to political art and activism born through her salon, history, and culture-making activities and mapped through personal memories of sojourning abroad demonstrates the complexities of her left-wing sensibilities over the twentieth century. As such, her reflections weigh the importance of social experiences in political identity formation—also a tenet of the social realist perspectives on art she shared with black Chicago renaissance contemporaries, such as Charles White, Useni Eugene Perkins, and others. For Burroughs, the combination of her South Side salon milieu and public-history labors, formative New Deal era experiences with the artistic milieus of black popular-front organizations, such as the South Side Community Art Center, and her anticapitalist viewpoints placed her activities within a Marxist frame just as C. L. R. James's writings in 1950s New York were reflective of "bolshevik sensibilities."[39] As Stacy I. Morgan indicates, the "African-American-controlled institutional anchor [of these older institutions born as they were in the 1930s and 1940s] helped affiliated artists and writers to sustain social realist cultural work in an array of disciplines well into the early Cold War era."[40] Indeed, the activism around the pursuit of related black public-history activities arguably sustained this "cultural work" the longest—right through the 1960s.

Margaret Burroughs was actually motivated (not deterred) by her troubles with McCarthyism in the 1950s to found a museum project. For example, she faced FBI surveillance and, most notably, Chicago Police Department harassment at her doorstep. This harassment led to her appearance before the Chicago Public School's Board of Education in 1952 where civic authorities attempted unsuccessfully to attain information from her about local Communists and their activities.[41] As one scholar notes, left-leaning Chicago teachers "faced further scrutiny from the Chicago Police Departments Subversive Unit, or 'Red Squad,' which investigated the political activities of all those who applied to or worked for the city, state, and county, and especially the Chicago public schools" in the 1940s and 1950s.[42] The Chicago Red Squad investigated Burroughs because she participated with Communists in a number of political activities and attended civil rights meetings and demonstrations in the 1940s and early 1950s.[43] A brief perusal of Burroughs's Red Squad file indicates the high level of surveillance she and many others were subjected to in Chicago (and other cities) by local city police departments—in addition to FBI harassment and monitoring. Burroughs's file includes entries on seventy-four public events she allegedly attended and/or publications she authored or was mentioned in between 1950 and 1968.[44]

Museum cofounder Feldman was also tracked by Chicago Police through this period and shared her commitment to socially committed art and politics. He was equally motivated by the very repressions he faced as a leftist. Feldman's Red Squad file charts his record of writing in the radical left-wing press, notably, for the *Daily Worker* and the *National Guardian* based in New York and the *Southern Newsletter* in Kentucky (the latter a newsletter that covered issues of civil rights and racial prejudice within organized labor in southern states). Feldman's file traces his activities through his relocation to Chicago and the Midwest in the late 1950s, where he continued to be involved with local progressive causes and labor and civil rights activism and where he became closely acquainted with Margaret Burroughs through the art fairs and black public-history works she promoted locally.[45]

Chicago's black public-history activists were certainly not alone among the many African Americans the FBI and local Red Squads monitored. As scholars such as Maxwell have shown with respect to African American cultural workers, these very registries of surveillance were designed to predict and prevent so-called radical unrest—a characterization that certainly applied to the broader liberal-left, as well. Local police forces, like those of the Chicago Police Red Squads who worked in alliance with conservative cultural organizations like the American Legion and the Legion of Justice, often shared their intelligence with the federal-level House Un-American Activities Committee (HUAC) and the FBI.[46] Indeed, Red Squad scholar Frank Donner indicates that urban police squads across the United States have "served as the protective arm of the economic and political interest of the capitalist system."[47] Historian John Lyons describes that the "red scare often turned into a black scare as Red Squads put African Americans from across the political spectrum who supported civil rights under suspicion of communism."[48] In Chicago, Red Squad surveillance combined with FBI surveillance and represented a profound violation of constitutional liberties for many citizens—not to mention the implicit support such infrastructures of surveillance represented for state-sanctioned violence and intimidation. However, because state security agencies monitored their subjects and targets so closely, an unintended consequence of these vast records was the creation of an archive for later public reception, dissemination, and study that literally helped to define a canon of dissident black American literary and cultural production over the twentieth century. Maxwell makes this point in his book *F.B. Eyes: How J. Edgar Hoover's Ghostreaders Framed African American Literature*. Individuals whose FBI files Maxwell was able to uncover for this study ran across the left spectrum: from itinerant and radical Chicago writer Wright to the decidedly liberal NAACP's Walter White. In the "depths of the Cold War . . . no fewer than twenty-two African American literary intellectuals were first tracked by the Bureau paperwork, among them Frank London Brown, Alice Childress, Harold Cruse, Shirley Graham Du Bois, Lonne Elder III, Ralph Ellison, E. Franklin Frazier, Lorraine Hansberry, Calvin Hernton, Lance Jeffers, Charles S. Johnson, Bob Kaufman, Julian Mayfield, Willard Motley, William Pickens, Saunders Redding, and William Gardner Smith." Notwithstanding the obvious surveillance of someone like W. E. B. Du Bois, whose FBI file exceeds 750 pages, the nation's Cold War registries clearly had a place for numerous dissident black American writers and thinkers from across the political spectrum. These included scholars engaged in many fields, from sociologist E. Franklin Frazier to iconoclastic cultural-studies pioneer Harold Cruse to left-wing playwright Hansberry.[49]

Like many of the above-mentioned figures, such surveillance and harassment did not completely impede Burroughs and many of her colleagues (both black and white) who were subjected to similar treatments. Despite "hard times" as a student of art education at Chicago's Institute of Art, where she had to balance part-time work with intensive study and when she was nearly kicked out for missing tuition payments and for sometimes low marks, Burroughs managed to complete a bachelor's degree and a master's degree in 1946 and 1948, respectively.[50] In fact there was hope for aspiring public teachers during this period, despite the hardships they faced if they were nominally left-wing and/ or progressive. Public teachers' salaries in Chicago steadily increased from the 1940s to 1953, from monthly minimums for elementary schoolteachers from $135 to $250 and for high schoolteachers from $200 to $288. Certainly, there were ongoing issues of racial discrimination in public schools regarding teaching appointments and social studies curricula. For example, black teachers were often assigned to overcrowded South Side schools and classrooms. However, reforms toward pay equity occurred in a period of expanding U.S. unionized workers' salaries over the post–World War II years—this was an era of overall affluence for the American working class (although blacks were invariably at the bottom end of this prosperity). Also, despite the anti-Communist leanings of Chicago Teachers Union (CTU) leaders, such as John Fewkes and Mary L. Herrick, the union generally supported teachers brought before government committees concerned with un-American activities. Teachers like Margaret Burroughs with leftist reputations would continue to teach despite the threat of reprimands that resulted from the Cold War climate.[51]

As such, instead of relinquishing her teaching job with the city under such pressures, Burroughs stepped back and applied for an enviable one-year sabbatical to Mexico. There, she sojourned with her family and joined other prominent African Americans (namely, Elizabeth Catlett and Charles White) to Mexico

City's Taller de Gráfica Popular arts school in 1952. In Mexico, Burroughs studied with renowned Mexican painters, muralists, and sculptors—notably, Leopold Mendez and Francisco Mora. She also met José David Alfaro Siqueiros. Through these experiences, Burroughs refined her skills in charcoal and stencil linocut forms—all of which became trademarks for her later visual art. For Burroughs, the year in Mexico "strengthened" her "in more ways than one—not only artistically, but morally and intellectually" so that when she "came back to Chicago," she "was in a fighting mood" determined to oppose any efforts to remove her from her teaching position in Chicago public schools. After her return, Burroughs notes, "Nobody ever called me in for questioning . . . again," and she was able to return to DuSable High School to resume teaching art and art history until she was eventually promoted as a teacher to community colleges by the late 1960s. Burroughs adapted many Mexican artistic aesthetics into her printmaking and linocut drawing techniques. American studies scholar Rebecca Schreiber suggests that a cohort of African American artists sought both temporary and permanent refuge through the Mexican art scene and distinguishes their approaches to modern art from the "universalist" abstract expressionism that had become more commercially viable in the United States during the 1950s.[52] Clearly, these experiences were not debilitating. Such experiences strengthened Burroughs and her cohort and provided them with motivation for continuing to take on the earnest labors for black public history.

Contested Public History

Despite Burroughs's and other teachers' successful negotiation of Cold War repressions, the role that public-history efforts had in Chicago appeared marginal. This was true if interest in public history was gauged solely on local activities associated with the ASNLH. Indeed, no local chapter of the ASNLH had been fully active in the city since the 1930s. Upon her return from Mexico in the mid-1950s, Margaret Burroughs and her friends attempted to revive a local chapter of the ASNLH as one way to continue the work of the NNMHF and the black public-history labors of past decades. However, their efforts were at least partially thwarted by Chicago clubwoman Gaines, who managed to convince the ASNLH's national office in Washington, D.C., to refuse Burroughs's group the right to charter a local chapter because of their left-wing associations and affinities. Burns writes that when the chapter application was revoked, "McCarthyism threatened" such organization in Chicago.[53] These challenges were paralleled by struggles that the South Side Community Arts Center faced over the same period. A more extensive treatment of this episode reveals a great deal about the stakes of black public-history activism in Cold War Chicago and the contested nature of public representations of black American identities.

The inconsistently active status of a local ASNLH chapter in Chicago ultimately continued until 1964 when one was finally reestablished. Indeed, a perusal of the ASNLH's community and public history–oriented publication *Negro History Bulletin* from the 1940s through the 1960s rarely featured Chicago in the bulletin's coverage of Negro History Week celebrations. In fact, the bulletin regularly features other mid-twentieth-century black metropolises, such as Detroit, Atlanta, and Washington, D.C., but Chicago's black-history activities are conspicuously absent.[54] People in Chicago still subscribed to the ASNLH's journals over this period, contributed to its publication, and generally supported the association's efforts. Indeed, the ASNLH had a long history in Chicago. After all, it was founded there in 1915 by Carter G. Woodson and his associates. Lorenzo D. Turner, Drake's colleague at Roosevelt College and an English scholar and pioneer in the study of Gullah dialect and African cultural survivals in the Americas, corresponded frequently with executives at the ASNLH over the 1950s about contributions he made to the association's efforts. The *Chicago Defender* and editor Morris Lewis also regularly featured and promoted the association's activities in both the newspaper's daily and national print editions, through the 1940s, especially.[55]

The fact that there was controversy over the establishment of an ASNLH chapter during the mid-1950s, however, reveals the significant levels of interest in the promotion of black public history in Chicago and how public history became an aspect of civil rights advocacy that underscored the complexities of African American cultural politics during the early Cold War era. In 1955 Margaret Burroughs and a group of local teachers and community activists that included local Communist leader Flory spearheaded efforts to reestablish the dormant ASNLH chapter. Initial responses from the association's staff in Washington, D.C., were positive about Burroughs and her "group" (who remained unnamed in correspondence). However, in the same year, clubwoman Gaines was appointed as an executive to the ASNLH's national council and decided to block the group from obtaining a charter for the chapter. As an executive, Gaines held the right to screen the background of applicants. She was also a civil rights activist in her own right and had been active during the 1940s with the collective work that went into the important curriculum-reform efforts carried out through Chicago's public schoolteachers and local black civic organizations. Gaines, president of the National Association of Colored Women (NACW) during the 1950s, was a key organizational figure in black Chicago's cultural renaissance during the postwar years. She was also a lifelong member of the Republican Party and, in this sense, represented a prominent and vocal political current in African American public life during the 1950s that firmly advocated for a form of Cold War racial liberalism. This political current promoted civil rights for blacks regardless of Democratic or Republican Party allegiances. In the spirit of the times, her racially liberal politics, nonetheless, included a healthy suspicion of left-wing, particularly, Communist, associations.[56] The reasons for the blocked local ASNLH chapter application had to do with the left-wing associations of Margaret Burroughs and her cohort as well as the high stakes involved in representing black public-history efforts during the Cold War.

Correspondence between Gaines, ASNLH staff, and Burroughs reveals much about the tensions that surrounded both Cold War and racial politics during this period. It also demonstrates the earnestness with which cultural activists from across the political spectrum approached black public history as a viable repertoire for civil rights activism. In a letter to Gaines that praised her for her nationally recognized work with the NACW, Albert Brooks (ASNLH national secretary-treasurer) initially thought Gaines would be "glad" to know about the formation of a local chapter by Margaret Burroughs; according to Brooks, Burroughs had retained Turner as an "advisor" for her group. An earlier letter from Burroughs to Turner indicates that her group had invited him to speak about the nature of ASNLH activities at the Washington Park YMCA. The ASNLH initially expressed enthusiasm in the fall of 1955 from both Gaines and the ASNLH toward Burroughs's application. However, under the direction of its then president, Charles Wesley, the ASNLH soon cited a "rather unforeseen development" that had "come up regarding certain officers and members" involved in the Chicago chapter application. The ASNLH, which wanted Turner to confer specifically with Gaines about the appointment of anyone interested in establishing a local chapter, felt it was to "be careful to avoid jeopardizing the future support of the Association . . . [that it] needs the help of all who believe in the fundamental rights and dignity of all mankind." Furthermore, the correspondence from Wesley implies that Burroughs would work with the more mainstream DuSable Memorial Club/Society as a compromise and that "gradually" through this parallel black history "club . . . these questionable people [Burroughs by implication] could be eliminated."[57]

In his reply to the ASNLH, Turner distances himself from any direct association with Burroughs's history group. Turner maintains he had met with them on only two occasions, one of which was to give an "illustrated lecture on African music and its influence on New World music." He indicates he had "no knowledge" of the members' political affiliations and that he was certainly not an "adviser to the group—whatever that term might mean." Moreover, Turner suspects that because of his "long connection with the [ASNLH] . . . members of the group have felt free" to ask "questions" about its work. He adds that he had "no knowledge" of the political affiliation of members in Burroughs's group, although he recalls that Flory had previously been a student at Fisk University when Turner worked there "several years ago" prior to his appointment at Roosevelt. In fact, while a student at Fisk, Flory helped organize a Denmark Vesey black-history club and organized pickets against a lynching that occurred near campus in 1933.[58] While he reaffirms his support of Gaines and her charge to scrutinize the chapter application, Turner emphasizes how Burroughs's group "appeared intensely interested in Negro History" and were "eager to learn . . . more" and that "[n]othing of a political nature was said at either of the meetings" he attended. The effect of this correspondence from both Turner and Gaines was enough to sway the ASNLH against the application. Indeed, the day after Turner clarified his position with the association, Albert Brooks wrote back to Burroughs in a manner that praises her interest in the association but underscores Gaines's authority on the matter: "Under the conditions heretofore stated, we find that the branch organization as set up in your area is not in effect a legally authorized branch. . . . It is with regret, therefore, that I must inform you that prior authorization to use the name of the Association is herewith withdrawn until such time when the proper procedures have been taken to set up a branch organization."[59] Clearly, the political stakes of the situation for the ASNLH's stature as the preeminent authority on black history, alongside the specter of left-wing political associations revealed in the application, were too high for the association to accept Burroughs's collegial overtures.

The failure to establish an ASNLH chapter in Cold War Chicago shows the political gulf between black cultural activists working on similar projects. For instance, Hadley, who worked closely with Burroughs on the museum, appealed to Gaines for a letter of support on a Ford Foundation grant application for a history project on black soldiers in American wars.[60] In 1956 Feldman's article about a Reconstruction-era black congressman was published in the ASNLH's *Negro History Bulletin*.[61] Margaret Burroughs and Turner were on a Negro History Week panel at the Kenwood-Ellis Community Center, and he was a reference on her application for a Guggenheim fellowship to write children's literature. Burroughs also sat on a diverse committee of Bronzeville's cultural activists who were part of an NAACP-sponsored black-history pageant in 1957. The committee was directed by South Side musicologist and organist Ruth Allen Fouche and included conveners like Hadley; Willoughby Abner, NAACP branch chair and United Auto Workers (UAW) organizer;

Turner and Drake, Roosevelt College professors; Sam Stratton, schoolteacher and public-history activist; and Faith Rich, a white CORE activist, DuSable High School teacher, and West Side resident.[62] These broad connections and interactions underscored the complexity of early Cold War African American cultural politics in Chicago and how figures with diverse political affiliations continued to work together.

Throughout this period, Burroughs maintained contacts within Chicago's teaching and artistic communities. Friends of hers with the SSCAC vouched for her with the board even after the center's board revoked her membership in 1956 on suspicion that she and her husband, Charles, were members of the Communist Party. Margaret and Charles Burroughs returned to Chicago at different times throughout the 1950s from their sojourns and continued to discuss plans for a black-history museum and politics, art, and culture with writers, intellectuals, artists, and civic leaders at the South Michigan Avenue home, which doubled as an exhibition space for black cultural artifacts from around the diaspora.[63] Through such social gatherings, Margaret Burroughs became increasingly involved with projects about the African diaspora and issues of anticolonialism.[64] By 1961 she helped found and launch _Freedomways_ magazine, based in New York City with, among others, Hansberry, author of _A Raisin in the Sun_, a play that offers yet another important post–World War II black left cultural expression set in Chicago and attuned to the profound changes taking place elsewhere in the African diaspora at midcentury.[65] _Freedomways_, which addressed issues of national reform, citizenship, and international struggles for anticolonialism, was an important black-led, leftist journal that convened an "intergenerational dialogue" that bridged "gaps" in the mid-twentieth-century black-freedom struggle. Burroughs relinquished her founding role as arts editor in 1965 to focus on museum and public-history work in Chicago.[66] She also became chairman of the National Conference of Negro Artists, started by Chicago artists, most notably sculptor Marion Perkins and first convened in Atlanta in 1959. The group aimed to influence the celebrations for the one-hundredth anniversary of the Emancipation Proclamation and to contribute to mainstream efforts at promoting public remembrance of the official end to U.S. slavery. Indeed, Burroughs eventually described her museum work as part of both the anticipation of the 1963 Emancipation centennial celebration and the work of the NNMHF "which extended into the early 1950s" and celebrated Black History Week every February.[67]

The 1963 Emancipation centennial exposition at Chicago's new McCormick Place convention center certainly demonstrated the conflicted nature of black public-history labors through the mid-twentieth century. It was primarily organized by ASNLH cofounder James E. Stamps and local businessman Alton A. Davis and backed by a committee of local businessmen and politicians, including state representative Corneal Davis. Over the summer, which also saw the March on Washington, the celebration attracted nearly twenty thousand people, including Martin Luther King Jr. Exposition organizers had hoped for over eight hundred thousand visitors; the *Chicago Defender*'s daily edition reported "capacity" audiences to many exhibits through late August 1963. Architectural studies scholar Mabel O. Wilson suggests that the exposition's sponsorship by big U.S. corporations, such as AT&T and Pepsi, "demonstrated how the Cultural Front's techniques of cultural production and representation through mass culture had been absorbed into corporate structures" and that the McCormick Place exposition marked the end of the "great" African American–led exposition movements, which dated from the late nineteenth century and paralleled mainstream industrial expositions.[68]

Burroughs played a central role at the 1963 exposition and drew on her experiences with the 1940 American Negro Exposition in Chicago. As she was in 1940, Burroughs was approached to arrange the exposition's main exhibits on black art and history, which featured her original paintings that "traced the Negro in Illinois" from "DuSable to Dawson." Burroughs also worked closely with fellow African American elementary schoolteachers Leo Sparks and Christine C. Johnson from the AAHA to exhibit African artwork. Johnson, a teacher at the Nation of Islam's University of Islam, had collected art on a 1957 trip to West Africa, where she met Nnamdi Azikiwe of Nigeria and Kwame Nkrumah of newly independent Ghana. As part of the Negro Hall of Fame exhibit at the 1959 African Heritage Exposition in New York City, the trio represented Chicago and displayed African art alongside the artwork of New York black artists.[69]

The Ebony/DuSable Museum project certainly connected with other black left organizations, such as the Afro-American Heritage Association in Chicago, the National Conference of Negro Artists in Atlanta in 1959, and *Freedomways* in New York. Indeed, Chicago became home to a groundswell of new public-history projects and organizations with radical left and liberal political affinities, especially by the late 1950s and 1960s. Some of the more significant local Chicago black public-history groups included the Frank London Brown History Club and the African American (or Negro) History Roundtable. These groups sought to memorialize the late novelist of *Trumbull Park* (1959), whose life as a radical trade unionist and civil rights activist was cut tragically short by cancer in 1962.[70] As Burns writes, the DuSable Museum's growth through the mid-1960s helped draw attention to such organizations, which otherwise might have had difficulty "garnering public attention or support—particularly after the divisive pressures of the McCarthy era."[71] Burroughs wrote in 1966 that the museum "tried to act as a clearing house or referral agency to publicize and direct the public's attention to such groups or institutions as The South Side Community Art Center; The Frank London Brown History Club; The Negro History Roundtable . . . and all other groups interested in the promulgation of Negro History."[72]

Collectively, these projects continued the black cultural fronts of previous decades. They complicate conventional chronologies for the Black Power and black arts movements and helped set the stage for these movements to emerge in Chicago. Furthermore, the work of figures such as Margaret and Charles Burroughs convened important intergenerational mentorships that materialized in the cultural resurgences of the late 1960s through the works of figures such as Haki Madhubuti, who helped found Third World Press (a major institution of the black arts movement), and historian Sterling Stuckey, whose writings helped pioneer black studies in the academy. Stuckey was the first president of the Amistad Society, a Chicago public-history group formed in the early 1960s by South Side and West Side public schoolteachers, such as Stuckey and James Wagner. The society hosted significant history lectures by prominent scholars, such as John Hope Franklin, and prolific activist icons, such as Malcolm X.[73]

The DuSable Museum founders ultimately used their black public-history labors to sustain civil rights activities from the 1950s into the 1960s. This period has been downplayed by historians who view Chicago's Democratic machine's takeover of the militant, protest-oriented leadership of the NAACP in 1957 and 1958 as a moment of declension for black activism and community vitality. Little has been written about the period between then and the more widely recounted open housing and school desegregation movements of the mid-1960s in much of the urban north. Historiographically, far-greater attention has been accorded these latter events as they occurred in Chicago, with special emphasis on when King and his associates brought the Southern Christian Leadership Conference's operations north in the mid-1960s.[74]

The city's main civil rights moments of the mid-1950s included demonstrations against white violence in the Chicago Housing Authority's public housing projects like Trumbull Park on the Far South Side and against the infamous murder of Chicago teenager Emmett Till in Mississippi. The local NAACP under union activist Abner was also involved in cultural-heritage projects as a tangent to its more prominent civil rights activism. The Chicago NAACP chapter's black heritage pageant during Black History Week, in Abner's view, underscored a worldliness through the "Negroe's cultural heritage" that contributed to "civilization in America and elsewhere in the world," despite the "barriers of segregation, discrimination and prejudice."[75] The NAACP's pageant commit-tee remained one example of how traditional civil rights organizations were significantly concerned with public history and cultural matters through the Cold War.

The DuSable Museum group was arguably in the vanguard of those who sustained this work, which maintained connections between civil rights and history activism. Burns comments, "The DuSable moved toward a radical ide-ology that deviated from the outwardly cautious politics assumed by earlier black cultural institutions and organizations, such as the NAACP, during the McCarthy era. Instead, the DuSable's programs and exhibits aimed to raise black consciousness."[76] To be clear, Margaret Burroughs and the museum group were not conventional civil rights leaders in this moment. They no longer carried on the marches and protests that would be undertaken by the prolific civil rights movements of this period—these were tactics her generation had followed in the 1930s and 1940s with groups, such as the NNC and NNMHF, who protested lynching in the South and boycotted segregation in the Loop. Still, Burroughs remained engaged with local discrimination issues during the mid- to late 1950s and 1960s. For example, she became the vice president of black history and culture of the Chicago League of Negro Voters, an understudied, black-led response to the independent Illinois Voters League, which positioned against Chicago's Democratic machine–dominated local politics. The independent but parallel League of Negro Voters would become a fixture of black civil rights activism in the city into the 1960s and was led by younger schoolteachers who would go on to be leading South and West Side community activists, such as Bennett Johnson, Gus Savage, Albert Janney, Herman Cromwell Gilbert, Robert P. Winbush, Brenetta Howell-Barrett, Carter D. Jones, Charles Armstrong, and others. Future Chicago mayor Harold Washington was a fellow traveler of this group, and Charles Burroughs and journalist Vernon Jarrett would often join the group at the Roosevelt College cafeteria, where they conducted much of their organizing and discussion. Margaret Burroughs also reflected on the city's heated school desegregation battles of the early and mid-1960s in an important article in the influential Chicago-based literary journal *Negro Digest*. Through this period, she was a member of CTU's powerful "independence Caucus" slate, a multiracial slate mainly of blacks and Jewish Americans who sought to dislodge an entrenched anti-Communist, largely white and male-dominated leadership that had historically avoided civil rights advocacy and the redress of equality issues for black and minority teachers in pay and appointment.[77]

If not still intimately involved in conventional civil rights activities, such as sit-ins and direct actions, Burroughs still saw her museum and teaching efforts to promote the missing pages of America's history as vitally important to redress racial discrimination. To negotiate the Cold War in Chicago, she and the other museum founders worked throughout the 1940s and 1950s to establish and maintain their presence in initiatives that promoted black public history. Such engagements culminated in a sustained vision for a museum on Chicago's South Side and highlighted significant interventions into black Chicago's shifting political cultures and geographies at midcentury. The museum founders maintained their commitment to left-wing cultural politics that engaged them with fellow-traveling cultural workers (particularly, in New York and Mexico). These experiences actually enabled their survival from Cold War repressions. The leftist affinities shared by the cohort who founded what became the DuSable Museum also demonstrate the importance of interrogating traditional chronologies, definitions, and categories for civil rights, black nationalist, and left-labor cultural front activities during otherwise repressive moments of U.S. history. This interrogation of traditional black-movement categories and ideologies can be furthered by examining the AAHA, founded by public-history activists closely associated with the DuSable Museum group. It was the AAHA that engaged most explicitly in resurgent expressions of black nationalism and that complicates many black social-movement categories of the period with its brand of public history.

CHAPTER THREE

Black-History Activism and the Afro-American Heritage Association

A Negro Emancipation Centennial celebration was held at Chicago's Dunbar High School at East Twenty-Ninth Street and South Parkway in 1958. For this event, DuSable Museum founder Margaret Burroughs worked closely with the Afro-American Heritage Association (AAHA) to organize a display of artwork by black Chicagoans at the South Side high school to commemorate the ninety-sixth anniversary of the Emancipation Proclamation's issuance. The AAHA was established in 1958 by Nation of Islam University teacher Christine C. Johnson and South Side Communist Party leader Ishmael Flory and emerged alongside the DuSable Museum as one of Chicago's key black public-history groupings. Events like the 1958 centennial helped demonstrate the creative ways radical civil rights and black nationalist–inflected efforts intersected through public-history observances in Chicago in the late 1950s in a moment generally viewed as quiescent within the black community. Indeed, the stated purpose of organizations such as the AAHA in much of their educational efforts was to promote accessible black history in the community that clearly stated how U.S. history to that point largely elided black American contributions to the nation. Moreover, by advancing a radical revisionist analysis of U.S. history, one that indicated the role white supremacy and racial ideologies played in the promotion of such faulty views of the past, the AAHA and its allies hoped they could encourage the development of a radical political consciousness among the city's African American working class.

As discussed below, Johnson worked to democratize the sexual politics of the University of Islam's parochial education in the late 1950s and connected these efforts explicitly to her public-history labors with the AAHA. Her compatriot with the AAHA, Flory, corresponded extensively with the elder scholar of black America W. E. B. Du Bois about the American Society of African Culture (AMSAC) and the politics of representing black history in the public sphere. Such interactions were significant and should be given equal treatment alongside more prominent perspectives on black-history matters highlighted by black Chicago's prominent concerns, such as Johnson Publishing Enterprises, over the same period (notably, the publication of what became the influential book *Before the Mayflower* by Lerone Bennett Jr.). Indeed, each endeavor demonstrated the richness of black American cultural repertoires related to public history over this period and the diversity of political modalities undertaken in black Chicago (from left-nationalist radicalism to entrepreneurial liberalism). Fellow-traveling figures in the orbit of the Communist Party of the United States of America (CPUSA), such as DuSable Museum founder Margaret Burroughs, certainly expressed pride in African American identity through their cultural activism and public-history work and were arguably also black nationalists in their own right. Collectively, these activists helped produce a windfall of interest in black public history for Chicago through the early 1960s.

The Afro-American Heritage Association

More than any other black public-history group in the city, the AAHA combined its black public-history activism with expressions of radical-left nationalism in the late 1950s. According to a perceptive Chicago Police file, the AAHA's major activities included both "celebrations and educationals (*sic*)" that stimulated "action around Afro-American History Week; Emancipation Proclamation Issuance Day, September 22, and Emancipation Day, January 1; DuSable Week [which memorialized Chicago's first settler]; cooperation with other Afro-American History Groups; action and mobilization in support of school demonstrations" by major national civil rights organizations; the "maintenance" of a community-focused bookstore called the Afro-American Bookstore; and interest in disseminating materials on African American history, and political pamphlets on "national and international affairs," as well as advocacy for "independent political candidates" and organizations. Above all, the organization placed "great stress upon history and heritage as an instrument for clear and effective action and struggle."[1]

Coverage of the AAHA in the *Chicago Defender* corroborated these connections between global activisms against racism and the promotion of history and heritage in the public sphere. For example, in 1959 the AAHA added itself to campaigns that opposed the activities of the House Un-American Activities Committee (HUAC)—specifically, subpoenas to members of the United Packinghouse Workers of America (UPWA) in the city who faced repression from government sources throughout the 1950s and early 1960s. Flory describes these actions by HUAC as "an attack upon an oasis in a desert of Chicago lethargy."[2] The AAHA called for a local work stoppage in 1960 as part of its African Freedom Day celebrations. AAHA president Johnson appealed to "all governments of the world to join in recognition" of African independence movements "not only to show solidarity with African independence, but also as a demonstration against racism anywhere in the world." The AAHA was at the forefront of activities in Chicago that protested the Central Intelligence Agency–orchestrated assassination of Patrice Lumumba, the exploits of United Nations–backed Belgium troops in the war-torn nation of the Congo, and connections between apartheid South Africa and southern U.S. racial violence. Like their contemporaries involved in the establishment of the DuSable Museum, the AAHA also worked to achieve civic recognition for Jean Baptiste Point DuSable, the city's first settler.[3] These collective activities demonstrate how the AAHA sustained a radical left-wing politics through public-history labors that impacted local black American working-class movements and engaged in observances of anticolonial liberation struggles.

Given AAHA's association with South Side community elites, African independence leaders, and intellectuals, some scholars have suggested that the AAHA represented a higher-brow form of activism. For example, reports on the AAHA by the Chicago Police Department's Red Squad considered the organization to be a Communist front on the South Side: "initiated for . . . cultured Negroes."[4] It is true that the AAHA's focus on culture and history in the public sphere was consistent with the "culture as weapon" approach encouraged by some black intellectuals within the CPUSA in the years after the CPUSA stopped advocating the "Black Belt Thesis" for self-determination of African Americans in the U.S. south (once advocated in the early 1930s when the CPUSA achieved its highest appeal to black communities nationwide). Still, through the 1950s, the "culture as weapon" approach was sustained as one of the more important CP strategies in the fight for racial equality in the United States given the restrictions placed on radical-left activism generally due to the nation's repressive Cold War climate.[5] In this sense, cultural works on the radical left seemed more possible, for example, than overt peace and labor protests. The Chicago Police

Red Squad characterization of the AAHA as an organization that catered to elite "cultured Negroes" also reinforces the belief of Roosevelt College professor St. Clair Drake that black Communists in Chicago made a deal with the local civic political machine to stay away from direct-action activism in the 1950s and focus on history. Indeed, such higher-brow characterizations seemed apt for a group focused on "culture" and "heritage." Still, their activities in public history had more to do with civil rights struggles in the city than merely a representation of higher-brow cultural politics.

The Dunbar High School event in September 1958 organized by the AAHA demonstrated the interconnectedness of civil rights, culture, and public history and how such activities could be construed as higher brow (or perhaps middle brow) in orientation. The event displayed artwork by Burroughs and prolific left-wing African American artists whose careers began in Chicago, such as Charles White, Bernard Goss, Fred Jones, and sculptor Marion Perkins. Moreover, a broad cross-section of Bronzeville's community leaders was featured speakers, including realtor Oscar Brown Sr. (father of radical activist and Broadway star Oscar Brown Jr.), Leon Beverly of the UPWA, Lutheran minister Massie Kennard, and representatives of the Negro Business Directory, as well as music and entertainment by the Vernon Duncan Dancers and dramatist O. Jean Ramsey, who offered poetry readings. The works of diverse black authors were also collected for display and included books by novelist Richard Wright, poet Gwendolyn Brooks, sociologists E. Franklin Frazier and St. Clair Drake, and world traveler and community scholar F. H. Hammurabi Robb.[6] As noted in chapter 2, Burroughs recalled these sorts of celebrations along with her museum work as part of the anticipation for the 1963 celebrations in the city that commemorated the centennial of the Emancipation Proclamation.[7] The event at Dunbar High certainly brought together a significant number of the black South Side's well-traveled intellectuals and politically inclined community elites. It also clearly gathered together disparate left-wing, liberal, and nationalist figures in the late 1950s.

Such a commemorative event and the related publications and local literatures promoted by the AAHA underscore the complexity of intraracial class politics in black Chicago from this period as well as the connected terrains of civil rights and public-history labors through the late 1950s. For example, at the 1958 proclamation-issuance observance, the AAHA presented merit awards to "individuals and organizations that . . . made significant contributions to the development and dissemination of Negro heritage and history." These awards recognized the efforts of local South Side business brokers and cultural elites, such as Claude and Etta Moten Barnett of the Associated Negro Press, local insurance executive Truman K. Gibson, and the publishers of Chicago's other renowned local black press outlets, John H. Johnson (*Ebony Magazine*), John H. Sengstacke (*Chicago Defender*), and Balm Leavelle (*Chicago Crusader*). Awards also went to local black artists and intellectuals like Margaret Burroughs for her artwork and writings as well as authors Frank London Brown, Gwendolyn Brooks, and local librarians and teachers Charlamae Rollins, Vivian G. Harsh, Marian Hadley, and Samuel Stratton. A film on newly independent Ghana was screened. In a keynote speech, AAHA secretary Robert Winbush suggested, "Negroes and all Americans . . . need to take a look back in order to charter a course away from disaster in the future." Clearly, the celebration also focused on using history in the service of U.S. civil rights as well as the freedom struggles of blacks around the world.[8]

In outlook, the Dunbar High School event presented a united front for black nationalism widely conceived. As such, the event featured local business and liberal civic leaders feted alongside radical artists, intellectuals, and local activists from organizations as diverse as the Nation of Islam (NOI) and the Communist Party. Just like the 1942 banquet celebrating the curriculum-reform measures of South Side teachers, a range of political affiliations and modalities at the event advocated for civil rights and black-freedom struggles. Each participant marked the importance of the celebration for signifying universal racial pasts within the black public sphere.

To consider the AAHA an elitist (or middle-class) undertaking, as Chicago's police monitors clearly did, missed the organization's larger vision and purpose as well as its efforts to work toward social change. From its inception in 1958, the AAHA demonstrated an earnestness to produce viable local historical knowledge for the community. The organization also appealed to a multifaceted constituency within the African American community as the event at Dunbar High demonstrated: from the South Side's working-class majority to its more elite cultural brokers. The AAHA, in fact, promoted diverse forms of black public history to those who wished to learn it and apply it.

It is true that, by and large, many civil rights organizations over the long mid-twentieth century were represented by middle-class segments of the African American community—a reality duly noted by scholars of black nationalism and racial politics during this period. As Jeffrey Helgeson notes in his recent and comprehensive history of black Chicago's community development over the twentieth century, black nationalist politics in the city "emerged out of a pragmatic black nationalist enterprise that had uneven benefits for black Chicagoans of different social classes and that never strayed far from interracial collaboration."[9] The complexity of class-based politics within the matrix of nationalist modalities and their connection to public expressions and discussions of African American identity from Chicago's black community is certainly underscored in *Black Nationalism*—one of two foundational and now classic studies of the Nation of Islam conducted during the 1950s.[10] In this study, E. U. Essien-Udom focuses especially on NOI's working-class appeal in Chicago and the lack of attention offered to issues of identity, collective pasts, and heritage elsewhere in the black public sphere. He feels the NOI went further than other groups in its attempt to appeal to blacks on the basis of group identity and shared pasts. Essien-Udom notes how black efforts in Chicago to "stimulate and foster pride in their heritage and in Africa" had "been minimal" and that "whatever information" was "available about their past" had "yet to reach the Negro masses." Moreover, Essien-Udom notes how Negro History Week stemmed "entirely from the Negro intelligentsia."[11] Overall, he remains apprehensive that organizations that promoted Negro History Week could bridge the experiential knowledge gap between classes within local black communities in the United States: "Even if such efforts were extended to the Negro masses, it remains doubtful that much would be changed unless they were matched with some evidence of solid Negro accomplishment in their present communities."[12]

In a revealing footnote to his study, however, Essien-Udom suggests there was hope for some nationalist formations that appealed to working-class blacks along the same lines as the NOI:

> Efforts to give the Negro a sense of a past, a myth, pride and confidence in the capabilities of his race have been made largely by the black nationalists, Garvey, Muhammad, etc. The works of J. A. Rogers and Carter G. Woodson have been inspired by the same objective. Groups such as the American Society of African Culture [AMSAC] cater to a small group of intellectuals who lack the vision or courage to relate and interpret their findings to the Negro masses. In recent years, however, other groups are beginning to show greater interest in disseminating information among the masses about their heritage and African kinship. The Afro-American Heritage Association in Chicago is one of these groups. Its effort shows some promise.[13]

In fact, AAHA cofounder Christine Johnson accomplished exactly what Essien-Udom anticipated. This was evident through her teaching labors on the South Side and with her principalship at the NOI's University of Islam in the late 1950s. A graduate of Loyola University in Chicago, Johnson helped democratize and internationalize aspects of the parochial education that the mainly working-class students of the University of Islam received. The NOI first established parochial schools in both Detroit and Chicago in the early 1930s, initially for students in elementary school. Scholars have not established a consensus on the exact number of NOI schools eventually established over the mid-twentieth century. As historian Edward E. Curtis IV indicates, an NOI newspaper "*Muhammad Speaks* copyeditor Charles 67X claimed in 1973 that there were forty-two such schools; scholar C. Eric Lincoln said that there were fourteen."[14] Certainly, a significant number were ultimately established in major cities across the United States. A high school was added to the Chicago location in 1954 (the year of *Brown v. the Board of Education*), and by 1959 the University of Islam had a total enrollment of 350 students from kindergarten through senior year. According to Lincoln, there were "600 students enrolled in Chicago, and 700 at Harlem's University of Islam."[15] In many ways, such vocational programs were hallmarks of the sorts of education and initiatives the NOI offered to black Americans over this period. Historian Helgeson notes, "In addition to offering revelations about the evils of white supremacy and black people's ascendance, the Nation also offered pragmatic aid for struggling individuals."[16] Johnson's involvement with the NOI also became emblematic of a gender shift in the education initiatives of the Nation, which by the 1960s became led primarily by female public schoolteachers. Curtis relates how "[f]emale members of the NOI brought educational experiences as public school teachers to their leadership of the Chicago school during the 1960s; they included Sister Christine Johnson, Effie X Pope, Zella X Prince, and Agnita X." *Muhammad Speaks* reports that the University of Islam "maintains a system of advancement on merit, rather than by sex."[17]

Johnson oversaw the integration of classes between girls and boys (the NOI kept boys and girls separate until 1959 when Johnson assumed her principalship). She also continued to oversee a diverse international faculty, notably two recent hires from Africa (Sierra Leone and Egypt) to add to a record of teacher hires from Nigeria, Egypt, and Palestine. Like her contemporaries, such as Margaret Burroughs, Madeline Stratton Morris, and Rollins (who were all South Side teachers), Johnson wrote about African American history for audiences of children and youth. In 1962 Johnson produced a first-grade textbook that treated "children at home, at school and at play" that included "the history of the black people, related in simple terms that the child can understand." Just like how Stratton Morris's efforts in the 1940s to reform local civic curricula worked as historical revisionism, Johnson perceived that standard American textbooks taught that "Africans and descendants of Africa are inferior and that white Christian missionaries went to Africa to educate the 'poor misguided heathens.' [Black students are] . . . taught that America was settled by civilized people from Europe, who came here seeking freedom. . . . Our children are taught America was discovered by whites even though the Indians were here." Just like the local curriculum reformers of earlier decades, Johnson's textbook was designed to correct these problems. Indeed, her new textbook "covered a number of subjects" that were not in standard U.S. history textbooks of the era, from "'Muslim religion,' the African American community in the United States, phonics, spelling, African art, black business in the United States, African heads of state, and African geography."[18] Johnson also felt skeptical of new government programs in the 1960s focused on single mothers and the unemployed. Rather, she favored the independent track record of the University of Islam that helped numerous black South Siders achieve college educations and vocational employment in technical fields, such as TV repair, as well as basic education.[19]

Through the early 1960s, the Nation of Islam offered some openings for African American leftists to continue to address a multiplicity of racial-justice issues—notably, through *Muhammad Speaks*. Not long after his tenure as a program department director of antidiscrimination activities with the UPWA through the early 1950s and a string of jobs on the political campaigns of local black civic leaders in the latter half of that decade, Richard Durham became a *Muhammad Speaks* editor. His wife, Clarice Durham, notes how he worked at the paper for nearly three years and helped steer its editorial direction "beyond the teachings of [NOI leader] Elijah Muhammad. To deal with arts and music and international affairs." According to Clarice Durham, *Muhammad Speaks* "became quite a good newspaper and circulation grew as a result."[20] As historian Peniel Joseph indicates, the newspaper became one of NOI's most "profitable enterprises" and reached a circulation of over five hundred thousand through the 1950s. *Muhammad Speaks*, of course, gave space to exaltations about NOI's leader Muhammad, but it also "provided coverage of local and national civil rights struggles, black militancy and corresponding white resistance, and African and Third World liberation movements, explaining how all the elements figured into the international politics of the Cold War era."[21] Helgeson notes how black Chicagoan Leon Forrest found opportunities writing for *Muhammad Speaks*, a job that enabled him entry to a position as a professor of African American studies at Northwestern University that won him "a level of personal success and cultural influence most black Chicagoans could not have imagined." As Helgeson indicates, Forrest's "influence remained tied to white-run institutions that were also undergoing profound transformations (in this case an elite academic institution [Northwestern University] that had clearly been changed by the Black Studies movement). Such mixed outcomes were characteristic of black nationalist ventures more broadly speaking."[22]

Even within the NOI through the 1950s, black nationalism was not simply a matter of men speaking militantly in public, wearing bow ties, or preaching about the specter of "white devils" in their midst.[23] As the actions and composition of the AAHA and figures like Johnson and Durham indicate, the coordinates for black nationalist activity extended into many spheres and are helpfully revealed through the rubric of black public-history activism. Whether they were writers, teachers, or trade unionists (or at some point all three of these stations), their repertoires for cultural work surely contributed to the diversity of black nationalist and political forms and modalities in 1950s and 1960s Chicago.

Du Bois, Flory, and AMSAC

E. U. Essien-Udom's analysis of black nationalism also included another organization, more national in scope than the AAHA. In the wake of U.S. participation at the Paris Peace Congress in 1956, the American Society of African Culture (AMSAC) was formed as a think tank of mainly university-educated, liberal, and moderately left-leaning African American intellectuals based in Washington, D.C. In some ways, AMSAC attempted to continue the intellectual projects advanced by the left-leaning Council of African Affairs headed by Du Bois and Paul Robeson through the late 1940s and 1950s, which disbanded under the pressure of U.S. government red scares. However, nearly a decade after it was formed, it was revealed that AMSAC had received substantial funds from the CIA to carry out its knowledge-producing efforts about Africa and its diaspora.[24] As such, it was part of the U.S. government's widespread endeavors to shape both the outcomes of Third World anticolonial struggles and the cultural fronts of black American activism during the Cold War.[25]

At the same time, recent scholarship shows that AMSAC's leadership and functions were complex. Because of AMSAC's wide appeal to black intellectuals of all ideologies, many U.S.-based leftists found important openings for their cultural and knowledge-producing labors through conferences and events it hosted. Historians Kevin Gaines and John J. Munro have written extensively about AMSAC. Munro notes how "AMSAC members were not automatons or dupes of [their] imperial master. [They were] without doubt concerned with ongoing radical expressions of African and African American solidarity." He adds, "AMSAC's directors wished to fill the gap left open by the demise of the Council on African Affairs while remaining opposed to its politics" but also "served other functions"—notably, "a space, however ideologically circumscribed, through which transatlantic discussion about colonialism could continue."[26] Moreover, Gaines relates, AMSAC "sought to promote cultural exchange, collaboration, and heightened mutual awareness between African and African-American intellectuals." While the organization's "leading intellectuals were Cold War liberals," such as John A. Davis, AMSAC "provided a space for radical and liberal black musicians, artists, and writers to independently enact their international visions of solidarity."[27]

Prolific African American intellectuals and artists known for their leftist affinities became involved with AMSAC through the late 1950s and early 1960s in the wake of the cultural left's organizational demise under various repressions. These figures included musicians Abbey Lincoln and Max Roach; writers John Oliver Killens, Rosa Guy, Maya Angelou, Audre Lorde, and Paule Marshall; *Freedomways* contributors Julian Mayfield and John Henrik Clarke; and black renaissance luminaries like Langston Hughes. All were associated at some point with AMSAC.[28] Chicagoans certainly attended AMSAC-supported events and activities, notably, writers Frank London Brown and Lorraine Hansberry, who were at a black writers conference the organization sponsored in New York in 1959. This event also featured Communists Lloyd Brown, author of the novel *Iron City* (1951), and Louis Burnham, a former executive of the CP-fronted Southern Negro Youth Congress, as well as more liberal figures, such as Roosevelt College and Chicago-based professor St. Clair Drake. Drake's colleague Lorenzo D. Turner also had the ear of AMSAC executives, who sought to arrange meetings through him when they passed through Chicago in 1959.[29]

Du Bois's academic accomplishments and ideas were widely recognized, if contentiously debated, in the circle of academics who headed AMSAC. Such contentions highlighted the divided terrain of Cold War racial politics in the black community. Du Bois's writings were featured in AMSAC publications, notably a reprint of a 1933 article on Liberia that appeared in the 1958 volume *Africa Seen by American Negroes*. Moreover, at the 1958 AMSAC conference, two of the organization's executives, Davis and Martin Kilson, argued vociferously over the significance of Du Bois's *Black Reconstruction*, a classic revisionist history of the years after the U.S. Civil War. As the quintessential black Cold War liberal, in line with the CIA's objectives for AMSAC, Davis lambasted the study as a "disservice" to truth and, pejoratively, "Marxist." Kilson supported *Black Reconstruction* as a "fine piece of historical interpretation." Munro indicates, "Such exchanges mattered because they demonstrated the continuity of Du Bois's influence, including precisely his Marxism, for the 1960s generation. And despite its conservative elements and CIA funding, it was AMSAC that operated as the vehicle through which intergenerational anti-colonialism could take place."[30] Still, AMSAC leaders, headed by their conservative president

Davis, published the conference proceedings in *The American Negro Writer and His Roots*, a volume that did little to reveal the diversity of exchanges and engagements that actually occurred at events the organization hosted. As Mary Helen Washington notes, the more radical views of figures such as Hansberry, Killens, Mayfield, and other black leftists who were at the conference in New York were actually omitted from the volume (especially the keynote speech Hansberry gave). Washington suggests these omissions provide yet "another example of the imaginative and ideological battles over representing race in the Cold War 1950s."[31]

The AAHA's local activities, much like the DuSable Museum's emergence over the same period, provide good examples of how and where else these representative "battles" were waged. During the same period that his ideas were being contentiously discussed through AMSAC, Du Bois expressed support for Flory and the AAHA's local work in Chicago. In his correspondence with Flory, Du Bois makes it known how aware he is of the problems with AMSAC, which in his view tended toward elitism and entrepreneurialism. Du Bois shares these sentiments alongside the prospective publication of the elder scholar's prolific writings on anticolonialism and world socialism through the AAHA. Du Bois cautions Flory and the AAHA about extensively publishing local literatures "by and about people of African descent" because this sort of knowledge production would be "very costly" and that there are already various "efforts in that line being made"—notably, those of the anticolonial and French-based journal *Présence Africaine* led by Alioune Diop and Leopold Senghor (founded at the 1956 Paris Peace Congress). Moreover, Du Bois indicates to Flory, "Some American Negroes have tried to steal the idea" through AMSAC, and he was "afraid they [had] investment in mind or personal position instead of scientific work. [I have] . . . heard of nothing yet worthwhile that they have done."[32] At this point in his life, Du Bois was becoming increasingly Communist in his politics and expressed great hope in an African institute founded "under the Soviet Academy of Science." But the true substance of Du Bois's letter to Flory is to encourage local Chicago efforts at producing "small, cheap pamphlets" that include his writings on anticolonialism, world socialism, and visions for racial equality.[33]

At this point in his career, Du Bois certainly expressed Soviet political orientations. He expressed the well-tread (and ill-fated) hope of ongoing Soviet-style nation-making experiments elsewhere in the world. There is also no doubt that such perspectives made his views highly suspect in the U.S. public sphere. But it would be a disservice to the broad circles of knowledge production that ranged across the left, liberal, and nationalist spectrums (discussed through

AMSAC or at local black-history events in Chicago) to dismiss Du Bois's ideas during this period outright simply because of his growing Communist affinities. Du Bois knew the currency of his work for the larger black-liberation struggle and sensed that not all avenues for publication energies merited contributions. Moreover, he worried about the elitist and commercial forms of knowledge that might continue to be transmitted through organizations like AMSAC, whose leaders were liable to dismiss radical viewpoints and ideologies (as evidenced by Davis's omission of Hansberry's keynote). It is crucial as well to recall that Du Bois wrote to Flory with his concerns well before it became known that the CIA had actually funded AMSAC as part of its cultural Cold War front.

Moreover, it is also helpful to recall that Du Bois remained a major intellectual figure for the emerging field of African studies in the late 1950s despite his increasingly radical-leftist leanings. Because of how prolific his writings and research were to this point, specialists in the field could simply not ignore his work despite the increasing repression he faced as a scholar-activist in Cold War America.[34] Eric Porter indicates how Du Bois continued to write voluminously from the 1940s until his death in 1963.[35] Moreover, scholars and biographers alike have deemphasized this extensive corpus because of the taint of leftism and Stalinism that marked Du Bois's intellectual labors later in his career. As such, Porter deftly suggests that Du Bois's midcentury work "cannot" be comprehended "without considering what [Du Bois] gained by being part of a radical intellectual milieu" but that his "leftist ideas and affinities," pronounced as they were by then, must not stand fully "determinative of his thought during these years in either positive or negative ways."[36] In an excellent recent study of Du Bois's internationalist thought, Bill V. Mullen notes that while the elder scholar "was a particularly vulnerable prisoner of Stalinism's dark magic" later in his career, Du Bois still maintained a "staggered and incomplete" understanding of Marxism, expressed a "lifelong aversion to political violence, and the congruent pull of competing ideological influence on his thought (from Pan-Africanism and Pan-Asianism to cooperative economics) evince marks of doubt, hesitation, and deviation from Stalin's Russian program up to the end of his life."[37] Rather, it is worth reading Du Bois and other similarly inspired intellectuals for their insights into how ideas about race and African American history were rapidly changing. Such knowledge production varied mainly between left-wing and nationalist idioms through the mid-twentieth century as white supremacy became increasingly and openly challenged worldwide through global anticolonial liberation struggles.

The local vantage point of Chicago offers an excellent case study for how African Americans sought to sustain such alternative forms of knowledge, especially those that remained consistently independent of U.S. government purse strings but connected in some way to leftist politics. For example, throughout this period, Du Bois felt more supportive about the Chicago-based AAHA's role as a producer of knowledge about black history than he did a well-funded organization like AMSAC through the late 1950s (based as the latter was in the diplomatic and knowledge nexus of Washington, D.C.).

While living in New York before he and his writer-activist wife, Shirley Graham Du Bois, moved to Ghana in the early 1960s, he corresponded frequently with figures on the radical black left in Chicago and elsewhere.[38] A notable correspondent was Flory, whose activism in the 1950s typified the strategic yet precarious role played by black leftists in these history-producing efforts. Flory was a mid-level CP-member of the South Side section and had been a community activist in the city for decades and previously a student activist at Fisk University and in Berkeley, California. He had also been a member of the defunct National Negro Congress and was an experienced trade unionist. In the 1930s, Flory worked with the UPWA in Chicago on various local civil rights campaigns through work in his own union, the American Federation of Labor–affiliated Dining Car Cooks and Waiters (from which he was expelled in the early 1940s for his CP affiliations).[39] Through much of the 1950s, Flory focused his attention on public-history efforts while he achieved a decent living selling cars for Pontiac. These efforts were certainly in the spirit of the affluent society and striving images of the 1950s. Such employment reflected the larger shifts away from militant trade unionism around the country where radical leftists were pushed out of the labor movement, but Flory's correspondence with a former CP comrade in New York shows he kept the acquisitive nature of his new employment in perspective. Flory felt the "automobile business so far [was] very good, relatively to what I have made as wages in the past." He felt "modest and humble" about the occupation and realized that "luck plays a big part." Moreover, he did not "have any illusions about the economic trend." He also noted he "never really" tried to sell his friends cars, instead, often telling "them how to buy at the greatest advantage" elsewhere. Flory's tone reflects how he had achieved economic security as a car salesman through an industry that typified America's affluence. But his tone demonstrated a critical lens on the sales role he now played through this particular occupation.[40] To Flory, such employment was still tangential to his public-history activism.

In the same letter, Flory is more earnest about his public-history work during the late 1950s and felt his efforts in public history were to try to "stimulate the emergence of some sort of Negro group that can speak out with deeper historical and theoretical clarity on issues on which the present crop of 'leaders' are speaking out, in the face of what really is a great opportune moment, the kind of statesman-like clarity that a Fred Douglass had in the Civil War period."[41] Flory (like his contemporaries Margaret and Charles Burroughs) sought to put public history directly in the service of social action for the black community as a whole.

With the AAHA, Flory worked through the late 1950s and early 1960s to publish affordable materials and pamphlets on African American history to distribute to the South Side's majority working-class population. The AAHA focused, especially, on the publication of small pamphlets of Du Bois's writings and thoughts, notably on the history of African colonialism and on world socialism. These two pamphlets originated as speeches that Du Bois gave in both Chicago and California while on speaking tours in 1958 and 1959, respectively. Du Bois's visit to Chicago in the fall of 1959 also helped raise funds for the Afr-Am Bookstore, run by Flory and his AAHA colleagues. In a 1960 letter to Flory, Du Bois suggests that Flory and the AAHA are "making it possible for Negroes and others at small expense to read parts" of Du Bois's recent work. In Du Bois's view, this is "more than is being done elsewhere in the United States. I appreciate it."[42] This support boosted the spread of black public-history activism in Chicago through the late 1950s and emphasized the city's centrality to racial knowledge production in the nation through midcentury.

Important recollections by Flory in 1982 further reflects on how public-history labors became viable forms of rights activism in Chicago through the repressive 1950s. The letter suggests the likelihood that Drake's views about black Communists going in for the study of "Negro history" were valid. In a lengthy letter to the CPUSA's longtime chairperson Henry Winston, Flory writes about his experiences with the AAHA in Chicago organizing public-history events as well as his earlier activism in the labor-based civil rights struggles of African Americans. He describes that the AAHA had worked "with what was new in the long history of Afro-Americans in the struggle for Afro-American History . . . [and] was able to deal not only with the rising independence movements in Africa, with Afro-American History Week, hold public meetings and present prominent speakers and extravaganzas, but it was also able to act on issues." Flory said that a similarly organized black workers' movement in the 1980s "under the banner of 'the history and heritage' [of African American labor] may be able to do many things."[43] Flory recalls very positively the experiences of doing black public-history activism in the 1950s, and, indeed, the prospect of emulating such activities in another repressive period of U.S. history (the Reagan 1980s) suggests the significance of these public-history projects in their time.

The AAHA's two pamphlets of Du Bois's Chicago speeches demonstrate the utility of circulating accessible and readable interventions on racial knowledge and public history through the mid-twentieth century. Sectioned by small paragraphs with headings such as "Legal Discrimination Fell on the Negro" and "Colonies: The Slums of the World," these pamphlets and others on Du Bois's writings were published by CP's local printer, Progressive Printers, 1153 East Forty-Seventh Street, on the South Side, and sold for fifteen to twenty cents each through Afr-Am Bookstore, 102 East Thirty-Fifth Street, which Flory kept running through the 1950s.[44] Correspondence between Du Bois and Flory suggests that the pamphlet *Socialism Today* already had four thousand copies run by early 1960 with another four thousand anticipated for circulation. The Chicago activist and the elder scholar exchanged proofs of Du Bois's prolific Chicago-based speeches, which demonstrated the openness Du Bois had for such local projects.[45] This was significant distribution for the U.S. black left in the late 1950s, since the influential civil rights journal *Freedomways*, based in New York (the urban intellectual epicenter of U.S. liberalism and left radicalism), only had a circulation of two thousand when first published under the direct tutelage of Du Boises in 1961.[46] Moreover, like *Freedomways*, Flory and his wife, Cathern Flory, sought to utilize Graham's extensive contacts in Africa to achieve transatlantic circulation for Du Bois's speeches from Chicago.[47] Although Du Bois's thoughts and ideas were obviously exchanged more prolifically through other venues, especially in later decades, it is significant that his work received erudite engagement for local distribution on Chicago's black South Side through the late 1950s.

Deeper analysis of the pamphlets and literature the AAHA produced in this period is further revealing. Flory offered a preface to each and added his own local filter to issues that were worldwide in scope. For example, the preface to the speech *Colonialism* is a plug for the AAHA's African Freedom Day celebrated in Chicago in 1960: "On this day . . . in Southern United States, in Africa, in Asia, people with more pigmentation in their skin than their western European and European-American cousins are in the forefront of preserving and extending all of the very best that has come down from history to the human race."[48] Flory's assertion mirrors the speech by Du Bois, who traces labor's degradation in the context of the modern era, industrialization in the nineteenth century, and the transatlantic African slave trade. For Du Bois, this history of labor's global degradations coincided with the "discovery" and "trade" of Europe with America and India—regions whose indigenous peoples had their wealth "brutally stolen" and were in various ways subjected to forms of European-led colonialism and imperialism. Du Bois offers a compelling expression of how racial knowledge by the mid-twentieth century had "nearly" completely debunked the pseudoscience of "inherent inferiority" faced by the "majority of the people of the earth who happen to be colored."[49]

This expression of how ideas of race had changed through the 1950s conceded that much work remained to be done to fully debunk the myth of racial hierarchies in the public sphere. In this sense, Du Bois's thought (while increasingly sectarian in political modes through the mid-twentieth century) still expressed important utopian and future ideals for social justice and racial equality that fundamentally challenged American exceptionalism in favor of radical internationalism. As Porter suggests, Du Bois's "quest for a fuller realization of democracy and his analysis of the present and future of the 1940s and 1950s were made possible by the political and analytical modes of popular front and statist Marxism, Keynesian economics, insurgent anticolonial nationalisms, social mobilizations against Jim Crow, and the state of civil rights and human rights discourse."[50] Moreover, as Mullen indicates, Du Bois's "most deeply affecting political lessons and analysis of twentieth-century history were drawn primarily—though not exclusively—from sources and events outside the United States."[51] Du Bois's intellectual outputs throughout much of his career, and especially later in his life, were informed by truly global sensibilities that extended well beyond the parochial parameters of American life.

Du Bois's thoughts on the connectedness of history and the prospect of global revolution from the "colonialism" speech were echoed at the African Freedom Fete, celebrated annually in Chicago. This celebration in 1962 attracted over three thousand people to the Parkway Ballroom on the South Side. Among the event's speakers were Christine Johnson; consul William H. Jones of Liberia; Fauzi Abadial, director, Arab Information Service; Issa Serag Eil Din [sic; Eldin], consul general, United Arab Republic; and Chimere Ikoku, president, Pan-African Students Organization in the Americas. Johnson told the audience about the connections between black struggles in Africa and throughout the diaspora and suggested that the "struggle" for black freedom would be "handicapped" until every "man, woman and child of African descent is made to realize and understand the relations of movements." For Johnson, this meant fostering awareness "of Africa and throughout the world, the long history of lies, distortions and misrepresentations about Africa which still debase our schools and institutions of higher learning." Until this situation changed, these problems of knowledge about race and history would engulf "the entire world." Johnson also read a message from Du Bois, in absentia, that global black freedom struggles would be victorious and "absolutely certain."[52]

Socialism Today also explicitly connects local social equality struggles in Chicago with racial knowledge production about African Americans, Africa, and the role of the United States in the world. Flory's preface notes how *Socialism Today* was an original publication by Afr-Am Books of Du Bois's work and that the AAHA was "deeply concerned with bringing to African Americans in the first place, and Americans in general, the scientific facts on race and on African-Americans or Americans of African descent." Flory emphasizes his view that white Americans were exceptional in the degree to which they bought into the "myth of race." This myth persisted "out of a long history of lies about Africans and Americans of African descent." In Flory's view, the form that U.S. exceptionalism took with regard to "racism and falsified history" had a lot to do with how the country was viewed globally and underscored its increasingly imperial role in the world. As such, local acts of U.S. racism registered "before the world" and made the country into the "land of over 5,000 lynchings; where 'free elections' don't exist for millions of black and white Americans; where at moments white men and women act like mad men from the caves as in the case of Trumbull Park in Chicago or Levittown in Pennsylvania, or Deerfield in Illinois."[53]

Du Bois's speech to a Chicago audience in November 1959 reflects Flory's local to global concerns about histories of race and racial injustice. He began with a recollection of the previous year's world travels that came with the reinstatement of his passport after nearly a decade of harassment from the U.S. government, which sought to deny his movements abroad.[54] These renewed travels took Du Bois from Western Europe to the Eastern bloc, the Union of Soviet Socialist Republics, and China. To Du Bois, this experience gave him "the right to say that the West, and particularly the United States [can] no longer ignore the world or consider themselves the center of the universe." More to the point, Du Bois looked to various socialist and social democratic experiments taking place around the world as models for future social change. He asked his audience what a "socialist country" looked and felt like and compared Moscow to Chicago. For example, in Moscow, there was "more planning . . . of streets and buildings; the people . . . are dressed in later styles, but the Moscovites are not in rags. They are satisfied with life and less worried than the people of Chicago."[55] These comparisons of regional contexts offered compelling examples to local audiences about the prospects for radical social change and/or reform in the United States, despite the obvious absence of democracy that accompanied Soviet realities.

Such observations clearly demonstrate Du Bois's increasingly Communist sympathies, but they also underscored important realities about the precariousness of urban social life for citizens of the United States during the post–World War II era and early Cold War—especially for citizens of color. Most Americans from all sections of society shared hopes for a prosperous future in an "affluent" consumer society driven by U.S. commerce and capitalism, but such hopes were not often reflected in material realities. This was especially true through the mid-twentieth century for African Americans, whose strivings for public accommodations and unattainable fruits of U.S. material progress have been well documented.[56]

More-prominent black Chicagoans of the 1950s and 1960s underscored how the terrain of local public-history labors were also an important site for articulating the entrepreneurial and striving character of civil rights activities throughout the nation. In his autobiography *Succeeding against the Odds* (1989), John H. Johnson, founder and owner of Johnson Publishing Enterprises, Chicago, recalls the cultural and political "awakenings" of black America at mid-century, which he characterized as a "quantum jump in black consciousness." Johnson, whose company published the successful *Ebony* and *Jet* magazines, explains that his multimillion-dollar companies "played a leadership role in this process" by creating the "foundations" of "struggle" in the "forties and fifties when the ground was hard and there were few laborers." Johnson insists that his magazines "anticipated the changes [of the 1960s] and gave focus and form to them." He recalls that in 1959 there was a "growing interest in Black history," and so among other efforts to publish books on black history and culture, he "authorized a pathfinding Black history series." Authored by *Ebony* staff writer Lerone Bennett Jr., the series was published in 1962 as a comprehensive book, *Before the Mayflower: A History of Black America, the Classic Account of the Struggles and Triumphs of Black Americans*. The book has since been revised numerous times to commemorate changes in the African American freedom struggle over the course of the 1960s and beyond.[57]

Ebony was definitely at the forefront of reporting progressive change throughout this period. For example, a report commissioned by the magazine (known for its glossy portrayal of African American lifestyles and consumption patterns) offered important information about structural changes in U.S. society and about how African Americans faced discrimination in many facets of their lives. As just one example, one key *Ebony* report highlights the slow but significant increase in the number of African Americans who worked in colleges and universities (by 1958, more than three hundred African American educators were teaching white students in 106 postsecondary institutions across the country).[58]

Johnson's boastful recollections about his publishing ventures privileged black entrepreneurialism as the engine for the cultural and social awakenings of the 1960s. Such recollections are problematic because they frame a two-decade period that casts the postwar struggles for civil rights by African Americans in very specific terms—as one of changing public culture and U.S. social life in light of changing forms of capitalist consumption and prevailing forms of consumerism. This is especially true if we consider how increased African American engagements with entrepreneurial and consumer cultures helped usher in the new media of the 1940s, 1950s, and 1960s (radio, television, etc.). For example, these decades saw the rise of pictorial magazines, radio, and television, which in many ways (as Johnson suggests in his autobiography) helped "anticipate," give "foundation" to, and "form" efforts toward social change underway by the 1960s. This was especially so given the long-tested strategies of consumer-boycotting campaigns and Johnson's own efforts to promote the notion of a black consumer market to larger white-owned advertising firms from the 1940s through the 1960s. Johnson describes how he approached potential advertisers by describing black consumers in the same way one might describe a "foreign market," defined in decidedly national parameters. He describes the challenges of convincing white advertising agencies about the incentives of advertising directly to African American publics.[59] Johnson's engagement with civil rights issues can also be understood as a reconstruction of collective grammars for black identity through the 1960s, which also implicitly combated racial prejudice. As historian Adam Green suggests, these grammars demonstrated a contingency about racial identities (in flux and ever-changing) that emphasized the preeminence of entrepreneurial forms in public efforts for African American recognition in the public sphere.[60]

The teleology Johnson employs in his autobiography is worth analyzing further given the "foundations" he saw within his business pursuits for public-history and civil rights activism. His autobiographical narrative obfuscates a complex field of political and intellectual exchanges in the late 1950s and 1960s about how images and representations of African American life, history, and culture were to be crafted, by whom, for what means, and to what ends. Bennett's *Before the Mayflower* as well as his many other writings became household and highly influential texts for many African Americans (and problematic white Americans, such as Bill Clinton). Given its prolific output through magazines like *Ebony*, *Negro Digest*, and *Jet*, Johnson Publishing itself became a shining example of African American enterprise and ingenuity.

Despite Johnson Publishing's prolific accomplishments, it remained only one significant enterprise representing black identities and pasts in the public sphere. The correspondence between Du Bois and Flory about organizations like AMSAC reveals the earnest concerns many had about the circulation and representation of African American identities in the public sphere. These concerns contrasted in form with the entrepreneurial foci of Johnson Publishing and its specific forms of cultural production (which, above all, emphasized making money). For her part, Margaret Burroughs has reflected on an incident the museum once had with Johnson Publishing because of the museum's use of the word "Ebony" in its original institutional name. Indeed, Johnson Publishing even threatened legal action against the museum when the institution was barely off the ground. Burroughs's reflection of the incident bristles with indignation. Unlike the magazines of Johnson Publishing, the museum and public-history labors Burroughs carried out were "not a venture."[61]

In fact, many people were concerned about how such cultural projects could be deployed in the service of civil rights alongside representations of black public identity through the mid-twentieth century. As the worries expressed by Du Bois and Flory about AMSAC and the reflections of Burroughs on Johnson Publishing make clear, public-history activism was at the center of vital conversations and contestations over how best to represent African American identities and pasts. The *Chicago Defender* documented Du Bois's visits to Chicago despite the neglect the African American press treated him with in the later years of his life.[62] Like the Emancipation Proclamation–issuance celebration in 1958, a birthday celebration earlier that year also held at Dunbar High School became an occasion for black Chicagoans to present a united front about representations of U.S. black history and identities in the public sphere. The Du Bois birthday salute, organized by the Chicago Du Bois committee in May 1958, received official recognition from Mayor Richard J. Daley and mirrored past Negro History Week celebrations in the city as well as the observances for curriculum reforms initiated in the early 1940s. Certainly, like past public recognitions, this event mirrored the local Democratic machine's attempts to co-opt black movement activities in Chicago.[63]

Like his predecessors had done during the early 1940s to recognize curriculum reforms, Mayor Daley "kindly" turned down the invitation to address the commemorative gathering in person at Dunbar High but, instead, offered sympathetic words about the elder, embattled scholar of black America. To the Democratic kingmaker Daley, Du Bois (by then a Communist and at ideological odds with Chicago's civic elites) was still a "renowned leader whose life span has encompassed much of the most significant stirring history of our nation."[64] The message was highly symbolic and ripe with the sort of disingenuousness that highlighted Daley's relationship with the black community. Still, such public recognition was rare in the United States, given Du Bois's exile status through the late 1950s.[65] More than anything, the recognition speaks to Du Bois's enduring popularity in black communities nationwide despite the repressions he faced for his politics during the Cold War.

Daley's token pronouncements notwithstanding, the Du Bois salute presented openings to African Americans in the city who used these occasions for carrying out civil rights activity as black-history celebrations. Like the Emancipation Proclamation–issuance centennial celebration later in the year, the Du Bois testimonial featured a who's who of black Chicago and its liberal and left-wing white allies. The event also further demonstrated the multiplicity of views held by local community leaders and activists: whether integrationist, entrepreneurial, liberal, leftist, *and* nationalist (and some combination of all these ideologies). The focus of Du Bois's speech at his birthday celebration shows how public-history, entrepreneurial, and nationalist modalities were articulated simultaneously. The title of Du Bois's talk was "The Negro in Business in a Changing World (1908–1958)." Local businessperson Truman K. Gibson chaired the committee that organized the Dunbar testimonial dinner. The event also served to aid Du Bois's efforts to continue to self-publish his writing and to distribute it as far and wide as possible in as affordable, accessible, and un-co-opted ways as possible. Other members of the birthday-salute committee included Golden B. Darby from the South Side Community Committee, Roosevelt College professor Drake, Northwestern University's Melville Herskovitz, the *Chicago Defender*'s and Urban League's Al Foster, local attorney and businessman Earl B. Dickerson, the white liberal Hyde Park couple Ed and Joyce Gourfain, and local high schoolteachers Timuel Black, Samuel Stratton, and Madeline Stratton Morris. Even more left-wing members of the committee known for their associations with CP circles included artists Marion Perkins, Margaret and Charles Burroughs, Fern Gayden, Dorothy and Charles Hayes, and Cathern Flory. The event also featured the support of Oscar Brown Jr.'s parents, Mr. and Mrs. Oscar Brown Sr., who had helped initiate a short-lived, forty-ninth-state movement from Chicago in the 1930s—a significant antecedent to later nationalist formations in the city and nation.[66]

Like the AAHA, the testimonial dinner also aided Du Bois's efforts to circulate and sustain in print through the 1960s the legacies of his ideas. The dinner's program indicates how the over $200 raised on the occasion for these writing and publishing endeavors would aid the resuscitation of Du Bois's "out of print" scholarship and get volumes recirculated, especially, to institutions he had taught at—namely, Fisk University in Nashville, Atlanta University, and Wilberforce University in Ohio.[67] Another member of the Chicago Du Bois committee was Margaret Burroughs. The event was certainly part of the broader public-history efforts she was at the center of in the city. Chicago native and prolific African American studies scholar Sterling Stuckey writes in the preface to Burroughs's autobiography, *Life with Margaret*, that she, indeed, led the "movement to have [Du Bois] brought to Chicago in 1958 to speak on the South Side." Stuckey notes how the famous Chicago poet Carl Sandburg was frequently honored by the city, and Burroughs felt "a great black figure should be honored as well."[68]

For Burroughs, these forms of recognition extended into areas of public education and the push through the 1960s for black studies on college campuses and in public schools. She recognized the challenges she and many of her generation faced building independent black-led cultural institutions through the 1940s and 1950s. The efforts of the AAHA to promote Du Bois and his writings and knowledge intimately paralleled her and many others' local labors as public schoolteachers who all sought far-reaching social changes in areas of curriculum reform and quality education for inner-city children. In an open letter in 1969 to "Black Students and Black Students Organizations of Chicago" that appeared in the *Chicago Defender*, Burroughs positions herself as a "pioneer in the black history, black pride and black is beautiful movement, (I wore a natural or 'Afro' fifteen years ago and have been rapping black pride long before you were born)." She felt she had "the right to issue" local youth a "challenge." Her letter speaks to the salience of self-determination in late 1960s Black Power and nationalist modes of that period. For example, Burroughs notes that while "schools, universities and libraries may . . . supplement" their studies of African American history, students had the responsibility for teaching themselves knowledge of "heritage and culture." At the same time, her challenge also served as a promotional appeal for financial support to older Bronzeville institutions like the South Side Community Arts Center and the DuSable Museum: "You demand your schools to set up black studies departments and black cultural centers when you have not even taken advantage of, or supported such related institutions which exist in your own black community."[69]

Burroughs's thoughts were very salient given the fact that African American college and university students in Chicago had long been advocating for black public-history recognition on their campuses and in their communities and ultimately helped lead the final push that established black studies in postsecondary institutions by the late 1960s and 1970s. As Ibram H. Rogers notes, University of Chicago students had been part of the early black-history movement in the city: A "Negro Student Club . . . organized balls, participated in Negro History Week activities, hosted a lecture by Howard's William Leo Hansberry on ancient Ethiopia, and hosted dancer Katherine Dunham and her cast, which performed 'Tropical Revue' in 1945." In 1945 University of Chicago students had even protested the existence of a segregated faculty club.[70] According to Rogers, it was "Black students [who] provided the vision for Black Studies. Their activism led to its institutionalization."[71] It has already been noted that significant pioneers of black studies from Chicago, like Stuckey and Haki Madhubuti, were mentored by the Burroughses, while other significant figures who were key student-movement leaders, like Abdul Alkalimat and Carol Adams, would go on to careers of significance in black studies. Indeed, Adams would transition from a faculty position at Malcolm X College to eventually become CEO of the DuSable Museum itself—a position she held from 2009 to 2014.[72]

Burroughs clearly expressed the generational tensions of the late 1960s in ways that revealed the complexities and richness of black nationalist–inflected modes of thought from this moment. She crafted a left nationalism through the late 1950s and 1960s that appealed to both older notions of radical civil rights integrationism and resurgent ideas for black self-determination and cultural nationalism. She had been active in the independent caucus of the CTU during the 1950s. The caucus pressured the union and the City of Chicago to adopt curriculum reforms and fairer hiring standards for blacks and minorities. Burroughs was also part of Teachers for Integrated Schools, a teachers group started in 1961 that was an important independent left-leaning organization made up of public school and city college educators who supported the Coordinating Council of Community Organizations on school-desegregation issues. The council and Teachers for Integrated Schools both worked with Martin Luther King Jr. when he and the Southern Christian Leadership Conference (SCLC) came to Chicago in 1966 and formed the Chicago Freedom Movement after a famous rally at Soldier Field to take on issues of open housing and public school inequities—focused mainly on the city's most poverty-stricken West Side wards.[73]

Burroughs offered ideological and intellectual support that helped frame the high stakes of struggles for racial justice in public education. In a 1966 *Negro Digest* article, she wrote of a need to "integrate" public school learning materials "NOW!" By integration she did not mean simply seating "Negro and white children" together in classrooms or the same schools. Instead, she urgently called for "additional [historical] research and much revision and rewriting." Burroughs noted how distortions about America's racial history in school textbooks contributed to the long-standing and willful disavowal of African American civic virtues in the public sphere, which also led to the prevalence of "white supremacist" views among many white Americans. To her, there was a "direct connection between the question of a positive image for the Negro American and the programs to aid . . . poverty stricken" blacks, who themselves were "culturally deprived" because they lacked "knowledge of self." Burroughs felt that the "millions of dollars" used in the vaunted War on Poverty of the mid-1960s and beyond would "go down the drain" unless the "positive self-image, heritage, Negro history—call it what you will—is faced up to." Such a perspective reflected the malleability of representing black American identities through the mid-twentieth century, their contested forms, and public receptions. For instance, Burroughs categorically collapsed notions of self-image, cultural heritage, and black history. But her suggestion that one could "call it what you will" also underscored the earnestness felt by many (from social reformers to left and nationalist revolutionaries) during the insurgent moments of the mid- to late 1960s and that surely emboldened many forms of global black politics. Burroughs concluded that the circulation and revision of America's "missing pages" of history were urgently needed to adequately redress the pressing racial grievances of African Americans.[74]

Burroughs's article offered a number of solutions to redress these gaps in public knowledge of America's racial past. More than just rewriting the "missing pages," she outlined a program that addressed a good deal of the innovative and creative cultural forms that highlighted the activities of black arts activists as well as African American educators through the late 1960s. Not only did revisions of curriculum units, "lesson plans, readers, language and historical texts" need to take place but also this knowledge needed to be "diagramed" into "pictures, charts, films, film strips, and recorded onto tapes, and records"—in other words, a whole range of new media for creative work available to cultural producers by the late 1960s. Many of these activities were central features of the black arts movement in Los Angeles, Atlanta, New York, and numerous other locales where African Americans partook in diverse cultural production of the late 1960s, especially.[75] Beyond the materials themselves, Burroughs notes how reforms would need to be initiated by "[c]ommittees of teachers, administrators and specialists in the field of Negro literature and history [to] review and make recommendations [for these changes]. Their aim should be to reflect . . . not only the [positive contributions] of the Negro to society, civilization and American history but of other ethnic groups who have been neglected or ignored."[76]

These solutions were acted upon through the DuSable Museum's efforts to promote public history as it expanded its programs through the 1960s. Beginning in 1965, the museum offered classes to schoolteachers and by 1967 had extended invitations to "youth leaders" and "other educators." These were introductory African American history courses that began with overviews of ancient Africa and histories of racial slavery and continued through to topics that dealt with "contemporary America." Coursework was designed to assist teachers in developing supplementary units for their classrooms.[77] When Burroughs announced the program in the *Chicago Defender*, she suggested, "Many [schools had independently introduced] African-American history to their students [but that] a large number of teachers [were] not prepared to introduce this subject to their students." For distribution in these classes, the museum's education committee prepared a range of materials, which included paperback booklets and brochures that featured 137 biographical sketches of "Figures in Negro History." These materials also featured such black Chicago "old settler" personalities as journalist and antilynching advocate Ida B. Wells and, of course, the city's first settler, Jean Baptiste Point DuSable, alongside Reconstruction-era officials like Mississippi's Hiram Revels and Alabama's James T. Rapier. The museum also used its extensive collection of artwork to make a filmstrip, *The African-American in the Making of America*, to supplement these materials.[78]

The focus of many in black Chicago who were closely involved in public-history labors, whether through teaching, public advocacy, or public-history endeavors, demonstrated the diversity of black political projects through the 1950s. Certainly, with its focus on AAHA's and its contemporaries' efforts, this chapter offers an important amplification of the idea that the African American public sphere remained vibrant throughout the entire post–World War II period and into the early 1960s. Public-history organizations, such as the AAHA, and figures, such as Flory, Christine Johnson, and their colleagues at the DuSable Museum, are also important because their labors demonstrated how black nationalism was also more than just the Nation of Islam during the 1950s. These expressions came from a range of organizations that represented the radical left, whose labors in public history emerged alongside those liberal entrepreneurs and strivers who helped publish about black history and life in *Ebony* or *Jet* magazine. The cultural projects undertaken by these organizations and institutions often varied—whether through pictorial magazines and journals as was the case for Johnson Publishing or through cheaper street-level pamphlets and publically accessible forums and celebrations as the AAHA did or that the DuSable Museum carried out.

These collective efforts used public recognition for black history as a way to advance civil rights in the United States and to circulate positive representations of African American identities in the public sphere. As such, black public history contributed to the diversity and richness of nationalist expressions beyond the conventional conservative and iconoclastically male variants that often still stand as definitive standards of black nationalism through the mid-twentieth century. This richness was demonstrated by the ongoing labors of South Side schoolteachers like Margaret Burroughs and significant figures who were a part of her museum-making cohort; and like Christine Johnson, who used her position as the University of Islam's principal through the late 1950s and early

1960s to democratize the forms of parochial education the NOI offered to South Side students; and like Flory, who helped circulate Du Bois's radical thought during a repressive period of U.S. history. The work that black public-history activists with the AAHA carried out through the mid- to late 1960s continued to demonstrate how public-history activism became central to important inter-generational engagements and discussions, as civil rights movements around the country shifted to Black Power and black art perspectives in light of urban rebellions, enduring issues of racial poverty, and conflicts that impacted Third World liberation struggles globally.

CHAPTER FOUR

Cultural Fronts and Public-History Activism in the Black Power Era

In a June 1968 editorial of the *Chicago Defender*, Margaret Burroughs echoes the nationalist leanings of her colleagues from the Afro-American Heritage Association (AAHA) in the early 1960s. Her entry appeared in response to a letter-writing contest the paper ran that prompted readers to answer the question: "Do you believe in black pride?" The paper offered a $5,000 cash prize as incentive for submissions to "help influence others for . . . better." Among the various letters published by the paper, Burroughs's piece was written in a critical (perhaps, sarcastic) tone and commented on the ubiquity and malleability of public assertions of black pride through 1968. "Certainly if such an influential newspaper as the *Chicago Defender*" felt it important to "run a contest," there was, in Burroughs's estimation, obviously a great "need for black pride."[1]

Burroughs continues the piece in a more earnest manner that situated her thought squarely in traditions of independent black politics but that also reflected her commitment above all to public-history activism. She suggests that a "knowledge" of "ancestral heritage, and the contributions that" blacks had "made to society" needed to be imbibed by younger generations through "any crash [*sic*] means possible."[2] Burroughs's assertions echo the sentiments in the 1960s of younger generations who revered the militancy of martyred figures like slain black Muslim leader Malcolm X, the figure most often viewed as the "forerunner" for Black Power in America. Peniel Joseph indicates, however, post–World War II political scenes in urban black metropolises, such as Harlem, "included openly Communist elected officials, Garveyites, trade unionists, and liberal integrationists."[3] Indeed, out of this diverse matrix of Black Power's forerunners, public-history activists certainly had space to express their own repertoires for activism. As such, Burroughs felt knowledge of black public history should be transmitted judiciously and generationally through parents to their children and further "nurtured" through traditional institutions, such as the "church, school, and indigenous community organizations."[4]

Burroughs's editorial was published just over two months after Martin Luther King Jr.'s assassination in 1968, when many African American neighborhoods around the country openly revolted. In Chicago, the West Side exploded after the news. Indeed, it was in this impoverished part of the city that King and his organization SCLC focused the bulk of their energies during the mid-1960s when they advocated for "open housing."[5] Burroughs's *Defender* editorial further analyzes an important speech given by King, only weeks before his death, at an at-capacity centennial celebration for the birthday of the acclaimed scholar-activist W. E. B. Du Bois at Carnegie Hall in New York City. The event had been sponsored by her left-wing contemporaries at the influential *Freedomways* magazine in February 1968 and highlighted King's important views against the Vietnam War and against racial poverty in America, which he frequently expressed in the late 1960s.[6] Indeed, as the DuSable Museum expanded its programs, its founders engaged with younger generations of Black Power and black arts movement activists energized by the widespread urban rebellions of many inner-city working-class communities of color and by various left-wing and nationalist currents equally emboldened by renewed affinities for Third World anticolonialism and revolution. Coverage in *Freedomways* demonstrates how these rebellions spread to over 257 cities across the United States in response to the ineffectiveness of voting-rights reforms, widespread white backlash to social reforms, and the starkness of urban poverty.[7]

Burroughs's editorial positions her own politics with an older generation of African American leftists and cultural activists because she tactfully enlisted black middle-class respectability alongside a radical teleology traced from Du Bois to King. As noted previously, Burroughs contributed to *Freedomways* magazine during the early 1960s, becoming the journal's first arts editor, and worked alongside general editor Shirley Graham Du Bois (Du Bois's wife) and other black popular-front leftists and fellow-traveling women, such as Esther Cooper Jackson. Throughout the 1960s, the editors of *Freedomways* established a politics of radical integrationism that enabled the magazine to partake in an "uneasy alliance" of left nationalists, leftists, and civil rights liberals who were part of the milieu of writers around whom the magazine coalesced.[8] Erik

McDuffie writes, "*Freedomways* signaled the long-standing effort of black left feminists to center women in the black radical agenda" as the magazine regularly featured the work of women who had been involved with the Communist left since the 1920s; these included Claudia Jones, Louise Thompson Patterson, Eslanda Robeson, Alice Childress, Dorothy Burnham, and visual artists Elizabeth Catlett and Margaret Burroughs.[9] The radicalism of such women predates the identity politics of the Black Power era and had been sustained through the repressive political settings of postwar and Cold War America. Recent scholars of black feminism note how many working-class African American women, unlike many of their black middle-class counterparts, struggled over the course of the whole mid-twentieth century to reshape "dominant notions of respectability as a vehicle to promote radical change."[10]

Burroughs was thus attentive to the idea of forging a united African American radical politics in the wake of King's assassination—especially through her work as a public historian in Chicago. In her *Defender* editorial, she notes how at the 1968 New York tribute to Du Bois, King remarked on the elder scholar's refusal to "apologize for being black." Burroughs adds that Du Bois's pride in his people was not because "their color endowed them with some vague greatness, [but, rather,] because their concrete achievements in struggle had advanced humanity in all its hues, black, white, yellow, red, or brown." Burroughs comments that Du Bois was a "fitting guide . . . for anyone seeking black pride." She concludes with a plug for the Museum of African American History, which had "taken upon itself the herculean task [of building] black pride" in the community and that its "founders [had] played some small part in focusing attention on the heroic black past [that also pointed] to a glorious future."[11] Overall, the editorial is a shrewdly worded positioning of both Du Bois's and King's connected and usable political legacies for the Black Power era. Seen in this light, Burroughs advanced a radical integrationism (humanity "in all its hues") that she heard expressed through King's revealing tribute to Du Bois. Such integrationism clearly invokes what scholars, such as Robert Korstad, Martha Biondi, and Jacqueline Dowd Hall, might call "civil rights unionism" or the "black popular front" from the 1930s and 1940s. Hall writes, "The civil rights unionism of the 1940s . . . combined a principled and tactical belief in interracial organizing with a strong emphasis on black culture and institutions." Rather than being fully "lost to memory" due to the disruptions of the Cold War 1950s, as Hall notes of civil rights historiography generally, figures such as the Burroughses worked to resuscitate these black radical pasts in the 1960s in ways that forecast their intergenerational impact on the shape that Black Power activism's diverse repertoires took through the late twentieth century.[12]

This chapter shows how, like many of her contemporaries, Margaret Burroughs and many of her colleagues at the DuSable Museum of African American History, such as Eugene P. Feldman, Ralph Turner, and other public historians, constructively engaged with younger generations of activists in Chicago who became interested in expressions of black cultural and political identity through the mid- to late 1960s. Chicago was certainly a site of tension between generations and political classes of black Americans. This tension often reflected the "typical" gap between young and old, militant and moderate, and integrationist and separatist and highlighted many forms of black radical and insurgent cultural politics during the 1960s. This contrasts with the generation gap greatly emphasized by most scholars, such as Sharon Monteith, David Farber, George Lipsitz, and others who have written on the youthfulness of many left social movements through the 1960s in national frames.[13] However, a conversation about this very generation gap and the related issue of black class politics between Margaret Burroughs and her elder colleague at the museum, Ralph Turner, reveals a great deal about the particular social visions black public-history activists had in Chicago. Turner, a former railway worker, was a Marcus Garvey supporter and later became a devoted volunteer lecturer at the museum. Both he and Burroughs expressed their own visions for how to achieve black liberation under U.S. capitalism and throughout the African diaspora. This chapter examines this revealing conversation between these DuSable Museum figures as a key source and shows how facile divisions between generations obscure what were, in fact, entangled cultural, political projects and contestations.

Through such conversations and through the work they each conducted at the museum, the DuSable staff demonstrated successful collaborations and interventions with local younger activists who made up Chicago's black arts movement (BAM)—the cultural arm of the Black Power movement. Although the Black Power and BAM are often discussed simultaneously, William L. Van DeBurg describes the arts movement as a "spiritual sister" of Black Power. For Van DeBurg, BAM was made up of "poets, playwrights, and artists in the late sixties and early seventies" who "sought to speed black empowerment via a 'radical reordering of the western cultural aesthetic.'"[14] However, any historical discussion of the arts and cultural dimension of power movements requires greater attention to local diversity and specificity. This chapter proceeds in the spirit of James Smethurst's suggestion that studies of the black arts movement, more than just the problematically gendered and spiritualized "sister" of Black Power, need special consideration of the movement's diverse manifestations. Rather, such studies need to be organized "regionally . . . to look at how connections between different groups of black artists and intellectuals took place on a grassroots level and to get a sense of the significant regional variations of the movement."[15] Smethurst builds on the methods of pioneer scholars of the black arts and cultural movements of the mid-twentieth century, such as Kalamu ya Salaam, who suggests that they "started out as disparate local initiatives across a wide geographic area, coalescing into a national movement with a sense of a broader coherence that, in turn, inspired more local, grassroots activities." Smethurst adds to Salaam's thoughts by suggesting that there was "a continuing, bidirectional interplay between the national and the local in which the national inspired the local, even as the local confirmed and deepened a sense of the national as truly encompassing the nation—both in the geographical sense of covering the United States and in the ideological sense of engaging the entire black nation."[16]

Black Chicago's history-museum endeavors were very much at the forefront of the commonly expressed idea that emanated from many local black arts movements: that it was in fact "nation" time. As the museum expanded its programs through the 1960s and 1970s, it began innovative work in local prisons and with local schoolchildren (black and white)—to reach younger generations of people as well as important segments of the black working classes. These efforts demonstrated how black public-history activists in Chicago continued both the interracial black cultural front and/or black left-labor coalition ideals earlier expressed by organizations such as the National Negro Museum and Historical Foundation from earlier decades well into the Black Power era.

Mr. Turner's History Lesson

Burroughs's thoughts on intergenerational black politics continued through the diverse public-history projects she carried out in the late 1960s. These projects helped further establish the context for the museum's physical expansion and its eventual need for relocation.[17] One unique endeavor in which she participated was a comprehensive citywide oral-history project co-commissioned by teachers at Chicago State College on the South Side. Through this project, Burroughs interviewed a number of elder African Americans in the community who had lived in Chicago since the beginning of the Great Migration.[18] In 1970 the museum continued the methodological approaches of the Chicago State College project and initiated Operation Awareness, its own oral-history program under the auspices of the Model Cities Program and federally funded. The project enlisted fourteen teams (each comprised one adult and two teenagers) from "remedial classes in South Side schools" to interview community members in a similar fashion. These students were trained in oral-history techniques and sent out to "interview black Americans of all ages, occupations and walks of life."

According to a *Chicago Tribune* article, the project worked in two ways. Student interviewers with portable museum exhibits visited fourteen South Side locations. These exhibits used a variety of media, from "films, slides, pictures and narratives" to convey the "story of Black American history" at a local level. After residents viewed the displays, students recorded their responses and documented the "ages, names, occupations, attitudes, memories and other important aspects of [their subjects'] day-to-day existence." The project's director, Archie Listenbee, notes that those who participated in the project included "a cross-section of people . . . from young . . . to a 111-year-old." The oral histories were ultimately archived at the museum and "made available to researchers."[19] These experiments with oral history and intergenerational exchange underscored the museum's significant and innovative role in promoting local public-history efforts in black Chicago through the late 1960s.

Though the full oral-history project was never completed or published by the college, Burroughs's interview with Turner was unique and deserves special consideration for its range and scope. Turner, the museum's founding treasurer and later a senior lecturer, moved to Chicago from Missouri and for most of his working life had been a railway worker and union organizer. He was also a Marcus Garvey supporter during the 1920s when Garvey's movement advocated emigration for black Americans under the banner "back to Africa." His politics shifted through the 1930s and 1940s to a more Marxist nationalism when he supported African American struggles in the interracial Congress of Industrial Organizations (CIO) union movements of those decades and visited socialist countries in the Eastern bloc to gain more critical perspectives on U.S. forms of racism and racial capitalism. He very much shifted toward the left-wing civil rights unionism that emerged in those decades. By the late 1950s, Turner became a key supporter of the Burroughses' efforts to buy the former railroad-workers club (also known as the Quincy Club) for their museum project.[20]

An interview with Turner that Margaret Burroughs conducted for the Chicago State College oral-history project reveals a great deal about how both these museum founders approached intergenerational concerns during the Black Power era. Throughout the conversation, Burroughs offers leading questions that prompt a wide-ranging discussion of the generation gap in ways that touch on everything from Black Power and nationalism to racial capitalism. For Turner, the first impressions of schoolchildren who came to the museum were conditioned by the fact of having first seen more impressive downtown museums, such as the Field Museum of Natural History. However, he observed that when young people walked around the DuSable Museum and viewed its many exhibits, they began to see how "black people" had made "a contribution to America" (figure 6). He and other volunteer staff members made sure to emphasize to visitors that the museum was "theirs"—a thought that projected a sense of community ownership and agency over the museum experience. In these instances, Turner felt there was "no generation gap." When he lectured to young people at the museum about black history, he was able to use his years of experience and a lifetime of autodidactic study and involvement with working-class African American social movements to "blend [his knowledge] with their thinking." To Turner, these interactions seemed especially significant given the dearth of African American history content in the curriculum of most public schools—even by the late 1960s.[21]

Others at the museum observed Turner speaking to students and felt his impact on visitors was a useful model for both teachers and local activists alike. Feldman describes Turner's teaching style as "down-to-earth" and "easy to understand. [Turner used] no platitudes, no terminology that sometimes people who are in a social movement use among themselves." His lectures commanded attention from students and were regularly interspersed by applause. This was usually followed by an open session for questions and comments that Turner welcomed. Turner's lessons were so captivating that the University of Illinois eventually made a film about them, *Mr. Turner's History Lesson*.[22]

Figure 6. Margaret T. G. Burroughs giving a tour to students at the original location of the DuSable Museum, 3806 South Michigan Avenue, ca. late 1960s. Eugene P. Feldman, *The Birth and the Building of the DuSable Museum* (Chicago: DuSable Museum Press, 1981), 56. Courtesy of DuSable Museum of African American History, Chicago, Illinois.

During the interview, Burroughs asks Turner to trace his role in twentieth-century black political traditions. She wanted to record his experiences in the history of the freedom struggle, his views of the "black problem," and his experiences in diverse radical African American–led movements of the twentieth century (particularly, the labor struggles of the 1930s and 1940s). For example, Burroughs asks if he recalled "early freedom fighters" and "organizations because many of the young people today feel that the fight for the rights of the people started in the '60s." She singles out figures like Edward Strong and Louis Burnham, national leaders with the National Negro Congress (NNC) during the 1930s and 1940s; singer and Communist activist Paul Robeson; former National Maritime Union head Ferdinand Smith; and Du Bois—all heroes of the African American radical left from the long mid-twentieth century and indicative of the black popular-front traditions Burroughs herself felt akin to throughout her life.[23]

Turner's reply returns their discussion to the issue of a generation gap in the late 1960s and he tells a specific history of the black-freedom struggle—one that emphasizes the accomplishments of black leftists alongside cultural tropes that connect to collective memories of the Great Migration experience. Turner expands on this: "I think I know what you have in mind. You're talking about the generation gap where we have young people who are saying to people of my age that had you people been doing your job, we wouldn't have the problems we have today, so since you haven't, get out of the way and let us do it." Turner bristles at this thought and suggests that "these people know nothing about history." He recalls his own activities in Chicago during the 1920s when he marched on South State Street for Garvey's back-to-Africa movement. He remembers the efforts of Chicagoans to protest laws against interracial prizefighting in light of the exploits of prolific African American boxer Jack Johnson in the 1910s and the later involvement of many South Siders in efforts to desegregate professional baseball. In Turner's account, these movements evolved into the militant civil rights organizations of the 1930s and 1940s, such as the NNC, and of the early 1950s, such as the National Negro Labor Council; each took up issues of wartime and postwar employment and economic discrimination, particularly. Though certainly left wing in orientation and at times dominated by the Communist left for better or worse, such organizations had been set up "by Black people" before they dissolved under the pressures and repressions of Cold War McCarthyism. For Turner, it was the militant leadership of figures, such as Robeson, from this earlier era that needed to be emulated in the Black Power movement of the late 1960s. Turner said Robeson "could not be made to run when the hounds began to see that the struggle for black dignity was coming in."[24]

Turner's metaphorical use of the term "hounds" also makes creative use of a famous blues music trope. He gestures to the struggles in blues lyrics of African Americans against the devil's hellhounds. Such use of the past signifies longer, more complex histories of black struggle against racism's many forms, particularly, the struggles of multiple generations of trans-Mississippi southerners, who made up the majority of participants in the Great Migrations to midwestern metropolises, such as Chicago. As blues historian Ted Gioia writes, the seminal lyrics of "Hellhound on My Trail" by the mysterious Delta Blues singer Robert Johnson suggest that listeners are "left to ponder whether the hellhound of the title is real or metaphorical, but the sense of being chased and hunted is powerfully evoked, as in those nightmares that leave you struggling to outrun some vaguely understood but deeply felt danger." The hound Turner evokes in African American vernacular is deliberately vague and metaphorical, yet also a fitting image to use as a way to indicate collective experiences of migration and struggle through the insurgent 1960s.[25]

Turner's reflection on the freedom struggle sidesteps the important roles played by mainstream civil rights and civic organizations, such as the Urban League and the NAACP. Instead, he offers an important statement about the complex relationship between African American old and new left cultural and revolutionary nationalisms during the mid- to late 1960s—namely, over the potential pitfalls of black capitalism, the conflicted outcomes of colonial independence struggles in the Third World, and ongoing Western-led wars abroad. Historian Van Gosse's more recent work on the new left and Black Power judiciously validates Turner's overtures here. Gosse demonstrates how tensions between the old and new left were overstated within the black community, especially because of the sustained popularity of iconic figures such as Du Bois and Robeson. Moreover, Gosse demonstrates how African American liberation struggles were the catalyst for America's new left social movements in the late 1960s.[26] Despite his old-guard leftism, Turner offers critical praise to cultural nationalists who supported racial separatism; these were "young people who [were] saying that we [African Americans]" had to "go it alone." They were, he concedes, "making gains." But, in Turner's view, the way to "bring about the greatest degree of equality in this country as black people" would be to deal with "economics. . . . As long as we're workers, we will have this problem." He extends this materialist analysis of power and "the black problem" to a consideration of the Vietnam War's hypocrisies and the peace movement that had only slowly attracted the support of civil rights organizations.[27] Finally, Turner also feels that the renewed interest in black capitalism by younger activists in the African American liberation struggle through the 1960s seemed untenable as a tactic for it would not benefit everyone due to the nature of capitalism. Turner doubts whether black capitalism alone could benefit the majority of African Americans and brings up the newly independent states of Africa as comparison. These states were mostly "politically independent" by the 1960s but had not attained "economic independence. Now, it might build up a few black businessmen who would want a front for the capitalists, but insofar as . . . [it might benefit] black people as a whole . . . [this appeared as] an impossibility."[28]

This expansive conversation between Burroughs and Turner stands as a significant intellectual statement by two veteran activists of the twentieth-century African American freedom struggle from Chicago. It further demonstrated how important ideas about generational exchange, political ideology and traditions, new movement tactics, and local knowledge of diverse racial pasts were discussed and framed through the many public-history activities supported by the founding members of the DuSable Museum.

Black Left Internationalism

Burroughs's conversation with Turner about longer traditions of black radicalism is further contextualized by her autobiographical reflections. These reflections specifically illustrate the coordinates for her and her husband's left-wing politics. Moreover, consideration of these expressions of personal and political identity helps situate the work that the Burroughses and their associates did through their public-history labors—geared as they were toward not simply uplifting black working classes but achieving their empowerment, as well. It was the intellectual legacies of earlier left-wing black radicalism that most impacted the outlook of the museum's early years and subsequent development despite the "sundering" of black politics from left traditions, generally noted by scholars about the McCarthyist moments of the mid-twentieth century.[29]

In her autobiography, Burroughs underscores the artistic and political sensibilities and feelings of camaraderie she and her husband shared with black cultural activists on the radical left (from her generation and older). Their collective travels to the Soviet Union, in particular, helped shape what were lifelong critical outlooks of the American scene:

> In the art of the times, there was a sort of coming together of influences that were multi-political, international and class conscious (in that they combined working class and rural Southern folkways), which resulted in the emergence of a new hybrid of black popular culture. Foreign influences, Russian included, became important to blacks, who felt they were treated better abroad than in their own country. The creation of a new Soviet citizen attracted African

Americans to the Soviet Union, where they could explore a national identity free from the kind of class, gender, and racial biases that pervaded America. Paul Robeson, Langston Hughes, W. E. B. Du Bois and Claude McKay all lived or traveled extensively in the USSR between the 1920s and 1960s, all of them using their Soviet experiences to rethink the practice of cultural exclusion and the ideas of citizenship and national belonging in the U.S. My late husband, Charles, spent much of his life there, as well. I think all these men traveled as much to obtain the proper perspective of distance, of awareness, as to gain a particular foreign perspective, in order to give them a vantage from which to consider the developing—or deteriorating—aspects of social and cultural life for black Americans back home.[30]

The Burroughses clearly saw themselves as fellow travelers with this older cohort of left-wing and internationalist African American cultural and intellectual icons. They eventually journeyed to Russia together in 1966 and 1967 and a year later made their first trip to Africa, visiting Ghana in 1968.[31] As noted in chapter 2, internationalism influenced the earliest stages of their visions for a museum project—politics that were highlighted by Cold War–induced sojourns to Mexico in the early 1950s and Charles Burroughs's own childhood experiences from Moscow. Salon discussions hosted by the Burroughses in the museum's formative years ranged widely in topic, from international socialism to educational method, and were essentially, in Feldman's characterization, "about the denial of Black history and culture in American and world life."[32] Such critical perspectives on American life and racial history were emboldened by the experiences of world travels that brought the Burroughses to Africa for the first time. Reflections from such black cosmopolitans about the effects that America's racial paradoxes had on issues of citizenship and national identity over the course of the twentieth century's long durée underscores why it is important not to overstate the racial uplift and/or social engineering impulses (and, hence, political homogeneity) of middle-class social actors.

Such a critique of middle-class intellectuals and artists is one of the major dynamics in Harold Cruse's monumental yet controversial *The Crisis of the Negro Intellectual*. The book offers a scathing condemnation of the African American intelligentsia from the 1920s through the 1960s. Cruse saves a good deal of his animosity for what he calls an "integrationist elite," particularly, African American leftists from New York; he aligns *Freedomways* editors alongside Hansberry, Robeson, and others, whom Cruse saw as disruptive to the labors of ostensibly genuine revolutionary nationalists (like himself). While Cruse gets at the strategic importance of culture industries to African American politics in the late 1960s that certainly helped express the black arts movement, his diatribe, which also lambasts other self-proclaimed "revolutionary" nationalists, obscures important political differences among middle-class social activists.[33]

Indeed, the black radicalism of Margaret Burroughs was especially attentive to racial, class, and gender oppression and, as such, defies the "integrationist elite" label a figure such as Cruse no doubt would have ascribed to her and her colleagues at the museum. In another piece of writing from the 1960s reprinted in her autobiography, Margaret Burroughs places herself in a longer tradition of mid-twentieth-century black feminism. She recalls how dancer Katherine Dunham (born in 1909 in Chicago), American folk singer Odetta Holmes, South African singer Miriam Makeba (born in the 1930s), and she each ascribed to natural hair aesthetics as a conscious rejection of European gender standards—well before such styles came into vogue by the late 1960s with the resurgent forms of cultural nationalism in the Black Power era.[34]

The Burroughses pragmatically incorporated these worldly and intersectional perspectives into their public-history work upon their return from many travels abroad. For example, they spoke at numerous South Side community events organized jointly with other local public-history groups, such as the AAHA, about their travels—some of which benefited the museum's expanding programs and physical relocation. Margaret Burroughs used her travels to West Africa, especially, to further professionalize as a museum specialist. She suggested that the field research she conducted in Ghana would "aid the work" she was trying to do at the museum. A year earlier, she told a *Chicago Tribune* reporter that she wanted to more accurately specify, in anthropological terms, "what part of Africa" a piece in the museum's collection was from, "from what time and who made it."[35] In her autobiography, Burroughs also notes how their travels were as much about research of "museological ideas" as they were about leisure, "split equally between relaxing and learning."[36]

Such desires for knowledge demonstrate how the DuSable's expanding functions accorded with democratic shifts taking place in both museum and academic disciplines through the mid-twentieth century. In the absence of professional expertise, earlier exhibits at the museum idealized and/or sentimentalized African and southern folkways. Still, Burroughs's strivings for education and further professionalization through global itinerancy are significant because she ultimately later worked through her museum and other public-history groups in Chicago to further revisionist scholarly efforts against tenacious Victorian legacies of biological and evolutionary racism, which still circulated in the public sphere. As Robert Rydell demonstrates, anthropological exhibits in world fairs and museums from the late nineteenth century through the twentieth century forwarded dangerous forms of racial knowledge and misinformation. Moreover, from the 1890s, Chicago's central role in staging such spectacles had always been recognized.[37] That the museum and its staff strove to professionalize their practices to work against such deep-seated fallacies in museum and exhibitionary fields further reveals the earnestness with which they undertook their labors to revise and represent the past.

Art and Politics

The mid- to late 1960s, of course, featured the upsurge of the black arts movement across the United States. The DuSable Museum's expanding programs and functions certainly contributed to the movement's growth. The museum showcased an emerging younger generation's role in the development of many old and new sites for African American cultural production by supporting young writers, artists, teachers, and historians.[38] This wider context for cultural production by black communities across the United States is one dimension of an important backdrop for understanding the expansion of the DuSable Museum's programs in Chicago over the same period and the degree to which the museum's staff engaged with younger generations who became active during the Black Power era. Arguably a close rival of New York, Chicago's black arts scene was equally vibrant and included visual arts, literature, and music that influenced the city's physical, cultural, and intellectual landscapes.[39] One very notable project for its impact on the aesthetics of inner-cityscapes nationwide was the Wall of Respect, East Forty-Third Street and Langley Avenue. The wall inspired numerous other mural projects throughout Chicago and in urban areas across the country. Collectively, these murals have reenvisioned African American urban spaces as empowered sites of community public history, autonomy, and cultural reflection. Though highly significant, the Wall of Respect was a project that also highlighted the conflicted nature of cultural politics during the Black Power era. A factional dispute between the artists who started the project (namely, William Walker and the artists who went on to form the Afri-Cobra collective) led to disagreements about how the mural was to be maintained and updated. In the wake of this charged political atmosphere, the Wall of Respect, devised by members of the Organization of Black American Culture (OBAC) and BAM in Chicago, was removed by city officials in 1973. Many of the young people who originally formed OBAC, such as Jeff Donaldson, first helped with the American Negro Emancipation Centennial Authority of the early 1960s and were known as the ANECANS.[40]

Certainly, OBAC was not the only significant BAM group in Chicago and was joined by others who worked on diverse artistic genres and media, notably,

Afri-Cobra, a group of visual artists who made up the majority of painters of the Wall of Respect. Theatrical projects included Val Gray's Kuumba Theatre and dance group and the Afro-Arts Theater, through which Theodore Ward mentored many younger aspiring black theatrical workers. Literary engines flourished, such as Third World Press, established by one of Margaret Burroughs's protégés, Haki Madhubuti; Lotus Press; and the journal *Negro Digest/Black World*, edited by Hoyt Fuller and owned by Johnson Publishing, which, of course, also published the very popular pictorial lifestyle magazine *Ebony* until 2016, when the company sold it. Acclaimed Chicago poet Gwendolyn Brooks ran creative-writing workshops that brought her into contact with numerous young BAM writers.[41] As Smethurst writes, "the most distinctive feature of the Black Arts Movement in Chicago is that it is difficult, if not impossible, to pick out a dominant artistic genre."[42]

All this activity paralleled other important midwestern institutions, such as the Karamu House in Cleveland and Dunham's performing arts center in the predominantly African American working-class town of East St. Louis in southern Illinois. These institutions were vibrant and supported a vast array of artistic endeavors and repertoires. Smethurst's encyclopedic work treats many of these figures and organizations in his BAM study, with separate chapters on regional centers in New York, the U.S. south, the Midwest, and the West Coast. Other scholars, such as Daniel Widener, are examining these regional centers even more closely in ways that further reveal the complexities of black arts activisms and repertoires and their extensive engagements with civic power structures, especially. Many of these new studies underscore the role that women, in particular, had in leading these forms of cultural and social struggle.[43]

Some of the OBAC artists who designed the Wall of Respect, perhaps Chicago's most prolific project from the black arts era, knew the Burroughses well and often exhibited their work at the DuSable Museum. Feldman, a former research director there, notes that at coffee seminars the institution hosted, two of the wall's central artists, Eugene Edaw and William Walker, discussed doing public artwork. Two large rooms in the museum's basement exhibited murals done by Eugene Edaw; Walker, the more senior of the artists, later completed the Worker mural outside the Packinghouse Workers union hall near East Forty-Ninth Street and South Wabash Avenue in 1974.[44] Like much of the artwork at the museum, these paintings treated iconic episodes and heroes of African American history, including the long history of racial slavery in the Americas "and the hard, harsh . . . work" and "killing of Blacks to force obedience" alongside images of hope, such as slave revolts; Harriet Tubman and the underground railroad; Sojourner Truth and "her abolitionist travels and lectures"; and the white abolitionist John Brown and "his efforts to free slaves" through martyrdom. Another Edaw mural from the same period depicts King and demonstrates the didactic aesthetics of such visual forms that connected black pasts to contemporary African American freedom struggles (figure 7). About twenty other paintings Edaw completed are of ancient West African kingdoms and remain housed at the museum.[45]

This artwork commemorating black pasts circulated well beyond the walls of the DuSable, notably, at important regional African American festivals and expositions. Such exchanges demonstrate that the museum's public-history work paralleled and, at times, overlapped with other significant expositional spaces African Americans developed around the city, which were also integral to cultural expressions from the Black Power era. For example, many of these paintings were exhibited at Chicago's Black Expo from 1969 through 1974. Black expositions were "promotional festivals" geared toward supporting local business ventures. Some were held at Chicago's International Amphitheater and boosted by institutions and organizations, such as the *Chicago Defender* and Operation Breadbasket, the latter headed by Jesse Jackson. The 1969 expo drew extremely large crowds to the three-day exhibits at the Chicago Amphitheater; the 1970 expo saw close to eight hundred thousand attendees. However, these massive spectacles were difficult to sustain financially when the U.S. economy faltered. As one historian notes, nearly half of Chicago's African American

Figure 7. Ralph Turner explaining a Eugene Edaw mural to students at the DuSable Museum, ca. late 1960s. Eugene P. Feldman, *The Birth and the Building of the DuSable Museum* (Chicago: DuSable Museum Press, 1981), 57. Courtesy of DuSable Museum of African American History, Chicago, Illinois.

businesses perished in the recession of 1974, along with Jackson's expo experiment. Edaw's paintings were also lent by the DuSable Museum for the Black Esthetics festival in 1973 at the Museum of Science and Industry in nearby Hyde Park, alongside paintings by other Illinois artists who had done the artwork for the 1963 Negro Emancipation Centennial at McCormick Place. The *Chicago Defender*'s coverage of these festivities and its inclusion of the DuSable's relocation to Washington Park reflect the museum's growing prominence in the local black public sphere. These efforts ensured that a space for the exposition of black history and culture could survive and be sustained through periods of hardship.[46]

The growth of African American–led expositions and festivals in Chicago and the Midwest became a significant part of a larger movement of widely attended black conventions that had increased with frequency across the United States from the late 1960s through the early 1970s. These conventions varied from region to region and in terms of emphasis (business, culture, or politics). Still, they certainly reflected the currency of black cultural politics to the public sphere as well as the historic twentieth-century migrations of black southerners to urban centers. Major conventions took place in Newark, New Jersey, and Atlanta, Georgia—but likely the most well-known was the 1972 convention in Gary, Indiana, not far from the boundaries of Chicago's Far South Side. These conventions brought African American political elites, civil rights leaders, and grassroots cultural and left nationalist figures together to form unified agendas for black politics nationwide.[47] It was at the Gary convention where Jackson famously delivered his provocative Nation Time speech and where poet-activist Amiri Baraka sought to convene a dialogue between diverse segments of the Black Power and BAM. The attempt to forge this united agenda revealed a major shift in African American political culture through the 1960s, wherein older divisions between militant black nationalists and civil rights integrationists had given way to new divisions, notably, between a putative "grassroots" and more elite elected officials. As Komozi Woodard argues, "the Modern Black Convention Movement was an essential component of the Black Power movement which included the cultural, political, and economic programs proposed and developed by the Black Arts Movement." The convention movement in Woodard's estimation included organizations as diverse as the "Black Panthers, US, Republic of New Africa, the Revolutionary Action Movement, the Nation of Islam [and] the League of Revolutionary Black workers," who all came to these conventions at some point: "Together these cultural and political formations galvanized millions of black people in the broadest movement in

African American history."[48] A precursor to the Gary convention occurred in 1971 in Northlake, Illinois—a western Chicago suburb near O'Hare International Airport. Manning Marable estimates that this meeting was "probably the only instance between 1965 and 1983 when representatives of virtually every major tendency of the black movement sat down together in the same room."[49] As such, the locus of many of these important convention-based discussions was in the Midwest in and around Chicago.

The DuSable Museum's expanding programs were certainly a part of this context, though much smaller in scale than the economically focused festivities of the black expositional forms of this period. The role that younger African American artists and activists had in the growing work of the museum does the most to situate the institution in this context. As noted above, the museum was also a major contributor to BAM in Chicago. It offered an important public history–focused site for the support of younger African American artists, intellectuals, and thinkers that highlighted their contributions to late 1960s black American culture and politics.

For example, as noted above, the Burroughses mentored prominent South Side poet and activist Madhubuti. Before he started Third World Press in Chicago in the late 1960s, Madhubuti (born Don L. Lee in 1942) volunteered as an assistant curator and membership director for the museum from 1962 to 1967 and worked closely with the Burroughses on their public-history labors through this period. Among his many activities with the museum, Madhubuti joined DuSable's research publications director Feldman to teach black-history classes for a parents' group in a member's home. In turn, the group, known as the Parents Guild, donated money and provided volunteers to carry out visitor tours so the museum could hold longer hours. Another important figure from the Black Power and black arts generation in Chicago and closely mentored by the Burroughses was poet, dramatist, and youth worker Useni Eugene Perkins, son of the late South Side sculptor and radical leftist Marion Perkins. Both Useni Eugene Perkins and Madhubuti volunteered at the museum in the mid- to late 1960s and were arguably deeply influenced by black Chicago's public-history milieu.[50]

The museum's founders worked to promote the poetry of Perkins and Madhubuti in ways that defied the late 1960s dissolution of traditional civil rights alliances (such as those between progressive Jewish Americans and African Americans). For example, in the *Chicago Defender*, Feldman reviewed the early poetry collections of both Madhubuti (under his original name) and Perkins. The reviews demonstrated the openness with which the museum's founders received new aesthetic ideas on black identity expressed by younger artists and activists from the late 1960s. Feldman quotes Lee's poetry to highlight the racial hypocrisies of America's involvement in the Vietnam War:

> Viet-brothers come give us a hand
> we fight for freedom,
> Give me my forty acres
> Broken promises and hypocri
> sies.

Here was a "young, Black poet of America," writes Feldman, "who belongs to the new generation of men and women who cannot be kidded any longer." He also reports the circulation of Lee's poetry in prolific BAM journals from New York City, such as *Kauri* and *Liberator* magazines, as well as through the Illinois Teachers College publication the *Torch*. Similarly, Feldman reviewed a poetry collection Perkins edited that included contributions from African American schoolchildren in summer writing workshops. Feldman's support for this work fit with his part-time contracts as a teacher for high school dropouts and in adult education in Chicago through the 1960s and his primary volunteer work with the museum. His reviews did not challenge the aesthetic cultural nationalism the younger poets expressed, for he recognized the imperative of understanding the "hearts and minds of Afro-Americans in 1967." These thoughts stand against the general indifference expressed (and, arguably, still expressed) by much of white America to the plight of inner-city African American youth over this same period.[51]

The public support that the museum's founders offered younger activists did not mean the founders completely transcended the generation gap. It is more accurate to suggest that relationships between BAM activists of different generations with working-class populations and movements were complex and need to be characterized in subtle terms. Smethurst demonstrates how intergenerational interactions of activists often consisted of "uneven" dialogues. For example, he points to a 1969 tribute hosted on the South Side for Chicago poet Brooks, an elder figure who fully embraced the black arts generation of the late 1960s through her mentorship of younger writers. At this tribute, Margaret Burroughs criticized the uncritical aesthetic forms for black pride she felt were expressed by younger artists and writers involved with BAM. To Burroughs, many younger artists lacked sufficient attention to questions of "craft" and, instead, embraced cruder visual and literary forms through their art that did not pay enough homage to older African American traditions and precursors. Such formalism alienated her and some of her generational cohort from younger

Black Power radicals who expressed more militant forms of cultural nationalism and whose creative work was more aligned with the "individual passions"
of America's avant-garde artists and intellectuals through the 1960s.[52]

It is also possible to view these intergenerational tensions through the prism
of shifting African American class politics and to consider these tensions in
light of one of the most traumatic events in black Chicago's history from the
late 1960s—namely, the police assassination of Illinois Black Panther Party
(BPP) leader Fred Hampton in December 1969. In Chicago, these divisions
manifested as neighborhood rivalries. This was especially true through the
1960s and 1970s, when poorer southern migrants moved to the city's West Side
neighborhoods, such as Lawndale.[53] It was, after all, no coincidence that in the
wake of King's assassination in 1968, the BPP expanded to Chicago through
these more working-class neighborhoods as a chiefly West Side organization
(despite the fact that under Hampton's leadership, the Illinois BPP chapter for
a time united South and West Side factions). The Panthers' local significance
to the more homogeneously "southern" folk on the West Side also highlighted
important differences with the larger and more class-divided African American South Side where the Panthers had less significance. Jon Rice relates, "A
minority of black South Siders had moved to the southern extremity of that
ghetto—the Chatham neighborhood—and found some financial success by
servicing the black poor as their schoolteachers, funeral directors, barbers, and
postmen. Thus, the South Side had a range of incomes much broader than those
on the West Side."[54] These neighborhood differences are to a degree supported
by the fact there is little evidence from local newspapers, museum records, or
the many interviews and reflective writings of the DuSable founders to indicate
that such groups as the Black Panthers (or even South Side youth gangs, such as
the Blackstone Rangers, with deeper roots on the South Side) had a great deal to
do with the museum and its activities. The DuSable Museum was a decidedly
South Side institution in a middle-class neighborhood between Washington
Park and Hyde Park and was likely not on the radar of organizations such as
the BPP.

When these dynamics between neighborhoods were taking place, routine
harassment from police and informants escalated against the black community and especially younger black activists who were in the BPP. These police
activities were encouraged by the local Federal Bureau of Investigation (FBI) and
its Counterintelligence Program (COINTELPRO), which FBI director J. Edgar
Hoover began in 1956. COINTELPRO, according to a recent historical dictionary
of U.S. intelligence, is the "FBI acronym for a series of covert action programs
directed against domestic groups. . . . In these programs, the FBI went beyond

the collection of intelligence and conducted clandestine operations to 'disrupt' and 'neutralize' target groups and individuals within the United States."[55] This form of government repression was essentially "vigilante" in nature. In 1969 Hoover stated that the BPP was "the greatest threat to internal security" of the United States. The program ended in 1971 "with the threat of public exposure."[56]

Most emblematic of this charged political atmosphere in Chicago was the fate that befell the Illinois chapter of the BPP. According to Illinois BPP historian Jakobi Williams, the charismatic and promising Hampton and the Illinois chapter "offered the best possible hope for stability as the national BPP attempted to overcome" its own crises during the late 1960s through a promising multiracial program the Illinois BPP had devised in alliance with Puerto Rican and white Appalachian youth groups. Indeed, for a couple of years in the late 1960s, the Puerto Rican Young Lords, Appalachian Young Patriots, and African American Black Panthers were a youth movement in Chicago that arguably was the nation's "original rainbow coalition" well before the one that emerged under Jackson in the 1970s on the left side of the Democratic Party. Hampton, an organizer with the youth branch of the Maywood, Illinois, NAACP in 1966 and 1967, had led campaigns against police misconduct and racial segregation in that suburban Chicago community. His leadership abilities situated him well to take on the role of leading a Chicago chapter of the BPP, founded in Oakland, California, in 1966. As Williams notes, by 1968 "the BPP was popular not only as a result of its defiance toward law enforcement but also because its socialist ideology resonated with African American youth." Hampton's intelligence and acumen for leadership helped unite nascent factions on both the South and West Sides, where significant and distinct black American communities now resided. In November 1968, Hampton was appointed the Illinois chapter's main spokesperson, "not only because of his oratorical prowess but because . . . [his] 'brain was like a sponge'; he was able to quickly read books and disseminate the knowledge he gained."[57]

Tragically, what afflicted the BPP nationally became true in Illinois. The fact the BPP and its allies were overwhelmingly targeted nationwide by COINTEL-PRO for elimination ultimately led to the party's dissolution from Oakland to New York City. In collusion with Chicago Police Department Red Squads, the FBI also targeted and ultimately assassinated Hampton and fellow BPP member Mark Clark in their sleep on July 31, 1969, in their West Side apartment, which had served as the Chicago Panthers' headquarters. The Illinois BBP's long-term efficacy was forever impacted by this tragedy even though, Williams relates, the Illinois chapter's "survival programs remained operative" after the chapter disbanded in 1974.[58]

In *When One of Us Falls*, Margaret Burroughs was part of a chorus of black Chicago leaders who eulogized Hampton and Clark after their murders.[59] Hampton's and Clark's assassinations took place only two months after they had met with the DuSable Museum and the AAHA. Clearly, the significance of the Black Panthers to the Black Power movement was recognized by an older generation of black radicals in Chicago even if they did not work closely together over the years.

During the time that the Panthers and other such groups were under vicious attack by city police and the FBI, the DuSable Museum continued to reach out to neighborhoods and schools on the more impoverished West Side. In 1969 Margaret Burroughs brought in a visiting exhibit for a bust of Jean Baptiste Point DuSable that Marion Perkins had created at the Emerson Branch of McKinley Upper Grade School. Students from southwest suburbs with large numbers of African American residents, like Harvey, Illinois, regularly took field trips to the museum and the South Side Community Arts Center.[60] Beginning in the mid-1960s, the museum offered "How to Teach African American History," one of the city's first courses for public schoolteachers. As Andrea A. Burns shows, twenty-two teachers enrolled in "Negro History for School Teachers," one of these courses in 1966, and the museum also managed to make connections with West Side schools, such as Malcolm X College (Crane Junior College until 1969). Margaret Burroughs recalls that the museum got "very good results from the people on the West Side who started to bring their children. Pretty soon, the yellow school buses were lined up in front of 3806 South Michigan, and people realized that something was going on in there."[61]

Many museum functions also sought to reach at-risk youth from local slums as well as prisoners in nearby penitentiaries. The Burroughses and Feldman became closely involved with prisoner education during the early 1970s, notably, at a state penitentiary in Pontiac, Illinois, where they conducted history and creative-writing classes.[62] By 1971 the museum had enrolled fifty prisoners statewide in a twenty-lesson correspondence course and supported poetry classes that solicited and published prisoners' writing in an anthology the museum's press produced. The correspondence course highlighted the contributions of African Americans to U.S. life and traced the history of "the earliest African civilization." Feldman felt he encountered some of his best students in prison through such programs. He donated regularly to the West Side–based Political Prisoners Defense Fund, "devoted to the welfare of the people."[63] Beyond his volunteer work with the museum, Perkins also became executive director of the Better Boys Foundation in Chicago in 1966 and worked closely with criminalized young people, a position that allowed him to gain special insight and access into local gang and prison cultures.[64] To Perkins, the anthology demonstrated "that people behind prison bars can and have developed literary talent" and emphasized that the project was "not a paternalistic endeavor."[65]

Both Perkins and Feldman received letters from prisoners they taught black-history classes to, which reveals the level of engagement these courses received from within the prison itself. One student Omar Rashaan, an inmate at Pontiac in 1972, wrote on behalf of "the other brothers" who attended the museum's history classes and said they were all "looking forward" to future classes and requested further reading materials.[66] One of the lessons Feldman conducted at Pontiac was about the history of the Harper's Ferry raid led by the radical abolitionist John Brown just prior to the U.S. Civil War. Rashaan asked why Feldman had focused solely on the story of Brown and not his "black" and "white" compatriots. Feldman conceded his omission and, indeed, noted how he was "hungup on the idea of the hero in history. When I was young I was fed heroes." Feldman re-read his lesson and wrote back that he felt "ashamed [to] have left out the names and the work and the sacrifices of the black and white men who were with" Brown during the raid.[67] Perhaps, Feldman overstated his enthusiasm for the material to boost Rashaan's esteem. But Feldman's pedagogy rings clear in this correspondence and demonstrates especially how he was focused on keeping prisoners in these programs engaged with their coursework and the pursuit of higher knowledge and inquiry.

Also in 1971, the museum and the South Side Community Arts Center sponsored West Side schoolchildren in pen-pal programs and visits to the two still-vibrant Bronzeville cultural centers along the 3600 block stretch of South Michigan Avenue. One student's sponsor commented that the project was designed to "build up their black pride by seeing the artifacts of their African culture and the historical documents of American blacks on display." The students appeared receptive to the project. When DuSable Museum lecturer Turner asked them, "Who freed the slaves?" the students managed to avoid the simple answer of Abraham Lincoln. Instead, they "cited Harriet Tubman, conductor of the Underground Railroad, and Frederick Douglass."[68] The students' answers remain significant, for they promoted African American heroes not yet accepted by mainstream U.S. history. One of the museum's many volunteer teachers, David Thula, an international graduate student from Sierra Leone attending Roosevelt College through the late 1960s, volunteered regularly for the museum and taught craft culture, such as raffia basket weaving and West African folklore. He seemed impressed with the many children who heard his lectures and was "encouraged to see the interest . . . [they had] . . . in their heritage and culture" and that their questions were "surprisingly sophisticated for their age." In contrast, Thula felt adults tended to be more "complacent about the past. It is the young person who really wants to know about the arts and crafts of the old country."[69]

The museum's activities in these settings certainly reflected the social-reforming impulses of many U.S. middle-class interlocutors in history. These activities clearly sought to reform student and prisoner behaviors through their engagement in projects that promoted black civic virtues and cultural heritage—all activities that point to the politics of respectability so often championed by the middle classes. Still, these diverse public-history activities engaged participants in fulfilling endeavors that were also not explicitly about racial uplift. For example, Perkins notes that the prisoners' poetry anthology was not "paternalistic," which seems to imply that participants had creative agency in their writing. Likewise, Thula observes that many young people in his classes were more receptive to learning about African folk culture than their parents and other adults, indicating that generational experiences also impacted these exchanges in diverse ways.[70]

Collectively, this work demonstrates the impact that black public-history efforts carried out through the DuSable Museum had at a local level and underscores how such activities bridged important knowledge gaps between generations during the era of Black Power. Through the museum's expanding programs that engaged with BAM activists and organizations, the progressive pedagogies and black popular front–style politics of past decades were sustained in black Chicago through much of the postwar period despite the restrictions and repressions of Cold War politics. Such conditions channeled important forms of political dissent into underrepresented public-history and related cultural endeavors. Even by the early 1970s, these instances of intergenerational and cross-class exchanges and collaborations represented significant political interventions on the part of museum workers in the late 1960s public sphere. As the museum and its programs continued to expand through the early 1970s, its need to develop larger physical spaces on the South Side conflicted with the city's priorities for urban gentrification. As the next chapter demonstrates, black public-history activism played an important role in signifying African American social places and spaces as white power sought to reassert its control over American urban areas. The DuSable Museum's expansion and relocation story tells much about how black American cultural workers whose lifework spanned the long mid-twentieth century creatively engaged with civic and federal power brokers to sustain vital public-history projects.

CHAPTER FIVE

The Washington Park Relocation

By the mid-1960s, the DuSable Museum of African American History was beginning to have trouble accommodating a growing range of programs and visitors to its historic mansion at 3806 South Michigan Avenue, the museum's home since it was founded in 1961. The museum's activities now included numerous tours of both the museum and surrounding South Side neighborhoods. Other activities were curatorial exhibits from Africa and from regional Afro-diasporic communities throughout the Americas, archival collections, and popular educational functions, such as regular black-history classes and lectures geared toward both children and adults. The museum attracted a little over 2,600 visitors in its first year, 1961–62. In 1966 it recorded 7,304 visitors and by 1971–72 well over 25,000 visitors annually. Most of these visitors were elementary-school students from surrounding Chicago areas. Given the spatial privations of the South Michigan Avenue mansion's Victorian living spaces, the museum could only reasonably accommodate fifty visitors at a time.[1]

In their discussions about expansion, museum staff considered other physical sites, including vacant properties beside its Bronzeville location. A group of local African American doctors who supported the museum hired an architect in 1967 to draw up designs for a new building. This initiative reached out to local writers and dignitaries, such as *Ebony* editor and popular history writer Lerone Bennett Jr., *Jet* magazine managing editor Robert Johnson, *Chicago Defender* news editor Dave Potter, local dentist Benjamin Coble, and South Congressional

Church pastor James Mack. This effort also sought unnamed representatives from independent African nations as consultants to the project. However, plans for this particular expansion effort fell through when the surrounding properties were sold to other buyers.[2] In the end, the museum did not follow the plans envisioned by the local doctors, dignitaries, and elites.

Though prominent black public figures would play a role in the museum's expansion, local college students actually provided the catalyst for moving the institution to Washington Park, where it remains to this day. This park site was first considered when Margaret Burroughs's students at Wilson Junior College (now Kennedy-King) alerted her to a vacant police building in the park across South Cottage Grove Avenue from the University of Chicago campus (figure 8). By then, Burroughs was an art history professor at Wilson after a lengthy career as a public schoolteacher on the South Side. As she recalls in her autobiography, the site "seemed like a perfect place for the museum to expand."[3]

Washington Park did seem like a natural site for relocation. For much of the twentieth century, it had been a space for African American cultural celebrations on the city's South Side. For example, it had been an end point of the Bud Billiken

Figure 8. The DuSable Museum of African American History today, 740 East Fifty-Sixth Place, Washington Park, Chicago, Illinois. Photo: Ian Rocksborough-Smith, 2009.

Parade (an annual Bronzeville cultural festival) for decades and a public space for community assembly dating back to at least the 1930s when the neighborhood (like many located outside of historic Bronzeville during and after the Great Migrations) became mostly African American in residency.[4] Since at least the Great Depression of the 1930s, community historians, radical orators, elders, nationalists of many persuasions, and griots lectured in Chicago's Washington Park on a variety of political and cultural subjects. The potentially militant tenor of these park scenes is recalled in the writings of figures such as Richard Wright and William L. Patterson and in the seminal urban study of the 1930s and 1940s, *Black Metropolis*, by St. Clair Drake and Horace Cayton.[5] The neighborhood was also significant for the strivings of upwardly mobile black Chicagoans through the mid-twentieth century. The notion of "striving" casts the neighborhood in more complex terms than the middlebrow enclave it is sometimes characterized as.[6] Robert Stepto, who grew up there and is a literary scholar, recalls how the neighborhood was home to many politically engaged folks who attended churches where figures such as W. E. B. Du Bois and James Weldon Johnson spoke when they came to town. The neighborhood residents were a diverse lot of "railroad workers and train porters, postal workers and social workers, small businessmen, schoolteachers, ministers, homemakers, and scant few doctors and lawyers." Washington Park residents insisted on making their neighborhood a "ceremonial ground" for uplift and striving in spite of the racism they faced, no matter their class position, from white residents and police forces.[7] In this sense, it was a neighborhood that promoted uplift and respectability and one that engaged many of its residents in significant political and cultural activisms—many of which revolved around public-history activism.

Given the political legacies that mark histories of Washington Park and its surrounding neighborhoods, this concluding chapter looks at how the DuSable Museum of African American History and the public historians who founded it negotiated its relocation into a former police station in the park. The city took approximately two years, to early 1972, to grant the museum the right to move into the park and another two years before the museum shifted its main programs there.[8] The museum's move reimagined a historically African American social space into the city's geography and can be considered alongside the highly diverse engagements of Black Power and black arts movements' activists around the country with civic-level politics.[9] Black Power historian Peniel Joseph, who has written extensively about the diversity of manifestations the movement took over the long twentieth century, suggests this diversity originated, especially, in post–World War II urban areas, such as Chicago, Detroit, Oakland, Newark, and New York, with large and growing black, southern, migrant populations and rising anxieties among settled white populations whose racial paranoia was provoked by their fears over job loss and neighborhood transformation. Detroit's story, from which Joseph traces the Black Power movement's earliest manifestations, represents a pattern that occurred to some degree in many other U.S. cities, including Chicago. For many African Americans, the move to Detroit for work and opportunity, especially after World War II, meant that direct engagement with civic politics seemed entirely possible. As Joseph writes, "the rising black population led to community, political, and corporate anxiety among whites that was only partially obscured by growing calls for urban renewal—a thinly disguised effort to clear African Americans from Detroit's darkening downtown." By the early 1960s, the "city's tensions created a nexus of religious, political, and cultural activity that highlighted the possibilities of Black Power."[10] Of course, as Black Power activist and theoretician Stokely Carmichael indicates in his now classic theorizations on the movement, which Joseph nicely synthesizes, it was not simply that Black Power instigated a "white backlash." Such perspectives "missed the point." Rather, for Carmichael, "Black Power was an integral part of a continuous dialectic of black struggle against racial oppression—specifically, violent, organized white opposition."[11] It is this nexus of diverse possibilities for Black Power activism that this chapter seeks to expand upon with an examination of black public-history activism and the politics of museum relocation.

The politics this expansion brought into play demonstrate how museum work and public-history activism continued to be a significant part of the broad repertoires of local movements for urban racial equality through the late 1960s and early 1970s. Such politics were expressed as many cities across the country grappled with new forms of discrimination, such as urban renewal and gentrification of erstwhile black cityscapes, and further reflected growing interest in African American heritage, culture, and local history and identities. Although most African Americans did not ascribe to ideologies of Black Power nor did they support political militancy, public interest in aspects of African American history and culture increased exponentially during this era.[12] As scholar William Van DeBurg notes, black Americans' "minimal support for the militant [of the Black Power movement] obscured the fact that when the various surveys are sifted more thoroughly, Black Power almost always is revealed to be more popular in its cultural aspects than it was as a political enthusiasm."[13] Moreover, such interest in African American culture helped push for black studies on many college campuses. In Chicago, student movements were prolific, such as the one at Wilson Junior that helped the DuSable Museum relocate to Washington Park. Historian Martha Biondi writes eloquently of student movements across the country but, especially, in Chicago at institutions such as Crane Junior College on the West Side (which in 1969 became Malcolm X College) and at the more elite and private Northwestern University in suburban Evanston. On "both campuses," relates Biondi, "disciplined and savvy organizers . . . championed campus improvement and greater African American access to higher education."[14] Although African American studies would increasingly become more associated in later decades with elite institutions that could afford more diverse programs, Biondi notes how these student movements for educational justice "began close to urban Black communities" and were "shaped, and galvanized by the broader Black Power upsurge."[15]

As this chapter shows, the museum's push for expansion and relocation constituted another similar example of how Black Power and public history worked as part of the nexus of diverse initiatives for social justice African Americans initiated during this period. By the late 1960s, Chicago was truly a symbol for a decade that began with redemptive promise but appeared to devolve into one of intractable urban decline. The usual local story of declension centers on Martin Luther King Jr.'s 1966 beleaguered efforts with the Chicago Freedom Movement to promote "open" housing in the poverty-stricken wards of the city's West Side. As was tradition in the Democratic Party machine–dominated city, dissent was quickly silenced. Mayor Richard J. Daley, a king maker in the Democratic Party during the 1960s, was quick to issue his famous "shoot to kill" orders in response to both antiwar demonstrators at the 1968 Democratic National Convention and to the West Side riots that erupted in the wake of King's assassination in the same year. Chicago's fall from grace was further marked by the tragic yet targeted assassination of local Black Panther leader Fred Hampton by city police and the Federal Bureau of Investigation (FBI) in December 1969. Scholar James Ralph, who focuses on King's and the Chicago Freedom Movement's campaign for civil rights and open housing in Chicago, points to broader movements in the city that had a lasting impact on the shift to an "independent black political" movement through the 1970s. This movement coalesced in the eventual undermining of Daley's civic machine, in part, through the efforts of organizations like Jesse Jackson's Operation Breadbasket, which closely associated with the work of the Southern Christian Leadership Conference (SCLC) but also reflected the initiative of many other local movements active in different neighborhoods of the city that frequently remain overlooked in typical narratives of the late 1960s and 1970s.[16]

The tragic denouement to the hopeful arc of mid- to late twentieth-century racial liberalism belies a far more complex story of social struggle for many local African American communities nationwide from at least the 1940s through the

1970s; this was especially true in cities as big and racially segregated as Chicago. The DuSable Museum's development and its associated public-history labors contributed to the diversity and range of the city's Black Power challenge to the U.S. liberal teleologies of the late 1960s and 1970s.[17] While the Black Power context of the museum's move provided important intellectual and organizational catalysts, the relocation efforts occurred as a series of specific engagements with local and federal power brokers, who were mainstream civil rights and black society figures, politicians, prominent businessmen, city officials, and liberal foundations ostensibly focused on black empowerment. Many of these elites were interested in promoting harmonious and pluralist race relations in light of late 1960s urban strife and wanted the necessary funds and legislation to achieve these ends. As this chapter illustrates, relationships with such elites, while conflicted and often problematic, also helped the museum move into a historically significant expositional space in one of Chicago's biggest public parks. More than anything, however, the DuSable's relocation moment demonstrates how black public-history activists continued to make their mark on local movements for racial justice. These movements ultimately helped shape the parameters for multiracial civic politics for much of urban America well into the 1970s.

Museums and Historiography

The DuSable Museum's expansion further underscores the uniqueness of history museums as a specific form (or repertoire) of public-history making and cultural activism. From their inception, museums like the DuSable functioned as important transmitters of cultural values and came to represent regional African American communities from Chicago to Washington, D.C., to Detroit, Michigan. As Andrea A. Burns notes, "African American neighborhood museums . . . took root in urban neighborhoods across the country after World War II and were created and staffed primarily by black community leaders rather than museum professionals."[18] She indicates that at their outset, these institutions were invariably situated in smaller storefronts or homes, rather than grand civic structures. As such, they became involved in the widespread efforts of African American communities to come to terms with the paradoxes of U.S. democratic ideals at the local level as urban communities sought to develop and strive on equitable terms within American society. To better grapple with many of these issues, black museums sought to become repositories of material culture and research for the African diaspora as well as regional knowledge centers for metropolises such as Chicago, which, of course, became central to northern, urban African American community formation through the mid-twentieth century.[19] The DuSable itself focused on "educational programs" that influenced "an audience believed to be in danger of slipping through society's cracks"— namely, "black children and teenagers."[20] According to its own records, DuSable Museum founders not only sought to serve students but also wanted to become "an instrument for community accord."[21]

In his history of the DuSable, museum cofounder Eugene P. Feldman comments, "A museum was not only a place for exhibits . . . but also for library, documents, musical records, the whole life of a people's culture, history, struggles and efforts."[22] Language about the "purpose" of the DuSable Museum of African American History from a promotional pamphlet reflects his recollection about its diverse functions:

> The purpose of the Museum is to develop a center of materials on the Negro to serve the research students and schools and universities of the Midwest. It gathers, preserves and displays books, relics, souvenirs, artifacts, documents, letters, pictures, art, sculpture, phonograph records, tapes and slides, relating to the Negro past and present. Pride and knowledge in the accomplishments of the past will instill confidence and security in the future.[23]

The brochure's rhetoric expresses the intent to develop local knowledge about pride in past and present cultures. In this sense, it accords with the recent findings of museum scholars. For example, Jennifer Barrett contends that the "contemporary museum often struggles to negotiate between the remnants of an earlier rhetoric of 'public' . . . and new practices and types of spaces designed to attract new audiences, engage new communities and respond to the locality or nation within which they are situated."[24] Without getting into an in-depth analysis of the museum's day-to-day activities (i.e., use of material culture, exhibit arrangements, etc.), it helps to consider how these democratic changes in museum practices provide another useful entry point to examine the cultural politics of representation that highlighted public-history activism in Chicago. As the DuSable Museum expanded from the South Michigan Avenue mansion to Washington Park next to the University of Chicago, tactical forms of museology were applied to its repertoires. These shifts in the museum staff's approach to their public-history labors situates this expansion not only in the politics of the Black Power era but also in crucial questions of how modern museums function and relate to the local communities they exist in, service, and claim to represent. As such, analysis of this expansion effort is aided by drawing upon the ideas of museum-studies scholars, such as Gustavo Buntinx and Ivan Karp, who write about community museums that have existed in "frictional relationship [with] either . . . established museums and/or to the broader social order," particularly, in South Africa.[25]

Why Relocation?

Why did the museum seek relocation? Ultimately, the need for relocation went beyond simply expanding programs and physical-space needs. The expansion was a highly political process and became, in effect, an expression of symbolic importance for representing an aspect of Bronzeville's identity through the Black Power era. The proposed site for the museum's relocation was an abandoned police headquarters located directly next to the University of Chicago. The city had moved the police station closer to the Dan Ryan Expressway (built in 1962), a highway that deliberately bisected and displaced some of the South Side's growing African American population through the mid-twentieth century and that represents yet another story of racist urban planning. As such, the DuSable Museum's relocation from a Bronzeville mansion into an even more distinguished former police headquarters in Washington Park next to a venerated global university demonstrates a small but significant victory in the many battles African Americans waged in urban politics through the mid- to late twentieth century. This was especially true given the history of the University of Chicago's predatory use of space on the South Side and the ongoing issues of police violence that continued to impact surrounding black communities. One could even invert the teleology of museum-studies scholar Tony Bennett's assertion that museums and fairs accommodated working-class publics by facilitating panoptic spaces that worked to self-police middle-class behaviors and discourage urban vice.[26]

The move into the Washington Park neighborhood next to a prestigious university and in a large urban park surely reflected an aspect of black Chicago's middle-class strivings for tidy cityscapes unmarked by vice and decay.[27] But the museum's very adoption of a former police headquarters also literally displaced a historic and overt site of racial surveillance, violence, and power and replaced it with a community-oriented space that promoted local black public history and knowledge. As such, while never explicitly stated by the museum's founders and supporters, the move was a highly political act for its time and for the local histories it evoked for its reclamation of social space. Indeed, as Burns indicates, part of the reason that the DuSable ultimately sought relocation from South Michigan Avenue was because in 1964 the city threatened to bulldoze the 3806 location. "Through her strenuous efforts," writes Burns, Burroughs "ultimately saved the mansion that originally housed the DuSable, and it has since been placed upon the National Register of Historic Places."[28] Both locations represented significant spaces for black Chicago's cultural vitality over the long twentieth century.

Many historians of the city's sordid housing policies have demonstrated how older neighborhoods, such as those closest to the South Shore and on large boulevards like South Michigan, also once contained the palatial homes of the city's richest white industrialists in the 1880s and 1890s. As African American southerners moved to urban areas during World War I and around World War II (many of them in the north), these same South Side neighborhoods transitioned from mainly white to mainly black, expanding the black metropolis's boundaries southward and westward. These changes took place despite the city's overall housing shortage through the 1930s and 1940s and the consistent attempts of urban elites to design local housing policies that restricted the movements of African Americans out of the boundaries of historic Bronzeville. As a result, many black southerners were forced to move into overly partitioned, cramped kitchenettes in the former homes of some of the city's earliest business elites— who had long since moved to northern or western suburbs. Recent scholarship demonstrates how these processes of racial change were complex and varied from neighborhood to neighborhood. Many white and black liberal elites benefited in certain ways from the different forms of racial segregation in housing. For example, Carl Hansberry, the father of Lorraine Hansberry, became a major real estate broker on the South Side because he was able to sell kitchenettes to many African American migrants who moved to Chicago and became desperate to find housing during the city's housing shortages—a situation that was exacerbated by the racial restrictions that existed elsewhere in the city. At the same time, Hansberry simultaneously and more famously challenged Chicago's notorious racial covenants that barred access to decent middle-class housing for many African American families in South Side neighborhoods, such as Washington Park, where his family had moved.[29]

The DuSable Museum's two locations defied these images of urban decay and also reflect the city's history of neighborhood change through the late 1960s. As such, even a brief appraisal of architectural styles from these South Side locations highlights the racial history of neighborhood change in the area and the race- and class-conscious aspects of the museum's relocation strategies. The architectural styles of the museum's buildings further underscore the importance of the institution's efforts to occupy symbolic city spaces connected to Chicago's civic modernity.

For example, the museum moved west from a mansion in Bronzeville to the majestic Washington Park building formally used as a police citadel that once guarded the University of Chicago. As such, it reimagined the local legacies and strivings of African Americans onto and near some of the city's most significant landmarks for high culture. The mansion, which became the primary residence of the Burroughses in the late 1950s, had been on one of the city's "premier" residential streets in the late nineteenth century. The home was designed in French Chateauesque style by one of Chicago's acclaimed architects, Solon S. Beman (who also designed the nearby railcar company town of Pullman). The South Michigan Avenue location was first owned by local development mogul John W. Griffiths, whose company built "many of Chicago's most iconic structures," such as Union Station, the Merchandise Mart, and the Civic Opera House. The Washington Park police armory had been part of architect Daniel Burnham's Beaux Arts developments from the World's Fair of the 1890s, which was a Jim Crow endeavor because it excluded African Americans from substantive participation. In this sense, it is significant that photographs of both the mansion and the old police station appeared on the museum's promotional materials. Such use of architectural imagery in the DuSable's public representations underscored black Chicago's indispensability to the city's modern history.[30]

This subversive reclamation of many of Chicago's historically white spaces for "high culture" were consciously promoted through the continuation of cosmopolitan and bohemian cultural activities along the South Michigan Avenue corridor in the 1970s where the museum had been founded. For example, Theresa Fambro Hooks reports in the *Chicago Defender* how Margaret Burroughs joined younger poets Haki Madhubuti and Useni Eugene Perkins in 1970 at a coffeehouse event at the closely associated South Side Community Arts Center (SSCAC), down the block from the original museum. Hooks asks her readers whether they could "dig" listening to poetry recited in a "scene where early in this century some of Chicago's wealthiest families gathered for grand balls, soirées and stuffy social occasions."[31]

The decision to relocate the DuSable Museum to Washington Park was then also highly symbolic and surely part of the cultural histories of these vital Bronzeville spaces. The move reclaimed a historically African American space in one of Chicago's largest public parks. Just as with the museum's first location, the move into the second and current location presents a subversive freeing of public space in an otherwise highly policed and racially controlled part of the city.

Museum and State

Museum making represents a greatly understudied facet of cultural forms during the Black Power era, especially in the institutionally vibrant settings of the Midwest. Indeed, to date, only a handful of books explicitly or extensively treat African American–led expositional activities in Chicago through the mid-twentieth century.[32] Early African American–led museum efforts, such as the DuSable Museum, are especially significant because they demonstrate the specificity of public-history work as an independent cultural form for black community knowledge production. In essence, these public-history efforts represented the beginnings of a nation-wide African American museum movement started by the mid-1960s. The Burroughses' museum work through the early 1960s connected them with Charles H. Wright in Detroit, a prominent medical doctor, who started that city's Museum of African American History in 1965.[33] In 1967 the Burroughses and Wright organized a series of forums and conferences together with their respective museum staff that culminated in a movement that eventually formed the Association of African American Museums in 1978. In September 1967, the first conference of African American museums attracted numerous delegates from museums and historical associations in Chicago, Boston, Washington, D.C., New York, Ohio, and Alabama and letters of support from organizers of a museum planned for San Francisco. The establishment of the first two major, independent, black-history museums in the United States in Detroit and Chicago broadens James Smethurst's suggestion that because of the "numerous direct exchanges" between both cities, these metropolises and the Midwest itself were among the most vital centers for the black arts movement in the United States, institutionally more diverse than New York City. Indeed, these connections between public-history projects paralleled important literary exchanges between writers at Broadside Press in Detroit, such as Dudley Randall and Margaret Danner, and writers at Third World Press and Lotus Press in Chicago—to say nothing of the very long history of jazz and rhythm and blues music in both cities.[34]

This movement toward a national association of black museums began as a critical response to federal officials who wanted to pass a bill to establish "a Federal Commission of Negro History" in the 1960s. Early discussions to form such a commission began in 1965. Its chief supporters in Congress were U.S. Representative James Scheuer, a liberal white Democrat from New York, and Gus Hawkins, an African American U.S. Representative from California. Scheuer wanted this commission to take the necessary steps of "collecting and preserving historical materials dealing with Negro history and culture" and to consider "the possibility of establishing a Museum of Negro History and Culture."[35]

As Mabel O. Wilson indicates, this commission was also a "response to the growing prominence of Black Nationalist organizations such as the Black Panther Party" and represented the fears among white government officials of "another hot summer of racial unrest," given the spread of urban rebellions through the late 1960s. The project was intended to help with the formation of a national "museum or center" that could devise broad "methods of distributing information" about African American history and culture in ways that "might be integrated into the mainstream of American education and life."[36] The idea of a federally mandated museum for these popular purposes attracted qualified support from diverse African American figures, such as writer James Baldwin; Betty Shabazz, Malcolm X's widow; Roy Innis, leader of the Congress on Racial Equality (CORE); and baseball icon Jackie Robinson, a lifelong Republican, who was often recalled as a moderate for his views on civil rights.

Despite this support, most of the African Americans who attended the commission's hearings adamantly emphasized the need for locally led "black educational institutions" to take the lead with this project in light of the failures to equitably integrate public schools after the *Brown v. Board of Education* decision of 1954.[37] The most vociferous speaker on this point was Innis. Although he supported the idea of a federal commission to oversee nation-wide initiatives in black history, he turned most of his testimony into a circular joust with Scheuer and Hawkins about the need for all-black representation on the commission. Innis's position was in line with the variant of cultural nationalism CORE had shifted to by the late 1960s, which nominally supported grassroots initiatives but whose programs became increasingly beholden to white liberal institutions, such as the Ford Foundation. Historian Karen Ferguson demonstrates how the Ford Foundation favored projects that boosted black capitalist strategies for the development and uplift of inner-city communities.[38] Most of the other African Americans asked to speak at the hearing disagreed with Innis's overt racial separatism but, nonetheless, shared his rhetorical qualifications about federal oversight on these matters. All agreed that judicious consultation with existing local black-led public-history and educational groups was required before any commission could establish a federal institution.

Those who firmly supported the idea of the commission were the most explicitly aligned with America's prevailing Cold War racial liberalism through midcentury. As such, they offered no real objections to the commission's ideas and saw it as fully complementary to their ongoing work—which was mainly academic. These Cold War liberals included John A. Davis of the American Society of African Culture (AMSAC) and Charles Wesley, president, Association for the Study of Negro Life and History (ASNLH). Davis's position was especially revealing given AMSAC's origins during the mid-1950s when a group of African American and Western-based intellectuals and scholars held a conference in Paris, France, about the histories of Africa and its diaspora as a way to serve movements for colonial independence. As Smethurst notes, the Central Intelligence Agency (CIA), which "secretly funded AMSAC to channel African

American anticolonialism and Pan-Africanism away from the Communist Left (and radical nationalists)," funded many cultural initiatives as a national strategy during the Cold War years. This had the effect of casting many avant-garde and abstract expressionist as well as other artistic and intellectual endeavors as avowedly anti-Communist. At the same time, the CIA deliberately set up a "long leash," which enabled many left-wing artists to occupy these tangentially funded spaces since it was easy to fashion oneself against the rigid aesthetics represented by Soviet art through Cold War–era lenses.[39] Fitting this cozy proximity to government power, Davis and AMSAC were given the opening remarks at the hearing. To his credit, Davis outlined the ways academics had misrepresented African Americans in national histories, notably through the work of figures, such as William Dunning, who perpetuated the "Sambo" misrepresentations of African Americans from post–Civil War Reconstruction. Davis pointed to a new generation of scholars, led by such figures as C. Vann Woodward, Oliver Cromwell Cox, and others who had been "setting the record straight" on these matters over several decades. Davis felt that a federal commission might help circulate such history to "all Americans" and thereby "rid America of the vulgar concepts of race." For his part, Wesley felt that no "local museum or library would be injured by any action on the part of a commission" and credited the work of the ASNLH in Washington, D.C., and the Schomburg Center for Research in Black Culture in New York but only briefly recognized the museum projects in Detroit and Chicago (perhaps, due to their presence at the hearing). While Wesley and Davis offered some useful appraisals of revisionist American history, they were each very comfortable with the idea of further government oversight in their respective fields of intellectual labor.

Opposition to the bill came from among African American public figures who were not asked to testify at the hearing. One columnist from the influential Harlem-based *Amsterdam News* doubted whether the bill would be "greeted by dancing in the streets" from many of Scheuer's own constituents in the Twenty-First Congressional District of upstate New York. The author Marietta J. Tanner felt the community (which included cities like Albany and Schenectady with large African American populations) had not been very well consulted on the matter.[40] African American congressmen Charles Diggs and Jon Conyers of Michigan along with Adam Clayton Powell, who represented Harlem, supported Wright's and the Burroughses' opposition to the bill. In the end, these public figures agreed to support the movement toward an independent African American museum association. It would take until an act from Congress in 2003 for a federally sponsored National Museum of African American History and Culture to be proposed and implemented. The museum, the nineteenth and newest museum of the Smithsonian Institution and devoted to African American public history and culture, opened in September 2016.[41]

Wright and the Burroughses had good reason to be concerned about the motives behind the bill. Scheuer made it clear in his testimony at the hearing that the underlying reasons for the bill were for the federal government to open another front in ongoing efforts to subdue racial strife in urban America. Just as the Kerner Commission report of the 1967 riots had "laid the responsibility squarely on the door of white America and placed the challenge where it belongs—with the Congress and the President," Scheuer had "the same hope" for a federal commission on black history that might produce a similar kind of actionable report.[42] The uncertainty caused by such ambiguous perspectives on urban issues eventually led black museum pioneers, such as the Burroughses and Wright, to form their own association free from the control of the federal government.

Ultimately, this top-down orientation to the proposed black-history bill was what figures such as Wright and the Burroughses opposed. Wright felt "such a bill" would have placed "in the hands of the President . . . the authority to appoint commissioners and to oversee, direct, and interpret matters related to our history"—and by implication influence the ideological and programmatic directions of local organizations, such as the museums in Chicago and Detroit. Along with the Burroughses, Wright took "a dim view of Scheuer's move and sought to arouse public interest in" their critical position on the proposed federal commission. For example, when the original bill was first discussed in 1965, Wright and the Burroughses approached the ASNLH at its annual meeting in Atlanta that year with concerns about the commission. They were advised to "wait and see how [the] measure fared." To echo Margaret Burroughs's mid-fifties- and Cold War–inflected dispute with Chicago clubwoman Irene McCoy Gaines and the ASNLH national executive's past admonitions, Wright noted how he and the Burroughses "did not take [Wesley's] advice."[43]

The other main concern that Wright and Charles Burroughs expressed at the hearing was the lack of consultation Scheuer's committee offered. Like many African Americans who participated, they felt that greater recognition for the longer struggles of many local groups in these fields was required. For example, Wright emphasized how the DuSable group was the "largest and oldest of its kind in the country" and criticized Scheuer for not adequately reaching out to them. For his part, Charles Burroughs clarified how Scheuer's office had contacted them in 1965 to submit information about their museum, but Burroughs noted that when he and Margaret promptly replied with materials detailing their public-history work, they never received an "answer" confirming their replies. In response to the criticism, Scheuer claimed he had since consulted "dozens" of organizations. Scheuer appeared to have little recollection (if any) of interactions with the DuSable Museum group. Moreover, Burroughs echoed many others at the hearing when he implored Scheuer to consider letting black leaders "in the field" appoint representatives to the commission because these local actors were better equipped to consult "with the broad mass of people" in Detroit, Chicago, Boston, and elsewhere who had been "working in the field."[44]

Such opposition was well founded. Those who formed the DuSable Museum had worked in public history for a long time and had been striving to connect their labors with diverse black political and cultural movements for decades. Their efforts predated the black arts–Black Power era of the late 1960s. The work of the DuSable group fits squarely into longer histories of activism that date back to Chicago's African American creative renaissance of the 1930s. As veterans of the city's left-wing and African American popular fronts, cultural workers, such as Margaret and Charles Burroughs, experienced many Cold War repressions, most notably, harassment from the FBI and local police Red Squads but also from public school board members and art center directors.[45] It was through the Burroughses' survival of such challenges that they remained engaged with educational and public-history work and came to mentor younger artists, writers, and educators in the 1960s.

In 1970, when time came to finally negotiate with civic officials for expansion in Washington Park, the DuSable Museum faced a difficult task. These officials made little effort to advertise the abandonment of the former police headquarters, let alone the possibility of its use by a small not-for-profit group of cultural workers from the South Side. This was especially true with Chicago Park District officials, such as its president, Daniel J. Shannon, who acted slowly in his response to early inquiries about relocation. After some initial enthusiasm from a mayor's assistant, Shannon answered the Burroughses' query with a terse letter in April 1970 that expressed a mildly worded intent to check into the "possibility" of the museum "using" the former Washington Park police-station building. That summer passed with little action from the park district on the matter.[46] At this early stage, the relocation process echoed the long history of bitter disappointment for local African American politics in the face of lethargic, corrupt, and frequently indifferent machine-driven civic officialdom.[47]

To gain momentum, the museum's directors reached out to local African American business and community leaders, namely *Chicago Defender* newspaper owner John Sengstacke, who supported black public-history work in the community, and U.S. Representative Ralph Metcalfe, who by then had fallen out with the civic Democratic political machine. Metcalfe rose through the ranks of the local African American Democratic submachine as an alderman in 1952 through 1971. However, his disaffection with the civic machine became a sign that its control over African American electoral politics in the city was disintegrating when he decided to fight back against Daley after Metcalfe became congressman of Illinois's First District in 1971.[48] Even John Hope Franklin, the eminent professional historian of African American history who became a full professor at the University of Chicago in the mid-1960s, lent his name to the campaign. The directors, who included figures closely involved with the museum's day-to-day work, such as Margaret Burroughs, Feldman, Eugene Ford, and Jan Wittenbar, were joined by significant community leaders, such as E. E. Hasbrouck, Archie Listenbee, Daniel Caldwell, Wendell Smith, Fitzhugh D. Dinks Jr., and journalist Vernon Jarrett. These figures reached out to civic officials as well as to directors of other Chicago museums, such as the Field Museum, the Art Institute, the Museum of Contemporary Art, and the Chicago Historical Society.[49]

More important, the prolific support of such civic figures helped with a widespread petition and letter-writing campaign led by many of Margaret Burroughs's college students at Kennedy-King College to create the necessary local political pressures for the DuSable's expansion into Washington Park. In his history of the museum, Feldman recalls that the petition campaign received "thousands upon thousands of signatures."[50] Significant letters from diverse patrons and supporters of the DuSable wrote to the Chicago Park District and echoed the proposal to underscore the museum's harmonizing role in the community. Ralph Turner, museum lecturer and old black left veteran, emphasized his background as a "long-time resident . . . most interested in" the city's "educational and cultural growth." Ruth Allen Fouche, a great supporter of the museum as well as an accomplished musicologist, church organist, and respectable local clubwoman, wrote that the museum was one of the most "educative places in Chicago" for it contained "items" that were "most precious to students of . . . Black Culture." Like the other appeals to city officials, Fouche felt the Washington Park location was appropriate because of its proximity to the University of Chicago and various public schools and because it was a "suitable house" for "Black Citizens" to store their "Heritage Collection." Forman Onderdonk, a white teacher from a western suburb, told a local CBS radio station how Margaret Burroughs visited his school district and was "warmly" received by students.[51]

Part of the effort to expand the museum required that its supporters make strategic appeals to city officials and the public at large. The museum's relocation proposal implies support for the harmonious accord of "race relations" and Chicago's role as a commercial gateway in the midwestern United States.

In the proposal, the supporters also subtly position black Chicago's rich cultural past—especially, in the fields of arts and intellectual production that most concerned cultural workers, such as Margaret Burroughs. The proposal document foregrounds the institution's role as a "bootstrap" project and "cultural resource." The resource designation came from the Chicago Board of Education and surely represents a term of endorsement that aided the museum's case for expansion. The proposal further highlights how the museum was a model institution that promoted peaceful human relations in Chicago "and the world." On the proposal's first page, a brief biography of Jean Baptiste Point DuSable, the city's first settler, emphasizes how DuSable saw the "commercial advantage of Chicago's location on the north banks" of a river that "joined Lake Michigan." In this reading, DuSable was the first to see the city "as a trade center and a crossroad." The proposal also highlights the service that the museum's founders had given to Chicago as "educators, artists, historians, and civic leaders who saw the need for an institution to preserve and promote the contributions of Africans and Afro-Americans to world culture"—a service that helped create interracial "goodwill" as well as black "pride."[52] Similarly, the petition that circulated for signatures and that was eventually sent to City Hall emphasizes how the use of the former Washington Park site would "help the cause of racial peace" and foster "much needed cultural education."[53]

The correspondence directed toward city officials hardly recalls the particularities of black Chicago's unique relationship to the Washington Park site and its neighborhood. While its location next to "the University of Chicago and the Museum of Science and Industry" is noted, the only indication of the community's relationship to the proposed site is that it is "surrounded by heavily populated residential" areas, whose "needs" could be satisfied due to their proximity. However, the proposal's summary contains an important caveat that linked the museum's relocation to local legacies of radical black intellectual and cultural production alongside traditions of middle-class racial uplift. The summary suggests the site might embolden a "new creativity in the inner city" of Chicago such as had not been seen since the "cultural upsurge of the 1920s" or the "cultural uplift of the 1930s."[54] As educational studies scholar Carline Williams Strong writes in her biography of Margaret Burroughs, the museum's main founder would "embellish" visits and negotiations with park-district officials by strategically bringing "knowledgeable supporters" to meetings—notably, a meeting on November 9, 1971, which reviewed the $175,000 in pledges obtained through the museum's relocation petition campaign. This figure alone was only halfway to a $300,000 figure stipulated by the city as necessary to renovate (and thereby grant use for) the Washington Park facility. Nonetheless, a decision came about shortly thereafter in early 1972 and well before larger foundations offered the museum their support.[55] Clearly, the strategic approach of the petitions and proposals helped move the negotiations forward. Margaret Burroughs recalls this process in succinct terms:

> When I came down, I brought a stack of petitions people had signed asking for money to help renovate the building. But I made my presentation about what we were doing and how we would utilize this building and so forth. So they voted for us to be allowed to have that building. We were the first community group that the Park District had ever given any building to. And so we made it into a museum and continued our fundraising to fix it up and so forth.[56]

The museum's relocation, in fact, represents an exceptional channel through which Black Power successfully engaged for a time with white, civic power structures. It is because of how and why this was orchestrated that it remains important to look beyond the self-reliant language of the "bootstrap" approach outlined in the museum's relocation proposals. The promotion of Washington Park as an expansion site for the museum effectively reimagines important social spaces for African Americans on the South Side of Chicago. The strategic selection of this location is evident in how the DuSable's directors went about their efforts to relocate and certainly impacted their choices for social space. Over the course of this expansion process, they used the public idea of a museum to attract political, legal, and financial support to successfully "free" an African American space without compromising their status as an autonomous organization.[57]

To be sure, like other cultural institutions of that era, the DuSable eventually sought greater sources of funding for its programs through foundations, private institutions, and government resources. The museum's first grant was for $9,000 from the Wieboldt Foundation in 1966 and was followed three years later by a $7,500 grant from the Albert Wadsworth Harris Fund. However, the museum did not receive larger grants until 1973—*after* the city's park district granted the rights to relocate to Washington Park. The grants include $100,000 from the Field Foundation in 1973, $100,000 from the Woods Charitable Trust, and $300,000 from the Chicago Community Trust. Most of these funds went toward the redevelopment and renovation of the Washington Park facility. During this later expansion phase, corporations, such as Bell Laboratories, Standard Oil, Oscar Meyer, and Sears, were approached to support extracurricular summer black-history classes for elementary schoolchildren, adult education classes, and correspondence history and creative-writing courses for inmates in local prisons.[58] When the museum received approvals from the city for relocation in the early 1973, Margaret Burroughs feted many of the civic and foundation officials who eventually supported the move. The park district president, who had responded slowly and tersely to the museum's initial proposal, only sent a representative to this event. But the heads of the Wieboldt Foundation and Chicago Community Trust attended, as did local black elected officials who backed the museum's efforts, including Representative Metcalfe and state representatives William Robinson, Richard Newhouse, and Corneal Davis.[59]

Interactions between community groups with powerful government bodies and/or foundations reflected complex engagements, relationships, and tensions. Such engagements offered important opportunities and openings to cultural workers and public-history activists, such as those who founded the DuSable Museum. Indeed, the number of awards Margaret Burroughs received during the late 1960s and 1970s helped validate the museum's expansion and relocation. In particular, she achieved an internship through the National Endowment for the Humanities in 1968 that allowed her to intern at the Field Museum and to gain professional training in museology, from "fundraising and development to curatorship and art management," which she drew on during her later field research in West Africa. Most important for the DuSable Museum's longevity, she learned about special laws in the state of Illinois that allowed citizens to apply for tax levies for local museum projects. In some 1967 revised statutes of an 1893 Illinois law, civic park districts could give museums money, provided the citizens groups behind them acquire the appropriate legal permissions for construction and development on state land.[60] The DuSable Museum did not receive these accreditations until the late 1970s, but the Washington Park relocation and the museum's not-for-profit status later allowed it to join a citywide consortium of museums that included the Chicago Art Institute, Chicago Historical Society, the Field Museum, and the Museum of Contemporary Art Chicago. Together, these institutions received federal funding to subsidize visitors passes for "inner city and/or low income citizens," a program that increased the accessibility and use of Chicago's museum spaces by broader publics. Within a year of beginning the program, the DuSable Museum had become the "most popular" of all five of the museums in the program.[61] Attracting this kind of support was necessary in order for the museum to sustain itself, let alone expand its programs. As late as 1966, the museum operated a deficit of nearly $3,000 yearly, almost half its operating costs for that year alone. It was also not until 1968 that the museum hired its first paid staffer. Until that moment, it was nearly entirely volunteer driven.[62]

The DuSable Museum's directors and supporters also recognized the dangers that many community institutions faced from large, white, liberal funding bodies (like foundations) through the early 1970s. For example, a 1970 appeal for museum membership in the *Chicago Defender* notes how the DuSable had received "no large foundation grants," and this statement was true at that time because the museum did not receive its first large grant until 1973. The *Defender's* appeal spoke to an awareness early on of the dangers that large foundations posed to local organizations.[63] In 1970 local television personality Vernon Jarrett, later a key member of the museum's relocation committee, penned an important editorial for his regular *Chicago Tribune* column. This editorial, "Beware! Here Comes the Foundation Black," indicates that some African Americans were well aware of the dangers posed by foundations to their movement's institutional autonomy. Jarrett wrote about a new, younger "militant neo-[Uncle] Thomas" who was masculine, "tough," and "revolutionary"; Booker T. Washington was a comparable race leader from history himself "allied" with "millionaire indus-trialists" because he helped fund the acclaimed vocational school in Tuskegee, Alabama. For Jarrett, Washington exemplifies an older style that surely "flat-tered Mr. Charley" just as it promised peace in the black community. Still, Jarrett felt that Washington's older style was in the very least "open and above board." The new militant leader, by way of contrast, met with "white sponsors" in the Loop and appeared "reasonable" and "sweet" to his backers. Yet, on the street or at a rally, he sounded like a "real 'soul brother from the ghetto' . . . 'a real black man . . .' who knows how to stop black rioters from destroying his heavy investments. The result [was] a . . . foundation grant to the guy who can talk the loudest and the strongest."[64]

With these deep roots on the South Side, the DuSable Museum's founders drew important ideological sustainers from community-based fund-raisers that doubled as black history celebrations and educational functions (figure 9). These events featured prominent keynote speakers who spanned the political spectrum but who were mainly left wing in orientation. The United Packing-house Workers of America's union hall, the Packinghouse Workers Center at South Forty-Ninth Street and South Wabash Avenue, was frequently used by the museum as a site for its earliest fund-raisers. Just down the street from DuSable High School, the union hall had been an organizing center for South Side Communists and unionists since the 1930s. As Smethurst relates, it was a "frequent site of militant black political and cultural events, embodying the intersection of black nationalists and leftists in Chicago as the Black Power and Black Arts movements took shape."[65] In 1963 Margaret Burroughs joined with the Afro-American Heritage Association (AAHA), led by her friends, local Communist activist Ishmael Flory, and University of Islam educator Christine C. Johnson, to organize a salute to W. E. B. Du Bois, who had recently passed away in Ghana. Another significant fund-raiser, the Jubilee Ball took place at the union hall in 1966 and featured an address by the union's district 1 leader

Figure 9. Margaret T. G. Burroughs, Ishmael Flory, Harry Belafonte, and Timuel Black, Committee to Defend the Bill of Rights fund-raiser, ca. 2002. Madeline Stratton Morris Papers, Vivian G. Harsh Research Collection, Chicago Public Library.

Charles Hayes.[66] The event was billed as a celebration of Negro History Week and combined the images of heroic figures, such as Abraham Lincoln, Frederick Douglass, and Du Bois. The benefit attracted over five hundred people and raised a few hundred dollars.[67]

The museum staged even more events near the end of the 1960s, which attracted supporters from black society. In February 1968, a benefit tribute to Harlem Renaissance poet Langston Hughes attracted a "near-capacity" audience at the Dunbar Auditorium on South Parkway. Important Chicago-based poets, such as Gwendolyn Brooks, Margaret Walker, and Margaret Danner, gave readings. Smethurst states that these prolific poets distanced themselves from the "Communist Left" but "maintained close, if sometimes tempestuous, personal relationships with active leftists, such as Charles and Margaret Burroughs."[68] Other benefits that directly supported the museum's relocation included one in 1968 featuring Chicago Cubs star Ernie Banks and the Chicago Bears' Gale Sayers. Another event featured the prolific acting couple Ossie Davis and Ruby Dee, who had each been involved in progressive arts organizations in New York City and around the country.[69] Funds from these local benefits and fund-raisers hardly compared to the foundation grants and civic tax levies the museum eventually received and that were critical to its expression. But those who participated in sustaining the DuSable's efforts through such events represented a good cross-section of the black public sphere, especially by the late 1960s when its efforts to expand programming and physical space were well underway.

Histories of black intellectual life and engagement in Chicago civic politics work well with the longer view scholars of museum studies have taken about questions of how public-history practices evolved over time. The efforts to expand and relocate the DuSable Museum to Washington Park and to promote the black museum movement nationally offer good examples of the "new practices" undertaken by modern museums through the mid-twentieth century. As such, the relocation moment validates some conclusions of museum scholars who feel museum practices and functions democratized through this period to reach and engage new publics.

The DuSable Museum's directors represented their project to local elites and civic power structures in ways that simultaneously reimagined African American social spaces in the city's South Side cultural geography. In this sense, the museum strategically attracted the necessary financial and political support for relocation and expansion. However, the move was more than simply about engaging local elites to grow the project. The museum's move also literally displaced a former site of racial surveillance to take back one of black Chicago's most significant and symbolic spatial sites for community knowledge production in Washington Park. The broader activities that fed into the relocation effort underscored the changing national and international coordinates for African American political culture through the late 1960s and early 1970s and highlighted the complex ideological and tactical discussions among local activists in Chicago and surely in other major urban centers who represented the diverse nexus of activities that characterized the Black Power movement in America. Museum projects such as the DuSable drew greater attention to the conflicted nature of top-down efforts that promoted racial diversity through the late 1960s and that sought to represent racialized working-class communities through government, business, and foundation resources. Through the strategic deployment of racial histories and the enlistment of local college students alongside significant South Side community supporters and leaders, the DuSable Museum was able to successfully negotiate its expansion with civic officials and confront the challenges of sustaining visions for a genuinely autonomous black public-history institution well into the early 1970s and in the decades to come.

Epilogue

In a recent interview, Margaret Burroughs noted how mid-twentieth-century civil rights movements and the work she and others did with public history were connected: "I think it's the civil rights movement that made us realize it's important to know about and document the history. To know where you're going, you have to know from whence you came."[1] As Burroughs's statement suggests, histories of twentieth-century U.S. urban, intellectual, and social life work well with the longer views, directions, and cultural repertoires and/ or forms that scholars of civil rights and regionally focused black-freedom struggles and activisms now turn to as areas of inquiry.[2] As *Black Public History in Chicago* demonstrates, important dimensions for these new directions can be reached through examining repertoires of black cultural activism that connected public-history labors, cultural activism, civil rights, black radicalism, and racial militancy in its many diverse forms and expressions. Indeed, the number of times historians come across an event called Negro History Week or a later Black History Month in literatures and archives that relate to twentieth-century black-freedom struggles suggests these very phenomena need to be taken seriously. Scholars of black expositions, emancipation celebrations, and Juneteenth recognitions during the mid- to late nineteenth century, such as Nathan Cardon and Kathleen Clark, now treat earlier periods of history in this manner.[3]

The very practitioners of these repertoires over the course of the mid-twentieth century collectively witnessed, analyzed, and helped shape the ways we can understand U.S. urban life and the many political contestations that shaped them as cities changed dramatically and diverse southerners and new-comers moved en masse to cities in the north and the west. It seems fitting then to consider such practitioners on a local level, as *Black Public History in Chicago* has done, given that the new Smithsonian National Museum of African American History and Culture opened in the fall of 2016. The museum's founding director, Lonnie G. Bunch III, has suggested the museum will be a place "where everyone can explore the story of the African-American experience"—a thought that is very much in the footsteps of local museum pioneers across the country like Margaret Burroughs.[4] The fact that the Smithsonian Museum has established an entire institution devoted to the African American experience certainly demon-strates how overdue such a development was. However, it would be well beyond the purview of this epilogue or book to discuss the political contestations that surely informed the decades-long process of developing this particular institu-tion in the nation's capital. Still, the Smithsonian museum's mere existence now also suggests, perhaps, that the independent movements for black American museum making that people such as Margaret Burroughs and Charles Wright helped initiate in Chicago and Detroit, respectively, had an impact on the public discourse that surely brought this long-overdue development about. Indeed, it was not that long ago, in the late 1960s, that Burroughs, Wright, and their colleagues were consulted through the first congressional hearing to discuss the possibility of establishing a national African American museum through a federal commission on black history and culture. The important interven-tions that these black public-history activists made in those hearings about the need for adequate local consultation with people "in the field" (as Burroughs put it) underscored how difficult a task it was (and surely remains) for African American communities around the country to have their voices and experiences accurately represented through public exposition and commemorations—no less one that aimed to represent an entire national experience.

The decades-long efforts to establish, build, and relocate the DuSable Museum from South Michigan Avenue to Washington Park fit nicely into these new paradigms of expositional and commemoration scholarship as well as renewed public discussions about how African Americans have interpreted and represented their pasts to the public now that a national museum is devoted to such an endeavor. The embattled campaigns to reform Chicago public school curricula through the mid-twentieth century fit into these discussions, as well. Curriculum reformers in the late 1930s and 1940s were at the forefront of dis-cussions about revisions to U.S. racial history particularly as the legacies of racial slavery were being rewritten by more acclaimed scholars and thinkers through the mid-twentieth century. Such projects surely also add dimension to the better-known school boycotts and racial desegregation battles over this same period led by figures in Chicago such as Al Raby and the Coordinating Council of Community Organizations.[5] Connected to these same energies for knowledge reform were the activities of cultural workers like Margaret and Charles Burroughs and their friends Ishmael Flory and Christine Johnson. These figures had been associated with the radical left and found ways to utilize their energy and passions for black history to promote their activism through vital museum and community organizations that ultimately became the DuSable Museum of African American History and the Afro-American Heritage Association (AAHA). They did this largely because of the political repressions they faced as black leftists who stayed to live, work, and struggle in Chicago through the mid-twentieth century.

Collectively, these endeavors presented excellent examples of the "new practices" and forms of public history examined by museum scholars, such as Ivan Karp, Gustavo Buntinx, Jennifer Barrett, Robert Rydell, and Tony Bennett. These museum studies scholars have shown how museum making took on more democratic forms and strategically engaged with local regions and communities throughout the mid-twentieth century.[6] As such, the DuSable Museum's directors tactfully represented their museum project as one that ultimately attracted the necessary support from civic power structures in ways that simultaneously and powerfully reimagined African American social and neighborhood spaces in Chicago's South Side cultural geographies. As discussed throughout *Black Public History in Chicago*, such projects fit neatly into the mid-twentieth-century history of the city's black cultural renaissance and engaged with the South Side's vibrant black civic culture through much of the mid-twentieth century. They became a significant part of the contestations over representing black American identities in the public sphere. These public-history activists also engaged with younger generations of artists and activists involved in the city's prolific black arts and Black Power movements, which produced such figures as local Black Panther leader Fred Hampton, Haki Madhubuti and Third World Press, and the Organization of Black American Culture (OBAC). Indeed, public schoolteachers, such as Margaret Burroughs and Madeline Stratton Morris, and clubwoman Irene McCoy Gaines, while each of differing political persuasions, were at the forefront of activities that unanimously supported the circulation of black history in the public sphere in some form or another.

Conflicts about who would lead and represent black public history emerged, as well. Both ideological and intellectual in nature, these conflicts over identity and public history underscored both the salience of creating black history materials for circulation in the public sphere and ongoing intraracial class and political tensions in the local black community. In particular, the failed attempts to charter a local ASNLH chapter during the mid-1950s demonstrated the deeply felt urgency and tensions that surrounded the establishment of such organizations and racial projects in the age of civil rights. Such projects simultaneously emphasized their connectedness to the racial politics of the Cold War (which so often adversely impacted anything that was nominally left wing in orientation). This sense of urgency was first reflected in the ultimately failed efforts of South Side teachers like Stratton Morris to advance the city's earliest attempts through World War II at curriculum reforms for civics classes. This sense of urgency was also mirrored in the correspondence AAHA founder Flory had with W. E. B. Du Bois about the merits of local racial knowledge production over the top-down foci of the American Society of African Culture (AMSAC). This latter organization had a progressive outlook but was eventually revealed as an appendage of the Central Intelligence Agency and thus an extension of the U.S. government's Cold War manipulations.

Black public-history projects fit into broader national and international coordinates for black political cultures during the Cold War, civil rights, and Black Power eras. In a large city like Chicago, these coordinates increasingly included other peoples of color who migrated to the region in greater numbers by the late 1960s, especially Mexican Americans and Latinos.[7] The sort of black public-history and civil rights–related endeavors that emerged through the mid-twentieth century in Chicago became part, no doubt, of the important multiracial coalitions that coalesced in the groundswell for Harold Washington's mayoralty in the 1980s and the Chicago-based presidential campaigns of Jesse Jackson. Moreover, these racial knowledge projects were mirrored to a degree in other black metropolises and major urban centers around the United States throughout the same period—notably, in New York, Atlanta, and Los Angeles.[8] In her position as a park board commissioner during the 1980s and 1990s, Margaret Burroughs consulted with Mexican Americans who sought similar forms of funding as the DuSable Museum had for what would become the National Museum of Mexican Art built in the Pilsen neighborhood. Working under Mayor Washington, Burroughs advised the Pilsen group to strategically call their project a "museum" so that they received similar tax levies to the ones that the DuSable had benefited from.[9] These strategies for museum making point to the democratic possibilities offered by such community knowledge-producing endeavors and how they could be sustained through complex engagements with civic power and political structures well past the DuSable Museum's relocation moment in the early 1970s.

At the same time, public-history institutions like the DuSable faced difficulties in the coming years that fundamentally challenged its founding vision for providing grassroots, intergenerational approaches to the promotion and expression of black history. Indeed, these issues continue to this very day.[10] This was especially true as the museum attracted more attention from foundations and the private sector for carrying out and expanding its programs. Andrea A. Burns has written on a series of crises that the museum faced in the late 1980s and 1990s—which prompted the emergence, largely from itself, of a local movement to "save" the museum. Much of this crisis amplified concerns about the processes, examined in this book, from the late 1960s and early 1970s as the museum expanded and relocated and sought to "professionalize" its programs and functions to compete with "mainstream" museums, like the Chicago History Museum (formerly, the Chicago Historical Society), and which risked losing its "grassroots" perspectives. As Burns describes, this "change was seen [by some over time] as an unforgivable betrayal of the community museum's original intent."[11] In some accounts, Burroughs was on the institutional side of these debates. She stated in the mid-1990s to a Chicago newspaper that the DuSable Museum was "in better shape than it has ever been" despite these tensions.[12] However, the record of her views over the 1990s period remains open to debate. Burns also analyzes Burroughs's public opposition to an exhibit that the Chicago Historical Society initiated about the black South Side Douglas/Grand Boulevard neighborhood in the early 1990s. Burroughs's opposition in such a moment needs to be understood as part of a longer fight "against the legacy of mainstream museums," which for decades (if not centuries) had misinterpreted and misinformed the public about black history "in favor of promoting 'stories' and artifacts."[13]

The DuSable Museum has faced similar issues again over the last decade that for many longtime members and supporters of the museum threatened its existence and its mission to continue the vision set forth by founders like Margaret Burroughs. A recent proposal by a University of Chicago visual arts professor to redirect the programs of the DuSable created conflict among the museum's board of directors and trustees, its staff, and museum supporters from the community. A *Chicago Tribune* article reports that the professor in question, Theaster Gates Jr. (who is in his forties), proposed that the University of Chicago "take over programming at the South Side Museum." Gates, who is listed as a trustee of the DuSable's board of directors, proposed creating a "DuSable Futures Committee" that would work to recruit "artists, scholars and curators for the museum, among other things" and work in a "two-year partnership" with the University of Chicago's Center for the Study of Race, Politics, and Culture and the university's Arts and Public Life Initiative, the latter of which Gates directed. The museum and its directors, responding to "community concerns" that the DuSable was about to be taken over by the University of Chicago, suggested that the Gates proposal was merely a "growth plan" for the institution and that the museum received "numerous" such proposals on a "monthly basis." It was reported that this particular proposal was only ever presented to the museum's executive committee and not its entire board.[14]

Gates answered the concerns by saying that the "content and ambition [of his proposal was based on his] experience as an artist . . . [and his] vision of the South Side as a world class arts and culture destination, with the DuSable being a leading force in representing and celebrating black culture and artists." Gates clearly sought to assuage his critics implying that the proposal had good intentions. For its part, the University of Chicago and its Center for the Study of Race, Politics, and Culture worked to distance themselves from the proposal after it was made public. The center noted that the proposal was merely a "rough draft" to be discussed with the museum and that it did not necessarily "approve of the content," while the university stood behind a faculty member's rights to engage autonomously "with external organizations."[15]

One *Chicago Sun-Times* article on the issue suggests that the tensions over Gates's proposal were generational. The newspaper notes how apart from his role as a university faculty member, Gates is also a local artist who reworks "discarded structures and turn[s] them into cultural artifacts." A recent work of his, Dorchester Projects, involved reclaiming two dilapidated buildings on South Dorchester Avenue in Chicago, one of which he lived in. Gates turned them from sites of "neglect" into a site of "vibrant cultural locus" and of "community interaction and uplift."[16] He maintains that his proposal was not made in his capacity as a professor at the University of Chicago or "as a pawn of a white person or white university" and suggests that the issue community members have with his ideas are generational: "The baton is rarely passed. As a result, our institutions often die, or they flounder."[17] Such generational contentions are, of course, nothing new historically, but they do not need to end with impasses. As discussed in chapter 4 of the current volume, it is possible to suggest that some of the most productive programs the DuSable Museum ever established, such as its prisoner-outreach writing programs, teacher-training modules for black history, and public school field-trip programs, involved extensive and innovative intergenerational exchanges and collaborations.

Despite good intentions, Gates's proposal, nonetheless, clearly "struck a nerve among some Southside residents" who feel that the DuSable needs to remain "independent" of the university at all costs. A group called the Concerned

Committee for the Support of Independent Black Cultural Institutions issued a statement in reply to Gates's proposal. The committee was made up of prominent and elder members of Chicago's African American community—some of whom figure significantly in *Black Public History in Chicago*—notably, author and journalist Lerone Bennett Jr. and local historian and former public schoolteacher Timuel Black. Other committee members included Alderman Willie Cochran, Northeastern Illinois University professor Conrad Worrill, and Chicago State University professor Kelly Harris. The committee felt that Gates's proposal "will result in the radical reconceptualization of the ideas, cultural focus, historical knowledge, and critical black direction of the DuSable Museum." It suggested that Gates's vision was not consistent with the activist spirit that Margaret Burroughs and her cofounders had envisioned for the institution. Indeed, the committee further stated, "The defining ideas of Dr. Margaret Burroughs and other co-founders of the Museum are being discarded . . . for 'new thought,'" and viewed the proposal as a "brazen attempt to deliver the DuSable Museum into University of Chicago management." As Harris suggests, the committee's concern was that "any reimagining of DuSable that doesn't prioritize its history is not the reimagining [they] want to see." The interest in the community about this issue was enough to attract over fifty residents, "educators, artists, and activists," on a Monday night in July to express their concerns.[18]

Indeed, such concerns make sense in light of the University of Chicago's long-standing role as a predatory real estate and land developer on the South Side.[19] The university's private police force, which numbers well over a hundred, is one of the "largest" campus forces in the United States. While the university and its police force have clearly kept out some of the violence that has plagued Chicago for many years (2016, for example, saw 762 homicides in the city), it has also worked to create a racist "wall" of private property around Hyde Park and parts of Kenwood, which disconnects the campus from surrounding communities that are predominantly black and poor. Moreover, much like the Chicago Police Department's sordid relationship with communities of color and in the context of the current nationwide epidemic of police shootings and brutality incidents and movements to oppose this violence, UC campus police have long been known for harassing young black men, in particular, who are regularly stopped and checked, often for no reason. According to Andrew Fan, "since its creation in the 1950s the UCPD has been dogged by accusations of racial profiling, leveled by both University of Chicago students and community members, primarily African Americans."[20]

Thus, concerns about the historical relationship of the university to surrounding black communities mixed with the ambiguous vision for collaboration with the DuSable expressed by Gates are clearly valid. Moreover, as *Black Public History in Chicago* makes clear, the very relocation of the DuSable Museum in the early 1970s to its current location on East Fifty-Sixth Place in Washington Park had a lot to do with the fact the institution was literally reclaiming a South Side black American community space that was in the shadow of the University of Chicago and in a former space of police surveillance. Given the important history and symbolic legacy of the DuSable's origins and its independent reclamation of a civic park building right under the nose of one of the most powerful universities in the United States, it is not surprising community members became alarmed by any discussion of extensive collaboration with the university on leadership matters and future visions for museum programs.

Another recent development presents the likelihood of further challenges to the DuSable Museum's historic mission as the main proponent of black public history in the city. Barack Obama's presidential library is, at the time of this writing, under construction in Jackson Park. The *Chicago Tribune* reports that the Barack Obama Presidential Center, backed by the nonprofit Obama Foundation, includes a museum that will deal with topics similar to those that the DuSable Museum currently does. It promises to "bring the prospect of economic revival, infusing long-neglected South Side neighborhoods with new businesses and investments that promise to generate $220 million a year and attract 800,000 visitors annually." DuSable staff interviewed by the *Tribune* said they are hopeful the DuSable Museum will survive and thrive with the arrival of the Obama library because it might attract more visitors to museums on the South Side. Troy Ratliff, the museum's current chief operating officer, indicates that the question for the DuSable to consider is how to get visitors to both places: "The question is: I came to the Obama library, what's going to make me leave the library and walk over to the DuSable?" The museum's future does look hopeful in terms of visitors. It experienced an increase in visitors from 102,603 in 2012 to 118,473 in 2014—which is more than a 15 percent increase. However, its financial picture is less sanguine. In 2011 the museum made $1 million more than it spent, yet in 2012 and 2013 its "expenses outpaced income by nearly $148,000" and $135,000, respectively. As the *Tribune* reports, these losses "paint a stark contrast to years like 2009, when DuSable cleared $3.5 million more in income over costs." Indeed, some of this financial shortfall is due to cuts in state funding to public museums—something that likely affects the entire museum sector. Paid memberships, which range from $40 to $1,500 a year, were approximately 1,400 in 2013 and 2014 and 1,850 in 2015. Other recent priorities had been finding a successor for Carol Adams, CEO and president, who retired in 2014. When the controversy about the Gates proposal took place in the summer of

2015, the museum had yet to appoint a successor, which created some concern about institutional leadership and directions.[21]

Recent developments for the museum have been quite optimistic. Perri L. Irmer is president and CEO, and the museum has a full complement of staff in many critical roles. High-profile appointments of South Side Chicago native Chance the Rapper (Chancelor Bennett), his father and former Obama administration aid Ken Bennett, and friend of the Obamas Eric Whitaker to the museum's board of directors over the last year will no doubt benefit the museum's ongoing fund-raising efforts. The recent opening of a $582,000 terrace and plaza designed for community groups is likely to boost visitor statistics and is part of an optimistic projection by museum administrators that the historic Roundhouse Wing (long under renovation) open prior to 2021, when the Obama library is due to be complete.[22]

Despite these positive directions of late, it is not unfair to suggest that like the scenario that developed with the recent Gates proposal, the DuSable Museum's future is tied to how it deals with change created by external forces. These forces are likely to continue being old powerful institutions like the University of Chicago, as well as new ones like the Obama Foundation or the DuSable's ongoing relationship with local political officials. Moreover, Gates's proposal and its controversial reception as well as the question of how the DuSable Museum relates to the establishment of Obama's presidential library on the South Side also speaks especially to the obvious yet enduring importance of openly discussing the political and historical representations and commemorations of Chicago's Bronzeville, the whole South Side, and the African American community nationwide. *Black Public History in Chicago* hopes in a small way to contribute to these ongoing and vital discussions by providing some historical context for how black public-history activists once engaged with these very questions.

In our current era of increasing, devastating cutbacks to public education (to say nothing of the mixed results of charter, parochial, and private schools), alternative pedagogical projects embodied by the activism that helped build the DuSable Museum deserve to be both encouraged and better understood historically. The same is true for the proposed curriculum reforms of public schoolteachers like Stratton Morris during the early 1940s and the early Cold War–era activities of local black-history groups like the AAHA who functioned during periods of intense political repression.[23] Indeed, it is not a stretch to suggest that understanding the historic legacies of black-history activism charted by the founders of institutions like the DuSable Museum might help to better understand the urgency behind the 90 percent of Chicago Teachers Union members who struck in 2012 to, among many things, oppose Mayor Rahm Emanuel's public-private partnerships and his initiating the closures of dozens of public schools in black and brown neighborhoods. Recent activism suggests Chicagoans are well aware of the potential impact that local public-private initiatives like the Barack Obama Presidential Center might have on displacing local communities, institutions, and initiatives. The CTU and the Service Employees International Union joined local activists in October 2017 to push for a "signed agreement on community benefits."[24] Had she lived to see it, Burroughs, a former South Side public schoolteacher and Chicago Teachers Union member, would surely have opposed such draconian measures enacted by the Daley dynasty's successor. These developments further underline the ever-present challenges faced by racialized populations and communities across North America in the building of viable, independent knowledge-producing institutions in a period when domestic racism and xenophobia are clearly on the rise once again.

In light of these ongoing issues, *Black Public History in Chicago* hopes to have provided a salient case study of a region that also took center stage in successive presidential campaigns during the historic administrations of Barack Obama. His campaigns, of course, openly invoked traditions for multiracial community organizing, the nonviolent tactics of civil rights icons like Martin Luther King Jr., and Abraham Lincoln's role as the Great Emancipator, given that Obama's first campaign was announced in Lincoln's hometown of Springfield, Illinois.[25] Indeed, such uses of the past demonstrate the importance of better understanding how public history has served and, perhaps, can still serve, as a form of political activism that successfully pushed for recognition by the highest political offices and figures in the country through the mid-twentieth century when such recognition was not easily won.

Black Public History in Chicago ultimately shows that there was a time that Negro/Black History Week was more than just a public relations opportunity for politicians and prolific figures during February.[26] It ultimately suggests that there are lessons to be learned about the ways that black pasts were utilized in the public sphere to convey aspirations for black American identity and citizenship. This was true especially given the repressive Cold War context that effected great numbers of black Americans and certainly those with radical left-wing political perspectives who were able to use public history as a viable repertoire of cultural activism. These lessons are helpful, given the prevailing triviality of proclamations about "black history month" in recent years, which can overlook the persistence of enduring racial inequalities in these times.

Notes

Introduction

1. Nahum D. Brascher, "Honor School Chief for New History Course Plan," *Chicago Defender*, national ed., June 20, 1942, 7; "History Teacher Pioneer to Be Honored at Annual Blue Ribbon Tea," *Chicago Defender*, daily ed., February 20, 1963, 15; Carter G. Woodson quoted in Knupfer, *Chicago Black Renaissance*, 82.

2. During the research and writing of the current volume, the archives and collections of the DuSable Museum of African American History were inaccessible to researchers due to building renovation and institutional transitions. This book is written in a spirit of open inquiry and in the hopes that future researchers and scholars will be able to build on and respond to its arguments to help sustain the legacy and traditions of the museum and its founders.

3. See Jerome, "Let Us Grasp"; Munro, *Anticolonial Front*, 111; Wilkerson, "Negro Culture." For more on Communists in Chicago, see Storch, *Red Chicago*.

4. Biondi, *To Stand and Fight*; Denning, *Cultural Front*, xviii–xix, and *Culture in the Age of Three Worlds*; Munro, *Anticolonial Front*; St. Clair Drake, interview with Robert Martin, July 28, 1969, transcript, Bunche Oral Histories Collection, 119–230; M. T. G. Burroughs, *Life with Margaret*, 14, 60–61.

5. Horne, *Communist Front*, and *Black and Red*; Lang and Lieberman, *Anticommunism and the African American Freedom Struggle*; Von Eschen, *Race against Empire*.

6. Denning, *Cultural Front*, xviii–xix; Biondi, *To Stand and Fight*.

7. See for example Von Eschen, *Race against Empire*; Plummer, *Rising Wind*; Dudziak, *Cold War Civil Rights*.

8. Singh, *Black Is a Country*, 172. For an excellent critical discussion of how racial liberalism has dominated the U.S. public sphere from the mid-twentieth century to the present and included the near merger of liberal and conservative impulses in American political thought in ostensibly "color-blind" critiques of multiculturalism, see Singh, *Black Is a Country*. Conversely, the clearest sympathetic interpretation of Cold War civil rights history and racial liberalism can be found in Dudziak, *Cold War Civil Rights*. For an articulation of consensus liberalism at midcentury aimed at the perceived excesses of mostly Republican-led conservatism, paranoid populisms, and other corruptions of ostensibly redeemable American political traditions, see Hofstadter, *Paranoid Style in American Politics.*

9. Dawson, *Blacks In and Out of the Left*, 2.

10. Ibid., 2–3.

11. Washington, *Other Blacklist*, 206.

12. Mullen quoted in Washington, *Other Blacklist*, 206; Mullen, *Popular Fronts*, 202. For useful discussions with similar conclusions about black cultural activism and intellectuals during the early Cold War, see S. I. Morgan, *Rethinking Social Realism*; Jackson, *Indignant Generation*.

13. Recent works on black Chicago's community formations over the mid-twentieth century include Satter, *Family Properties*; Garb, *Freedom's Ballot*; Reed, *Knock at the Door*; Helgeson, *Crucibles of Black Empowerment*; Kimble, *New Deal for Bronzeville*.

14. Helgeson, "Striving in Black Chicago," 3–4, and *Crucibles of Black Empowerment*, 18; Satter, *Family Properties*.

15. Grimshaw, *Bitter Fruit*, 119–21.

16. Helgeson, *Crucibles of Black Empowerment*, 2.

17. For more information, see Baldwin, *Chicago's New Negroes*; Best, *Passionately Human*; Courage and Bone, *Muse in Bronzeville*; Gilfoyle, "Making History"; A. Green, *Selling the Race*; Hine and McCluskey, *Black Chicago Renaissance*; Mullen, *Popular Fronts*; Schlabach, *Along the Streets of Bronzeville*; Tracy, *Writers of the Black Chicago Renaissance*.

18. Schlabach, *Along the Streets of Bronzeville*, xii, 19–21.

19. This was well before Graham's marriage and extensive sojourns abroad with the elder scholar-statesman W. E. B. Du Bois.

20. This literature is large and growing, though several recent titles show trends toward comprehensive national frames, for example, Gilmore, *Defying Dixie*; Hall, "Long Civil Rights Movement"; MacLean, *Freedom Is Not Enough*; Sugrue, *Sweet Land*. A growing number of case studies substantiate and engage in different ways with J. D. Hall's provocative 2005 *Journal of American History* essay and the Organization of American Historians address that posited a "long movements" paradigm from the 1930s through the 1970s as a framework for future research. See Biondi, *To Stand and Fight*; Countryman, *Up South*; Jones, *Selma of the North*; Lang, *Grassroots at the Gateway*; Phillips, *Alabama North*; Self, *American Babylon*; Sklaroff, *Black Culture and the New Deal*; H. A. Thompson, *Whose Detroit*; Trotter, *Black Milwaukee*. For recent comprehensive accounts of both Black Power, black arts, and black liberation struggle activisms that emphasize regional variations, see Gore, Theoharis, and Woodard, *Want to Start a*

Revolution; Joseph, "Black Power Movement" and *Waiting 'til the Midnight Hour*; Lieberman and Lang, *Anticommunism and the African American Freedom Movement*; Singh, *Black Is a Country*; Smethurst, *Black Arts Movement*; Smith, *Visions of Belonging*.

21. Grossman, *Land of Hope*; Lemann, *Promised Land*; Pacyga, "Chicago" and *Chicago*.

22. A. A. Burns, *From Storefront to Monument*, 18.

23. See also ibid.; Fleming and Burroughs, "Dr. Margaret T. Burroughs"; Rocksborough-Smith, "Margaret T. G. Burroughs"; Van Balgooy, *Interpreting African American History and Culture*; Wilson, *Negro Building*.

24. See Mullen, *Popular Fronts*, 192; Smethurst, *Black Arts Movement*. For more on the origins of the DuSable Museum, see Rocksborough-Smith, "Margaret T. G. Burroughs," and chapter 2 of the current volume.

25. Mullen, *Popular Fronts*, 192.

26. Maxwell, *F. B. Eyes*.

27. Dudziak, *Cold War Civil Rights*, 18–46.

28. Omi and Winant, *Racial Formation*, 185–210.

29. For a synopsis of how public history evolved into a subfield of professional history with its own associations and conferences, see Howe, "Reflections on an Idea"; Scaraville, "Looking Backward," 8. For useful discussions of Carter G. Woodson's role as a practitioner of public history and the establishment of African American history as an academic field in its own right, see Dagbovie, "Making Black History Practical and Popular."

30. Baldwin, "Black Belts and Ivory Towers;" Drake and Cayton, *Black Metropolis*; Myrdal, *American Dilemma*.

31. Clarice Durham, "Bronzeville's Venerable Historian," *Hyde Park (IL) Herald*, July 23, 2003, 1; Smethurst, *Black Arts Movement*, 193–200, 195.

32. "How Do We Define Public History?" *National Council on Public History*, 2017, http://ncph.org/what-is-public-history/about-the-field/.

33. See Hine, "Carter G. Woodson," 406.

34. Dagbovie, *Early Black History Movement*, 1.

35. Crew, "African Americans, History, and Museums," 81; Goggins, *Carter C Woodson*; Dagbovie, *Early Black History Movement*.

36. Dagbovie, *Early Black History Movement*, 99.

37. Knupfer, *Chicago Black Renaissance*, 82.

38. St. Clair Drake, interview with Robert Martin, July 28, 1969, transcript, 119–230, Bunche Oral History Collection.

39. For a recent discussion of the trivialization and tokenism that surround public reception and recognition of Black History Month, see Franklin, Horne, Cruse, Ballard, and Mitchell, "Black History Month."

Chapter One. Curriculum Reforms in World War II Chicago

1. Lyons, *Teachers and Reform*, 130; Timuel D. Black, interview with Erik Gellman and Ian Rocksborough-Smith, November 17, 2009, Chicago, Illinois.

2. M. T. G. Burroughs, *Life with Margaret*, 73.

3. Black, interview. The bracketed words are inferences because his words on the tape are unintelligible.

4. Dudziak, *Cold War Civil Rights*; Plummer, *Rising Wind*; Von Eschen, *Race against Empire*.

5. February is now, of course, Black History Month.

6. Mavis Mixon, "The Development of the Study Negro History in Chicago," *Chicago Defender*, February 7, 1942, 15; Lyons, *Teachers and Reform*, 162; S. I. Hayakawa, "Second Thoughts," *Chicago Defender*, national ed., October 9, 1943, 15; Mavis Mixon, "Galleon's Goal," *Chicago Defender*, December 16, 1942, 14; Mullen, *Popular Fronts*, esp. chap. 3; Wald, *Exiles from a Future Time*, 270; Hine and McCluskey, *Black Chicago Renaissance*; Davis, *Livin' the Blues*, 70.

7. Black, interview.

8. Madeline Robinson "married three times, divorcing Thomas Morgan (1926–43) and surviving Samuel B. Stratton (1946–72) and Walter Morris (1981–83)," and so to provide consistency, she is referred to as Stratton Morris hereafter. "Biographical Note," Madeline Stratton Morris Papers, *Chicago Public Library*, 2017, https://www.chipublib.org/fa-madeline-stratton-morris-papers/.

9. "History Teacher Pioneer," 15 (introduction, n1); M. R. Morgan, "Chicago School Curriculum," 120–23; Black, interview.

10. Knupfer, *Chicago Black Renaissance*, 81.

11. Ibid., 82.

12. For more on the *Brown* decision, see Kluger, *Simple Justice*; Scott, "Postwar Pluralism."

13. Homel, "Politics of Public Education," 180.

14. Two pioneering black American school principals from this period were Ruth Jackson and Maudelle Bousfield. Madeline S. Morris, "Autobiographical Sketch, c. 1943 (?)," Folder 4, Box 1, Stratton Morris Papers. See Danns, "Maudelle Bousfield."

15. "Informal CV Morris 1964?" Box 1, Folder 8, Stratton Morris Papers; M. R. Morgan, "Chicago School Curriculum," 120–23.

16. M. R. Morgan, "Chicago School Curriculum," 120–21; M. S. Morris, "Autobiographical Sketch"; Carter G. Woodson to Madeline R. Stratton, November 22, 1946, Folder 51, Box 6, Stratton Morris Papers.

17. M. R. Morgan, "Chicago School Curriculum," 121–22.

18. Montalto, *History*; Knupfer, *Chicago Black Renaissance*, 79; Mickenberg, *Learning from the Left*, 90–94; Drake and Cayton, *Black Metropolis*, 263–64.

19. Scott, "Postwar Pluralism," 72.

20. M. R. Morgan, "Chicago School Curriculum," 121–22.

21. Ibid.

22. Knupfer, *Chicago Black Renaissance*, 81.

23. Kelley, "Afterward," 168–69. Among the many classic works by Du Bois and Aptheker (who collaborated on numerous occasions, including Aptheker's role as one of the chief executors of Du Bois's papers), two of the most notable are Du Bois, *Black Reconstruction*; Aptheker, *American Negro Slave Revolts*.

24. "Education: Brown Studies"; Knupfer, *Chicago Black Renaissance*, 82.

25. M. R. Morgan, "Chicago School Curriculum," 123.

26. M. R. Morgan, "Autobiographical Sketch."

27. Woodward, *Origins of the New South*, 51; Du Bois, *Black Reconstruction*; Aptheker, *Negro Slave Revolts*.

28. Steinberg, *Turning Back*, 44–45; Baldwin, "Black Belts and Ivory Towers," 397–450.

29. Baldwin, "Black Belts and Ivory Towers," 400.

30. Garb, *Freedom's Ballot*, 11.

31. Reed, *Knock at the Door*, 2.

32. Stanley, "Schooling."

33. Robin Lindley, "Textbooks and History Standards: An Historical Overview," *History News Network*, August 29, 2010, http://historynewsnetwork.org/article/130766.

34. M. R. Morgan, "Chicago School Curriculum," 123.

35. A. Green, *Selling the Race*, 41, 45–47; Helgeson, "Who Are You America but Me?" For an extensive treatment of the Chicago Negro Progress exposition in 1940 as one of the main expositions conducted by black Americans through the mid-twentieth century, see Wilson, *Negro Building*, 191–241.

36. M. R. Morgan, "Chicago School Curriculum," 120.

37. Singh, *Black Is a Country*, 153.

38. "History Teacher Pioneer"; Nathan, "Classrooms against Hate," 7; M. R. Morgan, "Chicago School Curriculum," 123; "Education: Brown Studies."

39. Carter G. Woodson to Madeline R. Stratton, November 22, 1946, Folder 51, Box 6, Stratton Morris Papers; Dagbovie, *Early Black History Movement*, chap. 1; Earl Conrad, "Dr. Woodson Hails N.Y. School Anti-Bias Act," *Chicago Defender*, national ed., April 7, 1945, 3.

40. "History Group Warns of Bogus Literature," *Chicago Defender*, national ed., January 27, 1940, 12.

41. Dagbovie, *Early Black History Movement*, 51–52.

42. Travis, *Autobiography of Black Politics*, 124; "Negro History Week," February 4, 1939, 16, "Drippings from Other Pens," April 29, 1939, 22, "City-Wide Forum to Observe Negro History Week," February 10, 1940, 4, "A Page from Our History," February 10, 1940, 12, "Chicagoans Hear Dr. Woodson," February 17, 1940, 12, "Negro History Week," February 17, 1940, 14, "Women to Observe Negro History Week," February 17, 1940, 16, "Attend Negro History Week Tea," February 24, 1940, 6, all *Chicago Defender*, national ed.; "Democracy Parade Hits Defense Jim Crow," *Chicago Defender*, February 15, 1941, 7.

43. "Committee Ready for Historians," *Chicago Defender*, national ed., August 3, 1935, 4; "Morris Lewis Gives Address to Ministers," August 25, 1934, 23, "4-day Program Announced for History Meet," September 7, 1935, 5, "Race Life History Groups in Drive," January 11, 1936, 2, and "Race Study Unit Plans Anniversary Fete," July 13, 1940, 8, all *Chicago Defender*; "Revamp Negro History Group," *Chicago Defender*, daily

ed., October 13, 1964, 11. Also see chapter 2 of this volume for discussion of the partisan use of a local chapter.

44. Patterson, *Man Who Cried Genocide*, 148–49. For a less-sympathetic interpretation of these same Washington Park speaker scenes—a critique Patterson duly references alongside his own perspective previously cited, see Wright, *American Hunger*, 37.

45. Essien-Udom, *Black Nationalism*, 50.

46. F. H. Hammurabi Robb, "Hammurabi Robb Starts New Feature Series for Defender," August 1, 1936, 24, and "Women to Observe Negro History Week," February 17, 1940, 16, both *Chicago Defender*, national ed.; Nance, "Respectability and Representation."

47. "Map Plans for Annual Negro History Week," *Chicago Defender*, national ed., February 12, 1944, 15.

48. "Democracy Parade Hits Defense Jim Crow," *Chicago Defender*, February 15, 1941, 7. For more on the March on Washington movement, see Garfinkel, *When Negroes March*. Numerous studies and memoirs written with attention to both social and literary history methods have treated the diverse activities of the *Chicago Defender*'s talented editors, especially Enoch P. Waters, Ben Burns, Era Bell Thompson, and Metz Lochard. These studies examine these editors' subsequent dispersal to other regions and the employment of many (considered by some as a "raid") with Johnson publications (*Ebony* and *Negro Digest*) and other similar "cultural" enterprises through the late 1940s and 1950s. James Grossman's study of black migration to Chicago through World War I and the interwar years remains foundational for understanding the role of print media in shaping or facilitating cultures of migration from the American south as blacks sought greater opportunities in more northern regions because of information they partly received by reading and hearing about content discussed in *Chicago Defender* articles. See B. Burns, *Nitty Gritty*; A. Green, *Selling the Race*, chap. 4; Grossman, *Land of Hope*; Mullen, *Popular Fronts*, chap. 2; E. B. Thompson, *American Daughter*; Waters, *American Diary*.

49. Margaret Taylor Goss Burroughs throughout this volume is referred to as Burroughs.

50. Margaret Taylor Goss, "A Negro Mother Looks at War," *Chicago Defender*, national ed., August 31, 1940, 13. African American intellectual engagements at both the popular and academic levels with World War II anti-interventionism was more widespread and should be viewed beyond the vacillations of the Communist Left, which pivoted around the Nazi-Soviet pact of 1939—to which they are sometimes erroneously attributed. See Aldridge, "War for the Colored Races." Although it requires further examination and substantiation, the *Chicago Defender* did exhibit a militancy during the 1930s and early 1940s, especially that made it among the most receptive to left-wing perspectives among African American newspapers. See Mullen, *Popular Fronts*, 44–74.

51. "More Teachers, Texts Needed for Growth of Race History," *Chicago Defender*, December 28, 1935, 10; "History Group Warns of Bogus Literature," *Chicago Defender*, national ed., January 27, 1940, 12.

52. Chapter 2 of the current volume continues to deal with these concerns about authority in relation to public history activism and museum projects.

53. Woodson to Stratton, November 22, 1946.

54. "Informal CV Morris 1964?"; "Education: *Brown* Studies."

55. Nathan, "Classrooms against Hate," 7–8; Hilda Taba to Madeline R. Morgan, February 7, 1945, Folder 1, Box 2, Stratton Morris Papers. For more historical assessment of the Springfield plan, see Scott, "Postwar Pluralism."

56. Knupfer, *Chicago Black Renaissance*, 81.

57. Ibid., 82.

58. Rebecca Stiles Taylor, "Activities of Women's National Organizations," *Chicago Defender*, national ed., February 20, 1943, 17.

59. See Irons, *Jim Crow's Children*, 62–79.

60. M. R. Morgan, "Chicago School Curriculum," 123.

61. Taylor, "Activities of Women's National Organizations," and "Defender Washington Bureau Head 12 Others on NCNW Honor Roll," *Chicago Defender*, national ed., February 8, 1947, 3; Klein, *Cold War Orientalism*, 7–8.

62. "East Meets West," *Chicago Defender*, national ed., May 12, 1945, 15.

63. Herbert Aptheker to Madeline Morris [undated], Folder 14, Box 2, Stratton Morris Papers; Davis, *Livin' the Blues*, 290. See also Aptheker, "Autobiographical Note," 147–50; Aptheker and Kelley, "Interview," 151–67; Kelley, "Afterward," 168–71; Shapiro, *African American History*; Wald, "Narrating Nationalisms."

64. Mickenberg, *Learning from the Left*, 6.

65. M. T. G. Burroughs, *Jasper the Drummin' Boy*, 22–24.

66. See Feldman, *Figures in Black History*, 94; Mickenberg, *Learning from the Left*.

67. All these groups made up Chicago's historic ethnic enclaves and much of the rank and file in the city's basic industries through the 1940s. See Horne, *Black Revolutionary*, 88; Patterson, *Man Who Cried Genocide*, 149–55.

68. Patterson, *Man Who Cried Genocide*, 149–55.

69. See Mullen, *Popular Fronts*, 9; Reed, *Chicago NAACP*. Such tensions among professional classes echoed an earlier division among black Chicago business elites during the first Great Migration era (1910s and 1920s) who did not ascribe to integrationism or to traditional uplift strategies. These elites ultimately favored the growth of institutional "black self-sufficiency." See Spear, *Black Chicago*, 226.

70. Patterson, *Man Who Cried Genocide*, 149–55; Davis, *Livin' the Blues*, 283, xxii; "Abe Lincoln School Plans to Continue," December 6, 1947, 13, and "Him They Can Have," April 21, 1948, 20, *Chicago Daily Tribune*; "Paul Robeson at Chicago War Plant," *Chicago Defender*, August 7, 1943, 20; Langston Hughes, "Here to Yonder," *Chicago Defender*, national ed., October 30, 1943), 14. For a treatment of the Jefferson school in New York, see Gettleman, "No Varsity Teams."

71. McDuffie, *Sojourning for Freedom*, 138–40; "Rockwell Kent, Noted Artist, IWO Speaker," *Chicago Defender*, national ed., December 30, 1944, 17A; Smethurst, *Black Arts Movement*, 199.

72. Neary, "Crossing Parish Boundaries," 160–61; Knupfer, *Chicago Black Renaissance*, 82–83.

73. Meier and Rudwick, *CORE*, 3–5; "CORE Maps Out Summer Campaign against Bias," *Chicago Defender*, national ed., April 27, 1946, 3.

74. Knupfer, *Chicago Black Renaissance*, 83.

75. "DuBois Says Peace Terms Must Include Dark Races," April 26, 1941, 6, "Will Honor Play-Wright at Reception," October 5, 1940, 5, and "It Grew Up with Defender: Lincoln Center," August 13, 1955, 4A, all *Chicago Defender*.

76. Mixon, "Development of the Study Negro History in Chicago."

77. Ibid.

78. Homel, *Down from Equality*, 171.

79. "Biography: Candidate for School Board for Samuel B. Stratton," [undated], Folder 6, Box 1, Congress of Racial Equality (CORE); Mixon, "Development of the Study Negro History in Chicago." The NNMHF is further discussed in chapter 2 of the current volume.

80. See Black, *Bridges of Memory*, 129, 134–41, 167, 171, 178, 179, 180, 181–82, 190, 248, 409–10; Harold Washington quoted in Travis, *Autobiography of Black Politics*, 472; Homel, *Down from Equality*, 101–2, 142.

81. For some good appraisals of how racial inequities were exacerbated by the actions of Benjamin Willis in the late 1950s and 1960s, see Anderson and Pickering, *Confronting the Color Line*; Lyons, *Teachers and Reform*; Ralph, *Northern Protest*.

82. Mixon, "Development of the Study"; Nahum D. Brascher, "Honor School Chief for New History Course Plan," *Chicago Defender*, national ed., June 20, 1942, 7; Knupfer, *Chicago's Black Renaissance*, 79; M. R. Morgan, "Chicago School Curriculum," 120.

83. Lyons, *Teachers and Reform*, 50–53; Herrick, *Chicago Public Schools*, 271–73.

84. "History Teacher Pioneer"; Lyons, *Teachers and Reform*, 52, 65, 67, 160, 162.

85. "Study Negro History Says Stratton to Group," December 28, 1940, 19, "City-Wide Forum to Observe Negro History Week," February 10, 1940, 4, "Hold Symposium on Negro," February 14, 1942, 5, "Honor School Chief for New History Course Plan," June 20, 1942, 7, "Defender Washington Bureau Head 12 Others on NCNW Honor Roll," February 8, 1947, 3, all *Chicago Defender*, national ed.; Black, interview; Woodson to Stratton, November 22, 1946.

86. Mixon, "Development of the Study"; Knupfer, *Chicago Black Renaissance*, 81. For more on the NNMHF, see chapter 2 of the current volume.

87. For a useful treatment of black beautician work as a form of working-class black modernity during a period of rapid urbanization, see D. A. Baldwin, *Chicago's New Negroes*, 53–90.

88. Much like Bughouse Square on the Near North Side of Chicago was to white radicals before and during the Depression years, Washington Park became a fixture of soapbox lectures and forums as well as more official public events, like Black History Week celebrations for African Americans in Bronzeville. The Chicago Police Department's Red Squad surveillance units focused on a group of itinerant black labor

radicals that often organized demonstrations in the park from the Great Depression era through the Cold War period. Black, interview.

89. For more about the renaming of the museum, see chapter 2.

90. "DeSaible Society Makes Plans for Fund Drive," December 29, 1928, 7, "Chicago Honors Jean DuSable, Frontiersman," December 9, 1944, 10, and "Commemorate DuSable as Great War Leader," May 7, 1948, 7, all *Chicago Defender*; "DuSable City Founder, Honored," *Chicago Defender*, daily ed., December 4, 1957, 15; "National DuSable Group in Program," March 2, 1957, 10, "DuSable Society Holds Open House," December 30, 1958, 14, "Chicago Hails DuSable Society Founder-Spearhead," December 17, 1960, 14, and "DuSable Society Founder, Mrs. Annie Oliver, Dies," November 14, 1962, 8, all *Chicago Defender*, national ed. The Men's Division of the Chicago Urban League also had a DeSaible Club that commemorated the first Chicago settler. See Reed, *Rise of Chicago's Black Metropolis*, 21.

91. Mixon, "Development of the Study Negro History in Chicago."

92. Drake and Cayton, *Black Metropolis*, 379–80. Originally called Grand Boulevard, South Parkway is now called Martin Luther King Jr. Drive.

93. Knupfer, *Chicago Black Renaissance*; Mullen, *Popular Fronts*; Mickenberg, *Learning from the Left*, 102.

94. See Mickenberg, *Learning from the Left*, 101–2; Rollins, *We Build Together*.

95. Savage, *Broadcasting Freedom*, 260–70; Richard Durham, "Biggest Text Book Buyer Never Got to College," *Chicago Defender*, national ed., July 22, 1944, 2; MacDonald, "Radio's Black Heritage"; Satter, "Cops, Gangs, and Revolutionaries," 12–13.

96. Waters, *American Diary*, 267.

97. "Emanuel's First Job: Fix Chicago Schools," *Chicago Sun-Times*, May 16, 2011, reprint, Chicago Teachers Union, https://ctunet.com/media.

Chapter Two. Imagining a Black Museum in Cold War Chicago

1. Strong, "Margaret Taylor Goss Burroughs," 197; *Annual Report 1966*, submitted by Margaret Burroughs, director, and *Museum of Negro History Cultural and Historical Tour*, miscellaneous pamphlets, etc., Museum of African American History, Chicago History Museum; "Black Museum Seeks Park Site," *Chicago Daily Tribune*, November 10, 1971, A18; A. A. Burns, *From Storefront to Monument*, 20–22, 75.

2. Feldman, *Birth and the Building*, 12.

3. Brooks quoted in Schulman, "Marion Perkins," 87.

4. See Wilson, "Making History Visible," 308; Wilson, *Negro Building*, 242–49; Crew, "African Americans, History, and Museums," 98; M. T. G. Burroughs, interview with Ian Rocksborough-Smith, October 19, 2009, Chicago; *Profile of Black Museums*; "Negro History Museum Officially Opens Sunday," *Chicago Defender*, October 28, 1961, 16.

5. M. T. G. Burroughs, *Life with Margaret*, 85–86.

6. Terry Tatum, Susan Perry, and Brian Goeken, *Landmark Designation Site: Griffith-Burroughs House*, Commission on Chicago Landmarks, November 5, 2009, *City of Chicago*, https://www.cityofchicago.org/content/dam/city/depts/zlup/Historic_Preservation/

Publications/Griffiths_Burroughs_House.pdf; "Quincy Club Important for Railroad Men," *Chicago Defender*, national ed., January 6, 1962, 6; Ralph Turner, interviewed by Margaret T. G. Burroughs, Chicago, Illinois, 1969, Oral History Research Program Papers. For a useful history of African American Pullman porters and their influence on African American political culture in the early to mid-twentieth century in Chicago especially, see Bates, *Pullman Porters*. For an excellent history of African Americans as workers in the railroad industry, see Arnesen, *Brotherhoods of Color*.

7. For more information on Turner, see chapter 4 of the current volume.

8. Feldman, *Birth and the Building*, 11, 15; "Top, 'Unknown' Artists Exhibit," *Chicago Defender*, daily ed., June 20, 1957, 7; "Outdoor Art Fair Is Huge Success," *Chicago Defender*, national ed., July 6, 1957, 3; Biondi, *Black Revolution on Campus*, 227.

9. C. G. Burroughs, *Home*; M. T. G. Burroughs, *Life with Margaret*, 72; McDuffie, *Sojourning For Freedom*, 55–57; Solomon, *Cry Was Unity*; Maxwell, *New Negro, Old Left*; K. A. Baldwin, *Beyond the Color Line and the Iron Curtain*; Gilmore, *Defying Dixie*.

10. M. T. G. Burroughs, *Life with Margaret*, 29–30, 55–56, 85; Strong, "Margaret Taylor Goss Burroughs," 26.

11. Smethurst, *Black Arts Movement*, 193.

12. Crew, "African Americans, History, and Museums," 81; Goggin, *Carter G. Woodson*; Smethurst, *Black Arts Movement*, 196, 200. For the dispersion of the black literary left from Chicago, see especially Mullen, *Popular Fronts*. For useful, in-depth studies of black Chicago's cultural renaissance, see Knupfer, *Chicago Black Renaissance*, and D. Baldwin, *Chicago's New Negroes*.

13. On Margaret Burroughs's role with SSCAC, see Mullen, *Popular Fronts*, 75–105; Knupfer, *Black Women's Activism*, 5, 8, 19, 67; Mara Scudder, "DuSable Museum's Proud Growth," *Chicago Defender*, daily ed., May 7, 1974; Wilson, "Making History Visible," 299–300, and *Negro Building*, 245–47.

14. A. A. Burns, *From Storefront to Monument*, 21.

15. Gellman, *Death Blow to Jim Crow*, 4–5, 25.

16. Ibid. For an account of immediate post–World War II labor insurgency with an emphasis on cultural forms and fronts, see Lipsitz, *Rainbow at Midnight*, 99–156.

17. "National Negro Museum and Historical Foundation, Inc.," St. Clair Drake's Freedom of Information Act (FOIA) FBI File, 77, http://omeka.wustl.edu/omeka/exhibits/show/fbeyes/drake. Thanks to William J. Maxwell and the F. B. Eyes Digital Archive for making this file and others accessible to scholars.

18. John M. Gray to Glenn Taylor, January 4, 1947, and proclamation, City of Chicago, Mayor's Office, January 22, 1947, both Folder 15, Box 66, National Negro Congress Papers.

19. Bracey, "St. Clair Drake," 434–35.

20. Drake, interview with Martin, Bunche Oral History Collection, 119–230. For more on the subject, see chapter 3 of the current volume. The literature on Chicago's Democratic machine and African American politics is extensive and complex. For a focused political biography of William Dawson's career, see Manning, *William L.*

Dawson. Studies of black politics and their complex engagement with Chicago's Democratic machine over the twentieth century include Grimshaw, *Bitter Fruit* and *Negro Politics in Chicago*; Reed, *Chicago NAACP*; Cohen and Taylor, *American Pharaoh*, 57–61; L. Cohen, *Making a New Deal*, 251–89; Travis, *Autobiography of Black Politics*; "Kerner O.K.'s Negro History Week Feb. 11," January 24, 1962, 6, and "Kerner Backs History Week," January 31, 1962, 9, *Chicago Defender*, daily ed.; Smethurst, *Black Arts Movement*, 194.

21. Wilkerson, "Negro Culture"; Jerome, "Let Us Grasp the Weapon of Culture," 195–215; Munro, *Anticolonial Front*, 111.

22. "Louise Thompson Speaks on Spain," *Chicago Defender*, November 6, 1937, 24; Halpern, *Down on the Killing Floor*, 243–44; Rocksborough-Smith, "I had gone in there thinking."

23. Fleming and Burroughs, "Dr. Margaret T. Burroughs."

24. For a treatment of African American intellectuals and their struggles to advocate for peace during the early Cold War, see Lieberman, "Another Side of the Story"; Horne, *Communist Front?* and *Black and Red*.

25. Plummer, *Rising Wind*, 195.

26. For a more focused discussion of black nationalism and public history, see chapter 3 of the current volume.

27. "Negro History Week: Win a People's Peace February 10–17, 1946," Folder 16, Box 67, National Negro Congress Papers.

28. Gellman, *Death Blow to Jim Crow*, 173.

29. "Negro History Week: Win."

30. Ibid.

31. "Negro History Folder," February 1947, Folder 16, Box 67, National Negro Congress Papers; Gellman, *Death Blow to Jim Crow*, 173.

32. M. T. G. Burroughs, *Life with Margaret*, 100.

33. "Negro History Week: Win," "Make History! Negro History Week, February 10–17, 1946," and "Negro History Week: Eighty-Two Years of Freedom 1863–1945," Folder 16, Box 67, all National Negro Congress Papers.

34. "Loop Hotels Ban Race History Fete," February 9, 1946, and "Chicago Hotels Set Quota on Negroes at Banquets," March 2, 1946, 12, both *Chicago Defender*, national ed.; Travis, *Autobiography of Black Chicago*, 126.

35. Kimble, *New Deal for Bronzeville*, 9.

36. For a recent study of civil rights in Chicago and an excellent focus on fair employment practices activism, see Kimble, *New Deal for Bronzeville*.

37. Feldman, *Birth and the Building*, 13.

38. Anna Tyler interview with Margaret Taylor Burroughs, November 11–December 5, 1988, Chicago, Illinois, Smithsonian Archives of American Art, Washington, D.C., 33–34; Gilfoyle, "Making History"; M. T. G. Burroughs, *Life with Margaret*, 55, 122–23.

39. Brennan, *At Home in the World*, 230.

40. S. I. Morgan, *Rethinking Social Realism*, 52–53.

41. M. T. G. Burroughs, *Life with Margaret*, 193; Mullen, *Popular Fronts*, 181–91; Strong, "Margaret Taylor Goss Burroughs," 117–18; M. T. G Burroughs, interview with Rocksborough-Smith; Fleming and Burroughs, "Dr. Margaret T. Burroughs," 39.

42. Lyons, *Teachers and Reform*, 123–24.

43. Ibid.; "Convention Lays Basis for Advance in Negro Creative Arts," *New York Daily Worker*, January 30, 1952, 7.

44. "Burroughs, Margaret Goss," alphabetical file no. 1950, Investigators Report, Box 296, Red Squad and related records, Chicago Police Department.

45. "Feldman (DR.), Eugene," alphabetical file no. [blank], Investigators Report, Box 299, Red Squad Records, Chicago Police Department; Feldman, *Birth and the Building*, 11–15.

46. Lyons, *Teachers and Reform*, 123–24.

47. Donner, *Protectors of Privilege*, 1.

48. Ibid.

49. Maxwell, *F. B. Eyes*, 59.

50. Tyler interview with Burroughs, 49.

51. Lyons, *Teachers and Reform*, 108, 114, 117, 122, 130. For more on black teachers and curriculum reforms related to public history and racial knowledge, see chapter 1 of the current volume.

52. Mullen, *Popular Fronts*, 192; Schreiber, *Cold War Exiles in Mexico*, 5–6, 27–57; Caplow, *Leopoldo Mendez*; Tyler interview with Burroughs, 62.

53. A. A. Burns, *From Storefront to Monument*, 18. For more on the struggles that the SSCAC faced in this period, see Mullen, *Popular Fronts*, and Knupfer, *Chicago Black Renaissance*.

54. "Revamp Negro History Group," *Chicago Defender*, daily ed., October 13, 1964, 11; "Plans for Celebrating Negro History Week," 86; "How We Should Celebrate Negro History," 101–2; Reddick, "Twenty-Five Negro History Weeks," 178–79, "Negro History Celebrations," 182; "History Clubs and Branches," 186; "Summary History of the Detroit Branch."

55. W. M. Brewer to Lorenzo Turner, December 7, 1953, Folder 1, Charles H. Wesley to Lorenzo Turner, October 5, 1954, Folder 2, and W. M. Brewer to Lorenzo Turner, October 20, 1955, Folder 3, all Box 6, Turner Papers; Levine, *Black Culture and Black Consciousness*, 146.

56. Margaret Burroughs to Lorenzo Turner, September 1, 1955, and Nerissa Long Milton to Lorenzo D. Turner, November 8, 1955, Folder 3, Box 6, Turner Papers; Albert N. D. Brooks to Irene McCoy Gaines, October 11, 1955, and Albert N. D. Brooks to Margaret Burroughs, November 15, 1955, Folder 1, Box 5, Gaines Papers. For an extended treatment of Irene McCoy Gaines's career and activism as a clubwoman, see Knupfer, *Chicago Black Renaissance*, 6. For more on African American bipartisan Cold War liberalism, see Dudziak, *Cold War Civil Rights*; Laville and Lucas, "American Way." In Chicago, some of this current materialized in the bipartisan movement that opposed Chicago's black congressman, William Dawson, who was a Democrat Party stalwart

during the 1950s. See Knupfer, *Chicago Black Renaissance*, 96; Beito and Beito, *Black Maverick*; Grimshaw, *Bitter Fruit*; Travis, *Autobiography of Black Politics*.

57. Albert N. D. Brooks to Margaret Burroughs, November 15, 1955, Folder 1, Box 5, Gaines Papers; Nerissa Long Milton to Lorenzo D. Turner, November 8, 1955, Folder 2, Box 6, Turner Papers.

58. See Gellman, *Death Blow to Jim Crow*, 11. For more on Flory's work as a union and community activist during the 1930s, especially where he worked with black railroad and dining-car workers in Chicago, see Arnesen, *Brotherhoods of Color*, 99.

59. Lorenzo D. Turner to Nerissa Long Milton, November 14, 1955, Folder 2, Box 6, Turner Papers.

60. Marion Hadley to Irene McCoy Gaines, May 11, 1956; Irene McCoy Gaines to Max Rabb, secretary to the president's cabinet, January 24, 1956; and Maxwell M. Rabb to Irene McCoy Gaines, January 25, 1956, all Folder 2, Box 5, Gaines Papers.

61. Feldman, "James T. Rapier," 62.

62. "Brotherhood . . . that each may contribute to the common good; . . . That all may be enriched. First Annual Dinner in Observance of Brotherhood and Negro History Weeks," February 25, 1956, flyer, Folder 2, Box 5, Gaines Papers; Margaret Burroughs to Lorenzo D. Turner, September 8, 1956, Folder 5, Box 6, Turner Papers; "The Shadow of My Hand," souvenir program, sponsored by the NAACP Chicago Branch Pageant Committee, February 10, 1957, DuSable High School Auditorium, Folder 8, Box 1, Turner Papers.

63. "Interview with Margaret Burroughs and Charles Wright 12/26/84," 1, Folder 13, Box 6, Charles H. Wright Papers; M. T. G. Burroughs, interview with Rocksborough-Smith; Feldman, *Birth and the Building*, 11–13; S. Stuckey, foreword, 13; Lee Blackwell, "Off the Record," December 19, 1957, 10, "Top 'Unknown' Artists Exhibit," June 20, 1957, and Ted Stone, "Heard and Scene," June 12, 1958, all *Chicago Defender*, daily ed.

64. See Meriwether, *Proudly We Can be Africans*; Plummer, *Rising Wind*; Gaines, *American Africans in Ghana*; Parker, "'Made-in-America Revolutions'?"

65. An excellent analysis of the Cold War context in which Hansberry produced *A Raisin in the Sun* is found in Smith, *Visions of Belonging*, chap. 9.

66. O'Dell, *Climbin' Jacob's Ladder*, 30–31; Rocksborough-Smith, "Filling the Gap"; Smethurst, "SNYC, *Freedomways*," and *Black Arts Movement*, 124–27, 196.

67. Rich and Wright, *Wright Man*, 289–90; *Profile of Black Museums*, 3–5; "Interview with Margaret Burroughs and Charles Wright 12/26/84," 1.

68. "Ask Artists to Meeting in Georgia," *Chicago Defender*, national ed., February 28, 1959; Margaret T. Burroughs, "The People Speak: Community at Center," *Chicago Defender*, daily ed., October 21, 1959; Corneal A. Davis to Otto Kerner, memo, February 4, 1963, Folder 1, Box 3, Corneal Davis Papers; Wilson, *Negro Building*, 243–44; "Large Crowds View Exposition," *Chicago Defender*, daily ed., August 20, 1963, A2. For more on the 1940 exposition, see A. Green, *Selling the Race*, chap. 1.

69. "Chicago Teacher Tours Africa Guests with Nkrumah, Azikiwe," October 12, 1957, 14, and Bob Hunter, "Negro Progress Exposition Open," August 17, 1963, 1, both

Chicago Defender, national ed.; "Admire African Art," *Chicago Defender*, daily ed., August 18, 1959, 14.

70. See Washington, "Desegregating the 1950s," foreword, ix–x, and *Other Blacklist*, 205–38.

71. A. A. Burns, *From Storefront to Monument*, 77.

72. Margaret Burroughs quoted in ibid.

73. Smethurst, *Black Arts Movement*, 223–24; S. Stuckey, foreword, 14; Strong, "Margaret Burroughs"; *The History of Americans of African Descent for Teachers and Social Workers of the Chicago Area*, February 8, 1968, orientation program, Folder 7, Box 3, Elma Stuckey Papers; Haki Madhubuti, "Liberation Narratives Collected and New Poems, 1966–2009," lecture, Carter G. Woodson Regional Library, Chicago, Illinois, February 13, 2010, transcript in author's possession; Sterling Stuckey, interview with Ian Rocksborough-Smith, April 16, 2010, Chicago.

74. Ralph, *Northern Protest*; Anderson and Pickering, *Confronting the Color Line*; Garrow, *Chicago 1966*.

75. Travis, *Autobiography of Black Politics*; Satter, *Family Properties*, 56–59. The best assessment of Abner's tenure as head of the NAACP, which does not make this case, is Reed, *Chicago NAACP*, chap. 9. For good assessments of the Far South Side housing battles and of black public responses to Till's murder, see Hirsch, *Making the Second Ghetto*; A. Green, *Selling the Race*, esp. chap. 5. A useful fictional interpretation of the post–World War II Far South Side housing riots, based on first-person experience, can be found in Frank London Brown's excellent first novel, *Trumbull Park*. A recent scholarly account of the Westside housing struggles that took place in conjunction with the second major wave of African American migration (1940s to 1960s) from the U.S. south can be found in Satter, *Family Properties*; "Shadow of My Hand."

76. A. A. Burns, *From Storefront to Monument*, 20.

77. "Voter's League Elects Officers," December 1, 1958, 2, and "Credits League with Spurning Vote," December 16, 1959, A2, both *Chicago Defender*, daily ed.; Burroughs, "Identity for the Negro Child." For information on Burroughs's protest activities in the 1930s and 1940s, see Mullen, *Popular Fronts*, 87; Bennett Johnson, vice president, Third World Press, interview with Ian Rocksborough-Smith, December 6, 2009, Chicago, Illinois.

Chapter Three. Black-History Activism and the Afro-American Heritage Association

1. "The Afro-American Heritage Association," August 23, 1967, File 848, Box 118, Red Squad Files, Chicago Police Department.

2. "Afro-American Heritage Group Raps House Probers," *Chicago Defender*, daily ed., May 6, 1959, 4.

3. "Urge Airing of Racism in U.S.," March 28, 1960, 19, "Plan Work Halt on 'Africa' Day," May 31, 1960, A10, "Urges UN Meet on Congo Row," July 14, 1960, 26, "Chicagoans Blast Tshombe as an 'Uncle Tom,'" February 14, 1961, 1, "Lumumba Mass Meet Set

Friday," February 21, 1961, 8, all *Chicago Defender*, daily ed.; "Chicago to Honor DuSable, First Settler," *Chicago Defender*, national ed., August 17, 1963, 6.

4. "Flory, Ishmael," Investigators Report, Folder "Flory, Ishmael, 1968–1974," Box 299, Red Squad Records, Chicago Police Department.

5. As noted in the introduction, CPUSA intellectuals, such as Doxey A. Wilkerson and V. J. Jerome, advocated cultural activism as a valuable "weapon" in global struggles for human rights. See Wilkerson, "Negro Culture: Heritage and Weapon"; Jerome, "Let Us Grasp the Weapon of Culture," 195–215; Munro, *Anticolonial Front*, 111. For a good, concise treatment of the CPUSA's conflicted abandonment of the Black Belt thesis, see Horne, *Black Revolutionary*, 93–94.

6. "Works of Artists to Be Displayed," September 15, 1958, A7, "Presents Merit Awards at Emancipation Day Program," September 22, 1958, A15, "Photo Standalone 35—No Title," October 11, 1959, 13, "Photo Standalone 24—No Title," September 24, 1958, A15, "Kerner O.K.'s Negro History Week Feb. 11," January 24, 1962, 6, "Kerner Backs History Week," January 31, 1962, all *Chicago Defender*, daily ed.; Essien-Udom, *Black Nationalism*, 50.

7. The celebration of the Emancipation Proclamation's centennial in Chicago culminated in the Century of Negro Progress Exposition in that year at McCormick Place, which is downtown. Rich and Hughes Wright, *Wright Man*, 289–90; *Profile of Black Museums*, 3–5; "Interview with Margaret Burroughs and Charles Wright 12/26/84," 1, Wright Papers; Wilson, *Negro Building*, 242–47.

8. "Works of Artists to Be Displayed"; "Presents Merit Awards at Emancipation Day Program."

9. Helgeson, *Crucibles*, 203.

10. Essien-Udom, *Black Nationalism*, 95. The other study is C. Eric Lincoln, *Black Muslims in America*.

11. Essien-Udom, *Black Nationalism*, 95.

12. Ibid.

13. Ibid., 95n13.

14. Curtis, *Black Muslim Religion*, 153.

15. Ibid.

16. Helgeson, *Crucibles*, 210.

17. Curtis, *Black Muslim Religion*, 153.

18. Christine Johnson quoted in ibid., 155.

19. "University of Islam Graduates Tomorrow's Leaders" and "Textbook to Be Published," both April 1962, 13, and Sister Christine [Christine Johnson], "Education of Relief Clients Why Is Chicago Afraid?" May 1962, 20, all *Muhammad Speaks* (Chicago).

20. Clarice Durham, interview with Ian Rocksborough-Smith, March 18, 2010, Chicago.

21. Ibid.; Joseph, *Waiting 'til the Midnight Hour*, 15–16, 25–26; Satter, "Cops, Gangs, and Revolutionaries."

22. Helgeson, *Crucibles*, 203.

23. Recent studies about African American Islam have already underscored these gender tensions and dynamics. See, especially, McCloud, *African American Islam*, 135–62.

24. Gaines, "African American Expatriates in Ghana," 67; Munro, *Anticolonial Front*, 239; Jackson, *Indignant Generation*, 463; Washington, *Other Blacklist*, 242–44. For more on the dissolution of the Council on African Affairs in the mid-1950s, see Plummer, *Rising Wind*, and Von Eschen, *Race against Empire*.

25. For more examples of the U.S. government's cultural efforts during the Cold War, see Von Eschen, *Satchmo Blows Up the World*. The CIA also funded modern art as part of similar cultural front efforts on the part of the state. See Frances Stoner Saunders, "Modern Art Was CIA 'Weapon,'" *Independent* (London), October 25, 1995.

26. Munro, *Anticolonial Front*, 239.

27. Gaines, "African American Expatriates in Ghana," 67.

28. Ibid., 67.

29. "American Society of African Culture Discuss Role of Negro at N.Y. Meet," *Chicago Defender*, daily ed., July 3, 1961, 5; Munro, *Anticolonial Front*, 239–42; James T. Harris to Lorenzo D. Turner, December 17, 1959, Folder 1, Box 7, Turner Papers.

30. Quoted in Munro, *Anticolonial Front*, 244.

31. Washington, *Other Blacklist*, 239–40, 247–49, 253–65.

32. W. E. B. Du Bois to Ishmael Flory, April 16, 1960, Folder 4645, Box 249, Du Bois Papers. For a good appraisal of Présence Africaine and its role in promoting and circulating important discussions about black identity worldwide, see Graf, "Roots of Identity."

33. Du Bois to Flory, April 16, 1960. Du Bois did not join the Communist Party officially until 1961 when he moved with Shirley Graham to Ghana. See Porter, *Problem of the Future World*, 2.

34. Porter, *Problem of the Future World*, 4–5; Gosse, *Rethinking the New Left*, 24; Horne, *Black and Red*.

35. Porter, *Problem of the Future World*, 2.

36. Ibid., 10.

37. Mullen, *Un-American*, 11.

38. McDuffie, *Sojourning for Freedom*, 150; Munro, *Anticolonial Front*; Smethurst, "SNYC, *Freedomways*, and the Influence of the Popular Front"; Rocksborough-Smith, "Filling the Gap."

39. Gellman, *Death Blow to Jim Crow*, 11, 55–57; D. G. Gibson, "California State News," *Chicago Defender*, national ed., November 21, 1936, 9.

40. Ishmael Flory to John Pittman, October 2, 1957, Folder 30 Correspondence, 1956–1959, Box 1, Pittman Papers.

41. Ibid.

42. Du Bois to Flory, April 16, 1960; Eva Swan, secretary, to Du Bois, January 16, 1960, Folder 4645, Box 347, Series 1, Du Bois Papers; Du Bois, *Africa: In Battle against Colonialism, Racialism, Imperialism* and *Socialism Today* (Chicago: AfrAm, 1960), Folder

849 Exhibit, Box 118, Red Squad Files, Chicago Police Department; "Dr. DuBois to Speak Here Mon.," *Chicago Defender*, daily ed., November 23, 1959, A19.

43. Ishmael Flory to Henry Winston, January 9, 1982, Box 2, Folder 67, Communist Party.

44. Du Bois, *Africa*.

45. Flory to Du Bois, February 8, 1960, Folder 4645, Box 347, Series 1, Du Bois Papers.

46. Rocksborough-Smith, "Filling the Gap," 15.

47. Flory to Du Bois, February 8, 1960.

48. Flory, preface, "Africa Freedom Day 1960," to Du Bois, *Africa*.

49. Du Bois, *Africa*.

50. Porter, *Problem of the Future World*, 15–16.

51. Mullen, *Un-American*, 7.

52. "Thousands at African Freedom Fete," *Muhammad Speaks*, June 1962, 1.

53. Flory, preface, "A Word from the Publishers," to Du Bois, *Socialism Today*.

54. Plummer, *Rising Wind*, 204; Von Eschen, *Race against Empire*, 183.

55. Du Bois, "Socialism Today"; "Dr. DuBois to Speak Here Mon."

56. Cohen, *Consumers Republic*, 166–91.

57. Johnson, *Succeeding against the Odds*, 287; Bennett, *Before the Mayflower*.

58. Lee Blackwell, "Off the Record," *Chicago Defender*, daily ed., April 29, 1958, A10.

59. For useful studies of African Americans increasingly engaged in post–World War II consumer society's cultural fields, such as advertising, pictorial magazines, and radio, see Robert J. Weems, *Desegregating the Dollar*; Chambers, *Madison Avenue and the Color Line*. Lizabeth Cohen indicates the decade-long efforts by civil rights activists to conduct consumer boycotts. See Cohen, *Consumers Republic*, 275–76; Johnson, *Succeeding against the Odds*, 179.

60. A. Green, *Selling the Race*, 132, 175.

61. Margaret Burroughs, interview with Rocksborough-Smith; Weissman, "Civic Watcher."

62. Blackwell, "Off the Record."

63. Grimshaw, *Bitter Fruit*, 96.

64. Telegram from Truman Gibson to W. E. B. Du Bois, May 5, 1958, Correspondence 1958, Folder 4063, Box 217, Du Bois Papers.

65. Horne, *Black and Red*; Von Eschen, *Race against Empire*; Porter, *Problem of the Future World*.

66. Essien-Udom, *Black Nationalism*, 50; program, *Lecture Dr. W. E. B. Du Bois*, 8 P.M., May 21, 1958, Dunbar Auditorium, 3000 South Parkway, Folder 4578, Box 245, Du Bois Papers.

67. Program, *We, a Committee of Chicago Citizens, from All Walks of Life Salute Dr. William Edward Burghart Dubois in This the 90th Birthday and Take Pleasure in Presenting Him in a Public Lecture*, May 21, 1958, Dunbar School Auditorium, 3000 South Parkway, and Truman K. Gibson to W. E. B. Du Bois, December 3, 1958, both Folder 4578, Box 245, Du Bois Papers.

68. Burroughs, *Life with Margaret*, 14; "Lecture Dr. W. E. B. Du Bois."

69. Margaret Burroughs to *Chicago Defender*, big weekend ed., April 5, 1969, 17.

70. Rogers, *Black Campus Movement*, 23, 58, 70.

71. Ibid., 154.

72. Biondi, *Black Revolution on Campus*, 113; Dawn Rhodes and Nahleen Glanton, "DuSable Museum Braces for Change Ahead of Obama Library Arrival," *Chicago Tribune*, August 13, 2015.

73. Weinberg, "Marching in Marquette Park."

74. M. T. G. Burroughs, "Identity for the Negro Child."

75. See Widener, *Black Arts West*; Smethurst, *Black Arts Movement*.

76. M. T. G. Burroughs, "Identity for the Negro Child," 34.

77. Eugene Pieter Feldman, "Negro History Class Scheduled at Museum," *Chicago Defender*, national ed., October 16, 1965, 8.

78. Ibid.

Chapter Four. Cultural Fronts and Public-History Activism in the Black Power Era

1. Margaret G. Burroughs, "How to Build Black Pride," *Chicago Defender*, daily ed., June 12, 1968, 4. Margaret Burroughs also published a shorter but similarly themed letter in *Chicago Daily Tribune* later that year. See Margaret Burroughs, "African-American History," *Chicago Daily Tribune*, November 25, 1968, 20.

2. Burroughs, "How to Build Black Pride."

3. Joseph, *Waiting 'til the Midnight Hour*, 11.

4. Burroughs, "How to Build Black Pride."

5. Ralph, *Northern Protest*; Anderson and Pickering, *Confronting the Color Line*; Garrow, *Chicago 1966*.

6. "Du Bois Centennial Celebration Poster," February 23, 1968, Folder 30, Box 30, Clarke Papers.

7. Clarke, "Introduction"; J. H. Jones, "Revolt in the Ghettos"; Pittman, "Negroes Challenge the Jackboot"; Wheeldin, "Situation in Watts Today"; Boskin, "Historical Roots of the Riots"; Woodard, *Nation within a Nation*, 71; Pulido, *Black, Brown, Yellow*; Singh, *Black Is a Country*, chap. 5; Elbaum, *Revolution in the Air*.

8. Smethurst, "Poetry and Sympathy," 266.

9. McDuffie, *Sojourning for Freedom*, 202.

10. Gore, Theoharis, and Woodard, *Want to Start a Revolution*, 12. For good examples of this type of intersectional, left, feminist nationalism, see Smethurst, *Black Arts Movement*, chap. 4; Joseph, *Waiting 'til the Midnight Hour*, 45–53; McDuffie, "March of Young Southern Black Women"; McDuffie, *Sojourning for Freedom*.

11. M. T. G. Burroughs, "How to Build Black Pride."

12. Hall, "Long Civil Rights Movement," 1253–54.

13. Van DeBurg, *New Day in Babylon*, 64–111; Lipsitz, "Who'll Stop the Rain," 206–34; Monteith, *American Culture*, 153–54.

14. Van DeBurg, *New Day in Babylon*, 181.

15. Smethurst, *Black Arts Movement*, 9.

16. Ibid., 9.

17. The museum's expansion is discussed in chapter 5 of the current volume.

18. Henry E. Simmons to Archibald Carey, March 23, 1967, Folder 81, Box 1, Oral History Research Program Papers.

19. "Teens Trained to Record Current Black Experiences," *Chicago Daily Tribune*, August 23, 1970, S6; A. A. Burns, *From Storefront to Monument*, 76.

20. "Ralph Turner," labor leader, interview by Margaret Burroughs, 13–14, Folder 17, Box 4, Oral History Research Program Papers; Feldman, *Birth and the Building*, 4, 14–15, 67.

21. "Ralph Turner," 8–9. Chicago's Board of Education finally implemented an official African American history curriculum supplement in 1968. Lyons, *Teachers and Reform*, 174.

22. Feldman, *Birth and the Building*, 67.

23. "Ralph Turner," 12. See Duberman, *Paul Robeson*; Horne, *Red Seas*; Porter, *Problem of the Future World*.

24. "Ralph Turner," 12–14.

25. Ibid., 14. See Goia, *Delta Blues*, 182.

26. For a provocative treatment of the tensions and connections between the U.S. Old and New Lefts, see Isserman, *"If I Had a Hammer"*; Gosse, *Rethinking the New Left*, 121–22. See also Elbaum, *Revolution in the Air*.

27. "Ralph Turner," 15–17.

28. Ibid., 20, 21.

29. Dawson, *Blacks In and Out of the Left*, 72.

30. M. T. G. Burroughs, *Life with Margaret*, 71–72. For recent scholarship that details the activities of figures such as Du Bois and McKay in the Soviet Union, see Baldwin, *Beyond the Color Line and the Iron Curtain*; Gilmore, *Defying Dixie*; Maxwell, *New Negro, Old Left*.

31. Doris Saunders, "Confetti," March 20, 1967, 12, and "Catalyst Sets Afro Program as a Benefit," *Chicago Defender*, daily ed., September 23, 1968, 8; M. T. G. Burroughs, *Life with Margaret*, 88.

32. Feldman, *Birth and the Building*, 12–13; Singh, *Black Is a Country*.

33. Cruse, *Crisis of the Negro Intellectual*, 240–346.

34. M. T. G. Burroughs, *Life with Margaret*, 160; Ashley Farmer, review of Kimberly Nichele Brown, *Writing the Black Revolutionary Diva: Women's Subjectivity and the Decolonizing Text*, H-1960s, H-Net Reviews, September 2011, http://www.h-net.org/reviews/showrev.php?id=32916.

35. Carol Kleiman, "Working Woman: Learns to Run a Museum," November 15, 1967, C2, and "Get Scholarships for African Tour," *Chicago Daily Tribune*, June 9, 1968, SCL7.

36. M. T. G. Burroughs, *Life with Margaret*, 89.

37. For a synopsis of how exposition spaces treated nonwhite people in "evolutionary" exhibits from the late nineteenth century and how later, more democratic museums for the "people" risked sentimentalizing and idealizing folk cultures, see Bennett, *Birth of the Museum*, 83, 109–10; Rydell, *All the World's a Fair*, 7.

38. Smethurst, *Black Arts Movement*, 14; Widener, *Black Arts West*.

39. Widener, *Black Arts West*, 4.

40. Smethurst, *Black Arts Movement*, 210, 213–14; Donaldson, "Rise, Fall, and Legacy"; Alkalimat, Crawford, and Zorach, *Wall of Respect*.

41. Smethurst, *Black Arts Movement*, 180, 210, 213–14; Marable, *Race, Reform, and Rebellion*, 105–6. See, especially, Widener, *Black Arts West*; Gore, Theoharis, and Woodard, *Want to Start a Revolution*; Fenderson, "Journey toward a Black Aesthetic."

42. Smethurst, *Black Arts Movement*, 180.

43. Ibid., 179, 217–18, 220–21; Lang, *Grassroots at the Gateway*, 207.

44. See Smethurst, *Black Arts Movement*, 199.

45. Feldman, *Birth and the Building*, 57, 78–79; M. T. G. Burroughs, *Life with Margaret*, 96; Michael L. Culbert, "Black History Lives in the DuSable Museum," *Chicago Defender*, big week ed., March 24, 1973, 32; "Mural of Black History," *Chicago Daily Tribune*, June 28, 1970, SCL7.

46. "Expo '69: A People's Show," October 9, 1969, and "Expo Root," November 3, 1970, 4, *Chicago Defender*, daily ed.; Earl Calloway, "DuSable Museum Art Highlights Black Festival," *Chicago Defender*, big weekend ed., February 3, 1973, 20. Jesse Jackson's effort to promote the expo as a "festival for black business" and his "discreetly appropriated" funds for the affair from SCLC coffers led to his break with the parent organization of Operation Breadbasket. See Frady, *Jesse*, 263–64, 290.

47. For more on the complexities and regional diversities of cultural nationalism during the Black Power era, see Woodard, *Nation within a Nation*; Brown, *Fighting for US*; Smethurst, "Retraining the Heartworks"; Marable, *Race, Reform, and Rebellion*, 105–6.

48. Woodard, *Nation within a Nation*, 203, 184–223, 261.

49. Manning Marable quoted in ibid., 191.

50. Feldman, *Birth and the Building*, 44–45, 73, 82; "Parents Guild Backs Negro Museum," *Chicago Defender*, national ed., October 26, 1966, 31; *Annual Report 1966* (ch. 2n1).

51. Eugene P. Feldman, "Black Expression Stirs the Heart," September 16, 1967), 14, and "'Think Black' Reviewed," March 26, 1967, 11, *Chicago Defender*, national ed.; Eugene P. Feldman to Ann Campbell, May 8, 1969, Folder 5, Box 1, Eugene P. Feldman Papers; Feldman, *Birth and the Building*, 16. For a good assessment of *Liberator* magazine and the milieu of New York Black Power and arts journals, see Tinson, "Harlem, New York!"

52. Smethurst, *Black Arts Movement*, 198; Courage and Bone, *Muse in Bronzeville*, 230.

53. For good treatments of this process of neighborhood transition and intraracial class politics, see Grimshaw, *Bitter Fruit*; Satter, *Family Properties*.

54. Rice, "World of the Illinois Panthers," 43.

55. M. A. Turner, *Historical Dictionary*, 30–31.

56. Hoover quoted in Williams, *From the Ballot to the Bullet*, 172–73. See also Churchill, "To Disrupt, Discredit, and Destroy."

57. Williams, *From the Ballot to the Bullet*, 54–60, 125–66, 61, 64. Also see Lopez, "In the Spirit of Liberation."

58. Williams, *From the Ballot to the Bullet*, 8, 174–75, 192.

59. Lopez, "In the Spirit of Liberation," 275–76. For more on the history of youth organizations and gangs in Chicago, see Diamond, *Mean Streets*.

60. Fred Hampton grew up in the predominantly African American suburb of Maywood, Illinois, southwest of Chicago.

61. "A First for Emerson," *Chicago Defender*, big weekend ed., March 15, 1969, 3; "Photo Stand Alone 11—No Title," *Chicago Defender*, February 20, 1971, 12; "Conduct, Grammar Improve as Pupils Become Pen Pals," *Chicago Daily Tribune*, June 17, 1971, W3; Fleming and Burroughs, "Dr. Margaret T. Burroughs," 41; Eugene P. R. Feldman, "Negro History Class Scheduled at Museum," October 16, 1965, 8, and "'Negro History and Culture,' a Fine Introductory Manual," September 18, 1965, 6, *Chicago Defender*, national ed.; A. A. Burns, *From Storefront to Monument*, 76, 78.

62. Margaret Burroughs, "For Prisoners," *Chicago Defender*, daily ed., September 27, 1971; "Claudia Davis Wins DuSable Museum Contest on History," *Chicago Defender*, big weekend ed., March 17, 1973, 23.

63. Feldman to Campbell, May 8, 1969.

64. Perkins, *Explosion*.

65. "Museum's Literary Project for Convicts Funding Sought," *Chicago Daily Tribune*, August 5, 1971, S8; Useni Eugene Perkins and Antonio Lopez, in-person interview with Ian Rocksborough-Smith, Chicago, August 2012.

66. Omar Rashaan to Eugene P. Feldman, February 9, 1972, Folder 171, Box 23, Feldman Papers.

67. Feldman to Rashaan (c/o Thomas Williams), May 18, 1972, in ibid.

68. "Conduct, Grammar Improve as Pupils Become Pen Pals."

69. "Children Spark African to Continue Teaching," *Chicago Daily Tribune*, November 16, 1969, SCL5.

70. "Conduct, Grammar Improve as Pupils Become Pen Pals"; "Children Spark African to Continue Teaching."

Chapter Five. The Washington Park Relocation

1. Williams Strong, "Margaret Taylor Goss Burroughs," 197; *Annual Report 1966* and Museum of Negro History Cultural and Historical Tour; "Black Museum Seeks Park Site," *Chicago Daily Tribune*, November 10, 1971, A18; A. A. Burns, *From Storefront to Monument*, 75.

2. "Negro History Museum Planned," *Chicago Defender*, national ed., May 20, 1967, 3.

3. M. T. G. Burroughs, *Life with Margaret*, 155; Williams Strong, "Margaret Taylor Goss Burroughs," 123, 232.

4. Reed, *Rise of Chicago's Black Metropolis*, 28; R. Wright, *American Hunger*, 37; Patterson, *Man Who Cried Genocide*, 148–49; Mullen, *Popular Fronts*.

5. Clarice Durham, "Bronzeville's Venerable Historian," *Hyde Park (IL) Herald*, July 23, 2003, 4; Smethurst, *Black Arts Movement*, 193–200, 195; Drake and Cayton, *Black Metropolis*.

6. For more on the concept of striving in black Chicago, see Helgeson, *Crucibles of Black Empowerment*.

7. Stepto, "Washington Park," 273.

8. Feldman, *Birth and the Building*, 84; "Du Sable Museum to Begin Drive for Remodeling Funds," February 17, 1972, S4, "DuSable Museum's Move Fulfills Founder's Dream," February 7, 1974, S3, and "New Building for Museum Fulfills Dream," February 7, 1974, N6, *Chicago Daily Tribune*.

9. The literature about the U.S. Black Power and black arts movements is extensive and growing. For good examples, see Biondi, *To Stand and Fight*; Countryman, *Up South*; Joseph, *Waiting 'til the Midnight Hour*; Self, *American Babylon*; Smethurst, *Black Arts Movement*; Sugrue, *Sweet Land of Liberty*; Widener, *Black Arts West*.

10. Joseph, *Waiting 'til the Midnight Hour*, 54.

11. Ibid., 163.

12. See Harris, "Coming of Age," 107–8; Van DeBurg, *New Day in Babylon*; Dagbovie, *African American History Reconsidered*, 31.

13. Van DeBurg, *New Day in Babylon*, 17.

14. Biondi, *Black Revolution on Campus*, 79.

15. Ibid.

16. Anderson and Pickering, *Confronting the Color Line*; Cohen and Taylor, *American Pharaoh*; Farber, *Chicago '68*; Rice, "World of the Illinois Panthers," 49–50; Williams, *From the Ballot to the Bullet*; Haas, *Assassination of Fred Hampton*, 99. See Ralph, *Northern Protest*, 221–30.

17. Important works on Chicago that do demonstrate the diversity of independent black community initiatives include Danns, *Something Better for Our Children*; Gellman, "Stone Wall Behind" and "In the Driver's Seat"; Green, *Selling the Race*; Helgeson, *Crucible of Black Empowerment*; Satter, *Family Properties*, chaps. 8–10; *Teachers and Reform*, chap. 6. For excellent examples of this challenge in other regions, see Countryman, *Up South*; Self, *American Babylon*; Woodard, *Nation within a Nation*.

18. A. A. Burns, *From Storefront to Monument*, 3.

19. Fleming, "African American Museums," 1020.

20. A. A. Burns, *From Storefront to Monument*, 75.

21. Museum founders quoted in ibid.

22. Feldman, *Birth and the Building*, 80; Simpson, *Making Representations*, 96–98.

23. *Museum of African American History* (Chicago: Museum of African American History, ca. late 1960s), call no. E185.5.M9 Z, Miscellaneous pamphlets, etc., Chicago History Museum.

24. Barrett, *Museums and the Public Sphere*, 3, 12.

25. Buntinx and Karp, "Tactical Museologies," 219.

26. T. Bennett, *Birth of the Museum*, 28, 48.

27. For a recent study of neighborhood space and class in the black community, see Helgeson, *Crucibles of Black Empowerment*.

28. A. A. Burns, *From Storefront to Monument*, 24.

29. Hirsch, *Making the Second Ghetto*; Spear, *Black Chicago*, 148–50; Smith, *Visions of Belonging*, 284–89; Schlabach, *Along the Streets of Bronzeville*, chap. 5.

30. Tatum, Perry, and Goeken, *Landmark Designation Site* (ch. 2n6); Reed, *All the World Is Here*; Rydell, *All the World's a Fair*; "The DuSable Museum of African American History: Educators' Committee Second Annual Luncheon—Colloquium," February 16, 1974, Folder 416, Box 59, Salk Multicultural Collection; "Interview with Margaret Burroughs and Charles Wright 12/26/84," 2; Margaret Burroughs to Daniel J. Shannon, October 5, 1970, Folder 5, Box 184, Abbott-Sengstacke Family Papers.

31. Theresa Fambro Hooks, "Friday Eve Coffee House Is New Groove Mecca," *Chicago Defender*, big weekend ed., December 5, 1970, 20.

32. Wilson, *Negro Building*; A. A. Burns, *From Storefront to Museum*; Alkalimat, Crawford, and Zorach, *Wall of Respect*; Reed, *All the World Is Here*.

33. For an excellent treatment of black public history in Detroit and the founding of the Charles H. Wright Museum of African American History, see Wilson, *Negro Building*, 249–96; A. A. Burns, *From Storefront to Museum*.

34. "Interview with Margaret Burroughs and Charles Wright 12/26/84," 1. For another treatment of the collaboration between Burroughs and Wright, see Wilson, "Making History Visible," chap. 4; Smethurst, *Black Arts Movement*, 180; Charles Wright, "An Early History of the African-American Museums Association," undated, 1–2, Folder 21, Box 3, Wright Papers.

35. Meyer, *Integrating America's Heritage*, 1; C. Wright, "Early History," 1.

36. "Bill Would Establish National Commission," *New York Amsterdam News*, September 16, 1967, 6; Wilson, *Negro Building*, 284–85.

37. Meyer, *Integrating America's Heritage*, 26–27, 31, 32–33.

38. Ibid., 22–34. For excellent examinations of CORE and the Ford Foundation, see Ferguson, "Organizing the Ghetto," 70, and *Top Down*; Roelofs, *Foundations and Public Policy*, 95.

39. Smethurst also notes how "Leftists and nationalists, particularly in New York, used AMSAC as a vehicle for a more radical politics with some success." Smethurst, *Black Arts Movement*, 120. See also Welch, "Black Art and Activism"; Frances Stonor Saunders, "Modern Art Was a CIA Weapon," *Independent* (London), October 22, 1995. See chapter 3 of the current volume for a more extensive analysis of AMSAC.

40. Marietta J. Tanner, "Community Conscious," *New York Amsterdam News*, May 11, 1968, 13.

41. C. Wright, "Early History," 1. See Kim Severson, "New Museums to Shine Spotlight on Civil Rights Era," *New York Times*, February 19, 2012, nytimes.com; Beth Py-Lieberman, "Opening Day for the New African American History Museum Is

Announced," *Smithsonian.com*, February 2, 2016, smithsonianmag.com. For more on Powell's radicalism during the Black Power era, see Joseph, *Waiting 'til the Midnight Hour*, 13–14, 174–75.

42. Meyer, *Integrating America's Heritage*, 57.

43. Ibid.

44. Ibid., 98.

45. See, for example, Bone and Courage, *Muse in Bronzeville*; Green, *Selling the Race*; Hine and McCluskey, *Black Chicago Renaissance*; Knupfer, *Black Chicago Renaissance*; Mullen, *Popular Fronts*.

46. Erwin A. France to Margaret Burroughs, March 18, 1970, Daniel J. Shannon to Margaret Burroughs, April 1, 1970, Erwin A. France to Daniel J. Shannon, April 2, 1970, Margaret T. G. Burroughs to Daniel J. Shannon, October 5, 1970, all Folder 5, Box 184, Abbott-Sengstacke Papers.

47. For a selection of works on histories of black politics and their complex engagements with Chicago's Democratic machine during the twentieth century, see A. Cohen and Taylor, *American Pharaoh*, 57–61; L. Cohen, *Making a New Deal*, 251–89; Grimshaw, *Bitter Fruit* and *Negro Politics in Chicago*; Manning, *William L. Dawson*; Reed, *Chicago NAACP*; Travis, *Autobiography of Black Politics*.

48. Grimshaw, *Bitter Fruit*, 137–50; D. Green, ""Ralph Metcalfe."

49. Margaret Burroughs to Ralph Metcalfe, May 11, 1970, John Hope Franklin to Margaret T. G. Burroughs, October 20, 1970, Margaret Burroughs to Ralph H. Metcalfe, January 18, 1971, Margaret Burroughs to John Sengstacke, January 24, 1971, March 3, 1971, October 14, 1971, and June 28, 1972, all Folder 5, Box 184, Abbott-Sengstacke Family Papers.

50. Feldman, *Birth and the Building*, 84; Fleming and Burroughs, "Dr. Margaret T. Burroughs," 41; Williams Strong, "Margaret Taylor Goss Burroughs," 234.

51. Ralph Turner to Daniel Shannon, October 13, 1970, Ruther Allen Fouche to Daniel Shannon, October 20, 1970, and Forman Onderdonk to Lane Venardos, October 15, 1970, all Folder 5, Box 184, Abbott-Sengstacke Family Papers.

52. "A Bootstrap Project in Heritage and History," ca. 1971, in ibid.; "DuSable Museum's Move Fulfills Founder's Dream," *Chicago Daily Tribune*, February 7, 1974, S3.

53. Petition to Daniel Shannon, ca. 1970, Folder 5, Box 184, Abbott-Sengstacke Papers.

54. "Bootstrap Project in Heritage and History"; Margaret Burroughs to Ralph Metcalfe, May 11, 1970, Folder 5, Box 184, Abbott-Sengstacke Family Papers.

55. Williams Strong, "Margaret T. G. Burroughs," 233–34; "Black Museum Seeks Park Site."

56. M. T. G. Burroughs interview with Rocksborough-Smith.

57. Thanks to Ibram Rogers at the American Historical Association annual meeting, January 2012, in Chicago for his useful comments about "free" and "freed" spaces in African American political and cultural imaginaries through the Black Power era.

58. "Wieboldt's Gives $9,000 to African-American Museum," *Chicago Defender*, national ed., December 3, 1966, 12; "Museum Receives 7.5Gs Grant," *Chicago Defender*, daily ed., January 8, 1969, 8; Feldman, *Birth and the Building*, 106. Sears began its program Sears Heritage Scholars Workshop with the museum in 1963. "Afro-American Course Has 65 Students Enrolled," *Chicago Daily Tribune*, November 24, 1968, SA10.

59. "DuSable Museum Fetes 6," *Chicago Defender*, big weekend ed., February 3, 1973, 4; Williams Strong, "Margaret T. G. Burroughs," 229–30.

60. Fleming and Burroughs, "Dr. Margaret T. Burroughs," 42; Burroughs, *Life with Margaret*, 155; Kim Efird, Office of the Illinois Secretary of State, e-mail message to author, November 8, 2011; Carol Kleiman, "Working Woman: Learns to Run a Museum," *Chicago Daily Tribune*, November 15, 1967, C2. The law is found in chap. 105, sec. 8, 3, of revised statutes from 1967, according to the Office of the Illinois Secretary of State in 2011, and also referred to by Burroughs in her interview with Fleming.

61. N. Leland Webber to Brian O'Doherty, November 24, 1970, Folder 5, Box 184, Abbott-Sengstacke Family Papers; "DuSable Ahead of Other Museums," *Chicago Defender*, big weekend ed., September 11, 1971, 3; "Nancy Hanks Visits Chicago Arts Centers," *Chicago Defender*, daily ed., December 9, 1971, 18; Williams Strong, "Margaret T. G. Burroughs," 240.

62. *Annual Report 1966*; Feldman, *Birth and the Building*, 17, 79, 84–85.

63. "Cultural Unit Seeks Members," *Chicago Defender*, daily ed., December 21, 1970, 12.

64. Vernon Jarrett, "Beware! Here Comes the Foundation Black," *Chicago Tribune*, October 4, 1970, A5.

65. Smethurst, *Black Arts Movement*, 199.

66. Charles Hayes represented Illinois's first district in the U.S. Congress from 1983 to 1993.

67. Feldman, *Birth and the Building*, 62; "Memorial Program to Honor W. E. B. DuBois," *Chicago Defender*, national ed., September 21, 1963, 5; "Heroes to Be Honored," *Chicago Defender*, daily ed., February 10, 1966, 5; *Annual Report 1966*.

68. Smethurst, *Black Arts Movement*, 193.

69. "Du Sable Plans Drama Benefit for Anniversary," *Chicago Tribune*, May 13, 1971, 59; Rocksborough-Smith, "Filling the Gap," 7–8; "Famed Actors Perform for Black Museum," *Chicago Defender*, national ed., March 20, 1971, 35; "Meet Tonight on Testimonial Dinner Benefit for Museum," March 12, 1968, "Actors Offer Performance for Museum," April 13, 1971, 11, "Actors to Perform for DuSable Museum," May 3, 1971, 10, Earl Calloway, "Hundreds Attend DuSable Museum Luncheon," March 14, 1973, 16, and Raymond S. McGann, "Hughes Memorial Tribute Benefits History Museum," February 6, 1968, 7, all *Chicago Defender*, daily ed.; "DuSable Opening Eagerly Awaited," May 5, 1973, 13, and Margaret Smith, "Council Aids the DuSable Museum," August 4, 1973, 13, *Chicago Defender*, big weekend ed.

Epilogue

1. M. T. G. Burroughs, interview with Rocksborough-Smith.

2. Hall, "Long Civil Rights Movement"; Sugrue, *Sweet Land of Liberty*; Gosse, *Rethinking the New Left*; Widener, *Black Arts West*.

3. Cardon, "Dream of the Future"; Clark, *Defining Moments*; Wiggins, *O Freedom*.

4. "Opening Day" (ch. 5n41).

5. For more on Al Raby and Martin Luther King's beleaguered forays in Chicago to combat neighborhood segregation, slum conditions, and education inequities, see Ralph's excellent *Northern Protest*.

6. Buntinx and Karp, "Tactical Museologies," 219; Barrett, *Museums and the Public Sphere*, 3; T. Bennett, *Birth of the Museum*, 83, 109–10; Rydell, *All the World's a Fair*, 7.

7. Fernandez, *Brown in the Windy City*; Innis-Jimenez, *Steel Barrio*.

8. Smethurst, "Retraining the Heartworks"; Widener, *Black Arts West*; Purnell, *Fighting Jim Crow*; Welch, "Black Art and Activism."

9. M. T. G. Burroughs, interview with Fleming, 43.

10. Mary Mitchell, "DuSable Museum Fight Exposes Generation Gap," *Chicago Sun-Times*, July 18, 2015.

11. A. A. Burns, *From Storefront to Museum*, 133–43.

12. Margaret Burroughs quoted in ibid., 137.

13. Ibid., 142.

14. Dawn Rhodes and Dahleen Glanton, "DuSable Museum Proposal from U. of C. Professor Gets Heated Response," *Chicago Tribune*, July 20, 2015.

15. Ibid.

16. Mitchell, "DuSable Museum Fight Exposes Generation Gap"; Theaster Gates Jr., "Dorchester Projects," *WordPress*, July 28, 2015, https://artpublicsphere.wordpress.com.

17. Mitchell, "DuSable Museum Fight Exposes Generation Gap."

18. Ibid.

19. For excellent historical treatments of the University of Chicago's role in promoting real estate development in and around Hyde Park, see Hirsch, *Making of the Second Ghetto*; Satter, *Family Properties*.

20. Andrew Fan, "'A Wall around Hyde Park': The History and the Future of the UCPD," June 2, 2014, "The Gate: Political Analysis and Opinions from the University of Chicago," *University of Chicago*, Public Policy Institute, 2017, uchicagogate.com; Azadeh Ansari, "Chicago's 762 Homicides in 2016 Is Highest in 19 Years," *CNN*, January 2, 2017, http://www.cnn.com/.

21. Dawn Rhodes and Dahleen Glanton, "DuSable Museum Braces for Change Ahead of Obama Library Arrival," *Chicago Tribune*, August 13, 2015; Steve Johnson, "Chance the Rapper Joins Du Sable Museum Board," *Chicago Tribune*, January 6, 2017, http://www.chicagotribune.com.

22. S. Johnson, "Chance the Rapper"; Jay Koziarz, "Chicago's DuSable Museum Reveals New Terrace, Timeline for Historic Roundhouse," *Chicago.curbed.com*, September 5, 2017, https://chicago.curbed.com.

23. Noreen S. Ahmed-Ullah, "CPS Approves Largest School Closure in Chicago's History," *Chicago Tribune*, May 23, 2013; Diane Ravitch, "The Myth of Charter Schools," *New York Review of Books*, November 11, 2010.

24. Uetricht, *Strike for America*; Sam Cholke, "Teachers Union, SEIU Join Call for Written Agreement on Obama Center," DNAInfo.com/Chicago, October 11, 2017, https://www.dnainfo.com/chicago.

25. Rodan, "President Obama Again Turns"; Edward McClelland, "How Martin Luther King Jr. Inspired Obama," January 21, 2013, *NBC Chicago*, http://www.nbc-chicago.com.

26. For a recent discussion of the trivialization and tokenism that surround public reception of Black History Month, see Franklin, Horne, Cruse, Ballard, and Mitchell, "Black History Month."

Bibliography

Abbott-Sengstacke Family Papers, 1847–1997. Vivian G. Harsh Research Collection of Afro-American History and Literature, Carter G. Woodson Branch, Chicago Public Library, Chicago.

Aldridge, Daniel, III. "A War for the Colored Races: Anti-Interventionism and the African American Intelligentsia, 1939–1941." *Diplomatic History* 28:3 (2004): 321–52.

Alkalimat, Abdul, Romi Crawford, and Rebecca Zorach. *The Wall of Respect: Public Art and Black Liberation in 1960s Chicago*. Evanston: Northwestern University Press, 2017.

Anderson, Alan B., and George W. Pickering. *Confronting the Color Line: The Broken Promise of the Civil Rights Movement in Chicago*. Athens: University of Georgia Press, 1986.

Aptheker, Herbert. *American Negro Slave Revolts*. New York: Columbia University Press, 1943.

———. "An Autobiographical Note." *Journal of American History* 87:1 (2000): 147–50.

Aptheker, Herbert, and Robin D. G. Kelley. "Interview of Herbert Aptheker." *Journal of American History* 87:1 (2000): 151–67.

Arnesen, Eric. *Brotherhoods of Color: Black Railroad Workers and the Struggle for Equality*. Cambridge, MA: Harvard University Press, 2001.

Baldwin, Davarian A. "Black Belts and Ivory Towers: The Place of Race in U.S. Social Thought, 1892–1948." *Critical Sociology* 30:2 (2004): 397–450.

———. *Chicago's New Negroes: Modernity, the Great Migration, and Black Urban Life*. Chapel Hill: University of North Carolina Press, 2007.

Baldwin, Kate A. *Beyond the Color Line and the Iron Curtain: Reading Encounters between Black and Red, 1922–1963*. Durham: Duke University Press, 2002.

Barrett, Jennifer. *Museums and the Public Sphere*. New York: Blackwell, 2011.

Bates, Beth Tomkins. *Pullman Porters and the Rise of Protest Politics in Black America, 1925–1945*. Chapel Hill: University of North Carolina Press, 2001.

Beito, David T., and Linda R. Beito. *Black Maverick: T. R. M. Howard's Fight for Civil Rights and Economic Power*. Urbana: University of Illinois Press, 2009.

Bennett, Lerone, Jr. *Before the Mayflower: A History of Black America, the Classic Account of the Struggles and Triumphs of Black Americans*. Chicago: Johnson, 1962.

Bennett, Tony. *The Birth of the Museum: History, Theory, Politics*. New York: Routledge, 1995.

Best, Wallace D. *Passionately Human, No Less Divine: Religion and Culture in Black Chicago, 1915–1952*. Princeton: Princeton University Press, 2009.

Biondi, Martha. *The Black Revolution on Campus*. Berkeley: University of California Press, 2012.

———. *To Stand and Fight: The Struggle for Civil Rights in Postwar New York City*. New York: Harvard University Press, 2003.

Black, Timuel D. *Bridges of Memory: Chicago's First Wave of Black Migration*. Vol. 1. Evanston: Northwestern University Press, 2003.

———. Papers. Vivian G. Harsh Research Collection of Afro-American History and Literature, Carter G. Woodson Branch, Chicago Public Library, Chicago.

Bone, Robert, and Richard A. Courage. *The Muse in Bronzeville: African American Creative Expression in Chicago, 1932–1950*. New Brunswick: Rutgers University Press, 2011.

Boskin, Joseph. "Historical Roots of the Riots." *Freedomways* 7:1 (1967): 60–63.

Bracey, John H. "St. Clair Drake, the Roosevelt Years: Reflections and Analysis." *Journal of African American History* 98:3 (2013): 434–35.

Brennan, Timothy. *At Home in the World: Cosmopolitanism Now*. Cambridge, MA: Harvard University Press, 1997.

Brown, Frank London. *Trumbull Park*. Chicago: Regnery, 1959.

Brown, Scot. *Fighting for US: Maulana Karenga, the US organization, and Black Cultural Nationalism*. New York: New York University Press, 2003.

Bunche, Ralph J., Oral History Collection on the Civil Rights Movement. Civil Rights Documentation Project, Moorland-Spingarn Research Center, Howard University, Washington, D.C.

Buntinx, Gustavo, and Ivan Karp. "Tactical Museologies." In *Museum Frictions: Public Cultures/Global Transformations*, edited by Karp, Corinne A. Kratz, Lynn Szwaja, and Tomas Ybarra-Frausto, 207–18. Durham: Duke University Press, 2006.

Burns, Andrea A. *From Storefront to Monument: Tracing the Public History of the Black Museum Movement*. Amherst: University of Massachusetts Press, 2013.

Burns, Ben. *Nitty Gritty: A White Editor in Black Journalism*. Jackson: University Press of Mississippi, 1996.

Burroughs, Charles G. *Home*. Chicago: Culture Fund, ca. 1980s.

Burroughs, Margaret T. G. *Did You Feed My Cow? Street Games, Chants, and Rhymes*. Chicago: Follett, 1956.

———. "Identity for the Negro Child: Integration of Learning Materials . . . NOW!" *Negro Digest*, March 1966, 30–34.

———. *Jasper the Drummin' Boy*. 1947. Chicago: Follett, 1970.

———. *Life with Margaret*. Chicago: In-Time, 2003.

Caplow, Deborah. *Leopoldo Mendez: Revolutionary Art and the Mexican Print*. Austin: University of Texas Press, 2007.

Cardon, Nathan. "A Dream of the Future: Race, Empire, and Modernity at the Atlanta and Nashville Expositions, 1895–1897." PhD diss., University of Toronto, 2014.

Chambers, Jason. *Madison Avenue and the Color Line: African Americans in the Advertising Industry*. Philadelphia: University of Pennsylvania Press, 2008.

Chicago Police Department. Red Squad records and related records, 1930s–1986. Chicago History Museum, Chicago.

Churchill, Ward. "'To Disrupt, Discredit and Destroy': The FBI's Secret War against the Black Panther Party." In *Liberation, Imagination, and the Black Panther Party: A New Look at the Panthers and Their Legacy*, edited by Kathleen Cleaver and George N. Katsiaficas, 78–112. New York: Routledge, 2001.

Clark, Kathleen. *Defining Moments: African American Commemoration and Political Culture in the South, 1863–1913*. Chapel Hill: University of North Carolina, 2006.

Clarke, John Henrik. "Introduction." *Freedomways* 7:1 (1967): 34.

———. Papers. Schomburg Center for Research in Black Culture, New York Public Library, New York.

Cohen, Adam, and Elizabeth Taylor. *American Pharaoh: Mayor Richard J. Daley and His Battle for Chicago and the Nation*. New York: Back Bay, 2000.

Cohen, Lizabeth. *Consumers Republic: The Politics of Mass Consumption in Postwar America*. New York: Knopf, 2003.

———. *Making a New Deal: Industrial Workers in Chicago, 1919–1939*. New York: Cambridge University Press, 1990.

Communist Party of the United States of America. Biographical Files. Robert F. Wagner Labor Archives, Tamiment Library, New York University, New York.

Congress of Racial Equality (CORE). Chicago Chapter. Chicago History Museum, Chicago.

Countryman, Matthew. *Up South: Civil Rights and Black Power in Philadelphia*. Philadelphia: University of Pennsylvania Press, 2006.

Courage, Richard, and Robert Bone. *The Muse of Bronzeville: African American Creative Expression in Chicago, 1932–1950*. New Brunswick: Rutgers University Press, 2011.

Crew, Spencer R. "African Americans, History, and Museums: Preserving American History in the Public Arena." In *Making Histories in Museums*, edited by Gaynor Kavanagh, 80–91. New York: Leicester University Press, 1996.

Cruse, Harold. *The Crisis of the Negro Intellectual*. New York: William and Morrow, 1967.

Curtis, Edward, IV. *Black Muslim Religion in the Nation of Islam, 1960–1975*. Chapel Hill: University of North Carolina Press, 2006.

Dagbovie, Pero G. *African American History Reconsidered: New Perspectives on Black History and Its Profession*. Urbana: University of Illinois Press, 2010.

———. *The Early Black History Movement, Carter G. Woodson, and Lorenzo Johnston Greene*. Chicago: University of Illinois Press, 2007.

———. "Making Black History Practical and Popular: Carter G. Woodson, the Proto-Black Studies Movement, and the Struggle for Black Liberation." *Western Journal of Black Studies* 28:2 (2004): 372–83.

Danns, Dionne. "Maudelle Bousfield and Chicago's Segregated School System, 1922–1950." *Midwest History of Education Journal* 25:1 (1998): 3–16.

———. *Something Better for Our Children: Black Organizing in Chicago Public Schools, 1963–1971*. New York: Routledge, 2003.

Davis, Corneal. Papers. Chicago History Museum, Chicago.

Davis, Frank Marshall. *Livin' the Blues: Memoirs of a Black Journalist and Poet*. Madison: University of Wisconsin Press, 1993.

Dawson, Michael C. *Blacks In and Out of the Left*. Cambridge, MA: Harvard University Press, 2013.

Denning, Michael. *The Cultural Front: The Laboring of American Culture in the Twentieth Century*. New York: Verso, 1996.

———. *Culture in the Age of Three Worlds*. New York: Verso, 2004.

Diamond, Andrew. *Mean Streets: Chicago Youths and the Everyday Struggle for Empowerment in the Multiracial City, 1908–1969*. Berkeley: University of California Press, 2009.

Donaldson, Jeff. "The Rise, Fall, and Legacy of the Wall of Respect Movement." *International Review of African American Art* 15:1 (1998): 22–26.

Donner, Frank. *Protectors of Privilege: Red Squads and Police Repression in Urban America*. Berkeley: University of California Press, 1990.

Drake, St. Clair, and Horace R. Cayton. *Black Metropolis: A Study of Negro Life in a Northern City*. 1945. Chicago: University of Chicago Press, 1993.

Duberman, Martin. *Paul Robeson: A Biography*. New York: Knopf, 1988.

Du Bois, W. E. B. *Africa: In Battle against Colonialism, Racialism, Imperialism, and Socialism Today*. Chicago: AfrAm/Progressive, 1960.

———. *Black Reconstruction: An Essay toward a History of the Part Which Black Folk Played in the Attempt to Reconstruct Democracy in America, 1860–1880*. New York: International, 1935.

———. Papers, 1803–1999. Special Collections and University Archives, University of Massachusetts Amherst Libraries.

———. *Socialism Today*. Chicago: AfrAm/Progressive, ca. late 1950s.

Dudziak, Mary. *Cold War Civil Rights: Race and the Image of American Democracy*. Princeton: Princeton University Press, 2000.

"Education: Brown Studies." *Time*, June 21, 1943. http://www.time.com.

Elbaum, Max. *Revolution in the Air: Sixties Radicals Turn to Lenin, Mao, and Che*. New York: Verso, 2002.

Essien-Udom, E. U. *Black Nationalism: A Search for an Identity in America*. Chicago: University of Chicago Press, 1962.

Farber, David. *Chicago '68*. Chicago: University of Chicago Press, 1988.

Feldman, Eugene Pieter. *The Birth and the Building of the DuSable Museum*. Chicago: DuSable Museum, 1981.

———. *Figures in Black History*. Chicago: DuSable Museum, 1970.

———. "James T. Rapier." *Negro History Bulletin* 20:3 (1956): 62–66.

———. Papers. DuSable Museum of African American History, Chicago.

Ferguson, Karen. "'Organizing the Ghetto': The Ford Foundation, CORE, and White Power in the Black Power Era, 1967–1969." *Journal of Urban History* 34:67 (2007): 67–100.

———. *Top Down: The Ford Foundation, Black Power, and the Reinvention of Liberalism*. Philadelphia: University of Pennsylvania Press, 2013.

Fernandez, Lilia. *Brown in the Windy City: Mexicans and Puerto Ricans in Postwar Chicago*. Chicago: University of Chicago, 2012.

Fleming, John E. "African American Museums, History, and the American Ideal." *Journal of American History* 81:3 (1994): 1020–26.

Fleming, John E., and Margaret T. Burroughs. "Dr. Margaret T. Burroughs: Artist, Teacher, Administrator, Writer, Political Activist, and Museum Founder." *Public Historian* 21:1 (1999): 31–55.

Flory, Ishmael. "Africa Freedom Day 1960." Preface to W. E. B. Du Bois, *Africa: In Battle against Colonialism, Racialism, Imperialism*. Chicago: AfrAm/Progressive, 1960.

Frady, Marshall. *Jesse: The Life and Pilgrimage of Jesse Jackson*. New York: Simon and Schuster, 1996.

Franklin, John Hope, Gerald Horne, Harold W. Cruse, Allen B. Ballard, and Reavis L. Mitchell. "Black History Month: Serious Truth Telling or a Triumph in Tokenism?" *Journal of Blacks in Higher Education* 18 (1997–98): 87–92.

Gaines, Irene McCoy. Papers. Chicago History Museum, Chicago.

Gaines, Kevin. "African American Expatriates in Ghana." *Souls* (1999): 64–71.

———. *American Africans in Ghana: Black Expatriates and the Civil Rights Era*. Chapel Hill: University of North Carolina Press, 2006.

Garb, Margaret. *Freedom's Ballot: African American Political Struggles in Chicago from Abolition to the Great Migration*. Chicago: University of Chicago Press, 2014.

Garfinkel, Herbert. *When Negroes March: The March on Washington Movement in the Organizational Politics for FEPC*. Glencoe, IL: Free Press, 1959.

Garrow, David J. *Chicago 1966: Open Housing Marches, Summit Negotiations, and Operation Breadbasket*. New York: Carlson, 1989.

Gellman, Erik S. *Death Blow to Jim Crow: The National Negro Congress and the Rise of Militant Civil Rights*. Chapel Hill: University of North Carolina Press, 2011.

———. "In the Driver's Seat: Chicago's Bus Drivers and Labor Insurgency in the Era of Black Power." *Labor: Studies in Working-Class History of the Americas* 11:3 (2014): 49–76.

———. "'The Stone Wall Behind': The Chicago Coalition for United Community Action and Labor's Overseers, 1968–1973." In *Black Power at Work: Community Control, Affirmative Action, and the Construction Industry*, edited by David Goldberg and Trevor Griffey, 112–32. Ithaca: Cornell University Press, 2010.

Gettleman, Marvin E. "'No Varsity Teams': New York's Jefferson School of Social Science, 1943–1956." *Science and Society* 66:3 (2002): 336–59.

Gilfoyle, Timothy. "Making History: Interviews with Timuel Black and Margaret Burroughs." *Chicago History* 36:3 (2010): 52–64.

Gilmore, Glenda. *Defying Dixie: The Radical Roots of Civil Rights, 1919–1950*. New York: Norton, 2008.

Goggin, Jacqueline Ann. *Carter C Woodson: A Life in Black History*. Baton Rouge: Louisiana State University Press, 1993.

Goia, Ted. *Delta Blues: The Life and Times of the Mississippi Maters Who Revolutionized American Music*. New York: Norton, 2008.

Gore, Daya F., Jeanne Theoharis, and Komozi Woodard, eds. *Want to Start a Revolution? Radical Women in the Black Freedom Struggle*. New York: New York University Press, 2009.

Gosse, Van. *Rethinking the New Left: An Interpretative History*. New York: Palgrave, 2005.

Graf, Marga. "Roots of Identity: The National and Cultural Self in Présence Africaine." *Comparative Literature and Culture (CLCWeb)* 3:1 (2001): Article 5.

Green, Adam. *Selling the Race: Culture, Community, and Black Chicago, 1940–1955*. Chicago: University of Chicago Press, 2006.

Green, Daniel. "Ralph Metcalfe: Champion Sprinter and Free-Thinking Politician." *Encyclopedia of Chicago*. Chicago: Chicago Historical Society, 2005. http://www.encyclopedia.chicagohistory.org/pages/2199.html.

Grimshaw, William J. *Bitter Fruit: Black Politics and the Chicago Machine, 1931–1991*. Chicago: University of Chicago Press, 1992.

———. *Negro Politics in Chicago: The Quest for Leadership, 1939–1979*. Chicago: Loyola University Center for Urban Policy, 1980.

Grossman, James. *Land of Hope: Chicago, Black Southerners, and the Great Migration*. Chicago: University of Chicago Press, 1989.

Haas, Jeffrey. *The Assassination of Fred Hampton: How the FBI and the Chicago Police Murdered a Black Panther*. Chicago: Hill, 2010.

Hall, Jacquelyn Dowd. "The Long Civil Rights Movement and Political Uses of the Past." *Journal of American History* 91:4 (2005): 1233–63.

Halpern, Rick. *Down on the Killing Floor: Black and White Workers in Chicago's Packinghouses, 1904–54*. Chicago: University of Illinois Press, 1997.

Harris, Robert L., Jr. "Coming of Age: The Transformation of Afro-American Historiography." *Journal of Negro History* 67:2 (1982): 107–21.

Helgeson, Jeffrey. *Crucibles of Black Empowerment: Chicago's Neighborhood Politics from the New Deal to Harold Washington*. Chicago: University of Chicago Press, 2014.

———. "Striving in Black Chicago: Migration, Work, and the Politics of Neighborhood Change, 1935–1965." PhD diss., University of Illinois–Chicago, 2008.

———. "Who Are You America but Me? The American Negro Exposition, 1940." In *The Black Chicago Renaissance*, edited by Darlene Clark Hine and John McCluskey Jr., 126–46. Urbana: University of Illinois Press, 2012.

Herrick, Mary J. *The Chicago Public Schools: A Social and Political History.* Beverly Hills, CA: Sage, 1971.

Hine, Darlene Clark. "Carter G. Woodson, White Philanthropy, and Negro Historiography." *History Teacher* 19:3 (1986): 405–25.

Hine, Darlene Clark, and John McCluskey Jr., eds. *The Black Chicago Renaissance*. Chicago: University of Illinois, 2012.

Hirsch, Arnold. *Making the Second Ghetto: Race and Housing in Chicago, 1940–1960.* New York: Cambridge University Press, 1983.

"History Clubs and Branches." *Negro History Bulletin* 22:8 (1959): 186–99.

Hofstadter, Richard. *The Paranoid Style in American Politics and Other Essays.* 1952. Cambridge, MA: Harvard University Press, 1996.

Homel, Michael W. *Down from Equality: Black Chicagoans and the Public School 1920–1941.* Urbana: University of Illinois Press, 1984.

———. "The Politics of Public Education in Black Chicago, 1910–1941." *Journal of Negro Education* 45:2 (1976): 179–91.

Horne, Gerald. *Black and Red: W. E. B. Du Bois and the Afro-American Response to the Cold War.* Albany: State University of New York Press, 1986.

———. *Black Revolutionary: William Patterson and the Globalization of the African American Freedom Struggle.* Urbana: University of Illinois Press, 2013.

———. *Communist Front? The Civil Rights Congress, 1946–1956.* London: Associated University Presses, 1988.

———. *Red Seas: Ferdinand Smith and Radical Black Sailors in the United States and Jamaica.* New York: New York University Press, 2005.

Howe, Barbara J. "Reflections on an Idea: NCPH's First Decade." *Public Historian* 11:3 (1989): 68–85.

"How We Should Celebrate Negro History." *Negro History Bulletin* 10:5 (1947): 101–3.

Innis-Jimenez, Michael. *Steel Barrio: The Great Migration to South Chicago, 1915–1940.* New York: New York University Press, 2013.

Irons, Peter. *Jim Crow's Children: The Broken Promise of the Brown Decision.* New York: Penguin, 2002.

Isserman, Maurice. *"If I Had a Hammer…": The Death of the Old Left and the Birth of the New Left.* New York: Basic, 1987.

Jackson, H. C., Jr. "Summary History of the Detroit Branch of the Association for the Study of Negro Life and History." *Negro History Bulletin* 26:1 (1962): 0.

Jackson, Lawrence P. *The Indignant Generation: A Narrative History of African American Writers and Critics, 1934–1960.* Princeton: Princeton University Press, 2012.

Jerome, V. J. "Let Us Grasp the Weapon of Culture." *Political Affairs* 30:2 (1951): 195–215.

Johnson, John H. *Succeeding against the Odds*. New York: Warner, 1989.

Jones, John Henry. "Revolt in the Ghettos." *Freedomways* 7:1 (1967): 35–41.

Jones, Patrick. *The Selma of the North: Civil Rights Insurgency in Milwaukee*. Cambridge, MA: Harvard University Press, 2009.

Joseph, Peniel. "The Black Power Movement: A State of the Field." *Journal of American History* 96:3 (2009): 751–76.

———. *Waiting 'til the Midnight Hour: A Narrative History of Black Power in America*. New York: Owl, 2006.

Kelley, Robin D. G. "Afterward." *Journal of American History* 87:1 (2000): 168–69.

Kimble, Lionel, Jr. *A New Deal for Bronzeville: Housing, Employment and Civil Rights in Black Chicago, 1935–1955*. Carbondale: Southern Illinois University Press, 2015.

Klein, Christina. *Cold War Orientalism: Asia in the Middlebrow Imagination, 1945–1961*. Berkeley: University of California Press, 2003.

Kluger, Richard. *Simple Justice: The History of Brown v. the Board of Education and Black America's Struggle for Equality*. 1975. New York: Vintage, 2004.

Knupfer, Anne M. *The Chicago Black Renaissance and Women's Activism*. Urbana: University of Illinois Press, 2006.

Lang, Clarence. *Grassroots at the Gateway: Class Politics and Black Freedom Struggle in St. Louis, 1936–1975*. Ann Arbor: University of Michigan Press, 2009.

Laville, Helen, and Scott Lucas. "The American Way: Edith Sampson, the NAACP, and African American Identity in the Cold War." *Diplomatic History* 20:4 (1996): 565–90.

Lemann, Nicholas. *The Promised Land: The Great Black Migration and How It Changed America*. New York: Random, 1991.

Levine, Lawrence. *Black Culture and Black Consciousness: Afro-American Folk Thought from Slavery to Freedom*. Oxford: Oxford University Press, 1977.

Lieberman, Robbie. "'Another Side of the Story': African American Intellectuals Speak Out for Peace and Freedom during the Early Cold War Years." In *Anticommunism and the African American Freedom Struggle*, edited by Clarence Lang and Robbie Lieberman, 17–49. New York: Palgrave Macmillan, 2009.

Lieberman, Robbie, and Clarence Lang, eds. *Anticommunism and the African American Freedom Struggle: 'Another Side of the Story.'* New York: Palgrave Macmillan, 2009.

Lipsitz, George. *Rainbow at Midnight: Labor and Culture in the 1940s*. Chicago: University of Illinois, 1994.

———. "Who'll Stop the Rain: Youth Culture, Rock 'n Roll, and Social Crises." In *The Sixties: From Memory to History*, edited by David Farber, 206–34. Chapel Hill: University of North Carolina Press, 1994.

Lopez, Antonio. "'In the Spirit of Liberation': Race, Governmentality, and the Decolonial Politics of the Original Rainbow Coalition of Chicago." PhD diss., University of Texas–El Paso, 2012.

Lyons, John. *Teachers and Reform: Chicago Public Education, 1929–1970*. Chicago: University of Illinois, 2009.

MacDonald, J. Fred. "Radio's Black Heritage: Destination Freedom, 1948–1950." *Phylon* 39:1 (1978): 66–73.

MacLean, Nancy. *Freedom Is Not Enough: The Opening of the American Workplace*. New York: Sage, 2006.

Manning, Christopher. *William L. Dawson and the Limits of Black Electoral Leadership*. DeKalb: Northern Illinois University Press, 2009.

Marable, Manning. *Race, Reform, and Rebellion: The Second Reconstruction in Black America, 1945–1990*. Jackson: Mississippi University Press, 1991.

Maxwell, William J. *F. B. Eyes: How J. Edgar Hoover's Ghostreaders Framed African American Literature*. Princeton: Princeton University Press, 2016.

———. *New Negro, Old Left: African-American Writing and Communism between the Wars*. New York: Columbia University Press, 1999.

McCloud, Aminah B. *African American Islam*. New York: Routledge, 1995.

McDuffie, Erik S. "The March of Young Southern Black Women: Esther Cooper Jackson, Black Left Feminism, and the Personal and Political Costs of Cold War Repression." In *Anticommunism and the African American Freedom Movement*, edited by Clarence Lang and Robbie Lieberman, 81–113. New York: Palgrave Macmillan, 2009.

———. *Sojourning for Freedom: Black Women, American Communism, and the Making of Black Left Feminism*. Durham: Duke University Press, 2011.

Meier, August, and Elliott Rudwick. *CORE: A Study in the Civil Rights Movement, 1942–1968*. Urbana: University of Illinois Press, 1975.

Meriwether, James. *Proudly We Can Be Africans: Black Americans and Africa, 1935–1961*. Chapel Hill: University of North Carolina Press, 2002.

Meyer, Howard N., ed. *Integrating America's Heritage: A Congressional Hearing to Establish a National Commission on Negro History and Culture*. College Park, MD: McGrath, 1970.

Mickenberg, Julia L. *Learning from the Left: Children's Literature, the Cold War, and Radical Politics in the United States*. New York: Oxford University Press, 2006.

Montalto, Nicholas V. *A History of the Intercultural Education Movement, 1924–1941*. New York: Garland, 1983.

Monteith, Sharon. *American Culture in the 1960s*. Edinburgh: Edinburgh University Press, 2008.

Morgan, Madeline R. "Chicago School Curriculum Includes Negro Achievements." *Journal of Negro Education* 13:1 (1944): 120–23.

Morgan, Stacy I. *Rethinking Social Realism: African American Art and Literature, 1930–1953*. Athens: University of Georgia Press, 2004.

Mullen, Bill V. *Popular Fronts: Chicago and African American Cultural Politics, 1935–46*. Urbana: University of Illinois Press, 1999.

———. *Un-American: W. E. B. DuBois and the Century of World Revolution*. Philadelphia: Temple University Press, 2015.

Munro, John J. *The Anticolonial Front: The African American Freedom Struggle and Global Decolonisation, 1945–1960*. New York: Cambridge University Press, 2017.

Musacchio, Humberto. *El Taller De Gráfica Popular*. Mexico City: Fondo de Cultura Economica, 2007.

Myrdal, Gunnar. *An American Dilemma: The Negro Problem and Modern Democracy*. New York: Harper, 1944.

Nance, Susan. "Respectability and Representation: The Moorish Science Temple, Morocco, and Black Public Culture in 1920s Chicago." *American Quarterly* 54:4 (2002): 623–59.

Nathan, Raymond. "Classrooms against Hate." *Common Sense* 14:9 (1945): 6–8.

National Negro Congress. Papers, 1933–47. Manuscripts, Archives and Rare Books Division, Schomburg Center for Research in Black Culture, New York Public Library, New York.

Neary, Timothy B. *Crossing Parish Boundaries: Race, Sports, and Catholic Youth in Chicago, 1914–1954*. Chicago: University of Chicago Press, 2016.

"Negro History Celebrations." *Negro History Bulletin* 19:8 (1956): 182–87.

O'Dell, Jack. *Climbin' Jacob's Ladder: The Black Freedom Movement Writings of Jack O'Dell*. Edited by Nikhil Pal Singh. Berkeley: University of California Press, 2009.

Omi, Michael, and Howard Winant. *Racial Formation in the United States: From the 1960s to the 1990s*. 3rd ed. New York: Routledge, 1994.

Oral History Research Program Papers. Archives and Special Collections, Chicago State University, Chicago.

Pacyga, Dominic A. *Chicago: A Biography*. Chicago: University of Chicago Press, 2009.

———. "Chicago: City of the Big 'Little' Museums." *Journal of American Ethnic History* 28:3 (2009): 55–64.

Parker, Jason C. "'Made-in-America Revolutions'? The 'Black University' and the American Role in the Decolonization of the Black Atlantic." *Journal of American History* 96:3 (2009): 727–50.

Patterson, William L. *The Man Who Cried Genocide: An Autobiography*. New York: International, 1971.

Perkins, Useni Eugene. *Explosion of Chicago's Black Street Gangs 1900 to the Present*. Chicago: Third World, 1987.

Phillips, Kimberley L. *Alabama North: African-American Migrants, Community, and Working-Class Activism in Cleveland, 1915–45*. Urbana: University of Illinois Press, 1999.

Pittman, John. "Negroes Challenge the Jackboot in San Francisco." *Freedomways* 7:1 (1967): 42–53.

———. Papers. Robert F. Wagner Labor Archives, Tamiment Library, New York University, New York.

"Plans for Celebrating Negro History Week." *Negro History Bulletin* 9:4 (1946): 86, 93.

Plummer, Brenda Gayle. *Rising Wind: Black Americans and Foreign Affairs, 1935–1960*. Chapel Hill: University of North Carolina Press, 1996.

Porter, Eric. *The Problem of the Future World: W. E. B. DuBois and the Race Concept at Midcentury*. Durham: Duke University Press, 2010.

Profile of Black Museums: A Survey Commissioned by the African American Museums Association. Washington, DC: African American Museums Association, 1988.

Pulido, Laura. *Black, Brown, Yellow, and Left Radical Activism in Los Angeles*. Berkeley: University of California Press, 2005.

Purnell, Brian. *Fighting Jim Crow in the County of Kings: The Congress of Racial Equality in Brooklyn*. Lexington: University Press of Kentucky, 2013.

Ralph, James. *Northern Protest: Martin Luther King, Jr., Chicago, and the Civil Rights Movement*. Cambridge, MA: Harvard University Press, 1993.

Reddick, L. D. "Twenty-Five Negro History Weeks." *Negro History Bulletin* 13:8 (1950): 178–79.

Reed, Christopher. *All the World Is Here: The Black Presence at White City*. Bloomington: Indiana University Press, 2000.

———. *The Chicago NAACP and the Rise of Black Professional Leadership, 1910–1966*. Bloomington: Indiana University Press, 1997.

———. *Knock at the Door of Opportunity: Black Migration to Chicago, 1900–1919*. Carbondale: Southern Illinois University Press, 2014.

———. *The Rise of Chicago's Black Metropolis, 1920–1929*. Chicago: University of Illinois Press, 2011.

Rich, Wilbur C., and Roberta Hughes Wright. *The Wright Man: A Biography of Charles H. Wright, MD*. Southfield, MI: Charro, 1999.

Rice, Jon. "The World of the Illinois Panthers." In *Freedom North: Black Freedom Struggles Outside the South, 1940–1980*, edited by Jeanne Theoharis and Komozi Woodard, 41–64. New York: Palgrave Macmillan, 2003.

Rocksborough-Smith, Ian. "'Filling the Gap': Intergenerational Black Radicalism and the Popular Front Ideals of Freedomways Magazine's Early Years, 1961–1965." *Afro-Americans in New York Life and History* 31:3 (2007): 7–42.

———. "'I had gone in there thinking I was going to be a cultural worker': Richard Durham, Oscar Brown, Jr. and the United Packinghouse Workers Association in Chicago." *Journal of the Illinois Historical Society* 109:3 (2016): 252–99.

———. "Margaret T. G. Burroughs and Black Public History in Cold War Chicago." *Black Scholar: Journal of Black Studies and Research* 41.3 (2011): 26–42.

Rodan, Maya. "President Obama Again Turns to Lincoln in State of the Union." *Time*, January 12, 2016. http://time.com.

Roediger, David. "The Retreat from Race and Class." *Monthly Review* 58:3 (2006). https://monthlyreview.org/.

Roelofs, Joan. *Foundations and Public Policy: The Mask of Pluralism*. Albany: State University of New York Press, 2003.

Rogers, Ibram H. *The Black Campus Movement: Black Students and the Racial Reconstitution of Higher Education, 1965–1972*. New York: Palgrave, 2012.

Rollins, Charlamae, ed. *We Build Together: A Reader's Guide to Negro Life and Literature for Elementary and High School Use*. 1941. Champaign, IL: National Council of Teachers of English, 1967.

Rydell, Robert. *All the World's a Fair: Visions of Empire at American International Expositions, 1876–1916*. Chicago: University of Chicago Press, 1995.

Salk, Erwin A., Multicultural Collection. Special Collections and University Archives, University of Illinois at Chicago.

Satter, Beryl. "Cops, Gangs, and Revolutionaries in 1960s Chicago: What Black Police Can Tell Us about Power." *Journal of Urban History* (2015): 1–25.

——. *Family Properties: Race, Real Estate, and the Exploitation of Black Urban America*. New York: Holt, 2009.

Savage, Barbara. *Broadcasting Freedom: Radio, War, and the Politics of Race*. Chapel Hill: University of North Carolina Press, 1999.

Scaraville, Michael. "Looking Backward toward the Future: An Assessment of the Public History Movement." *Public Historian* 9:4 (1987): 34–43.

Schlabach, Elizabeth Schroeder. *Along the Streets of Bronzeville: Black Chicago's Literary Landscape*. Urbana: University of Illinois Press, 2013.

Schreiber, Rebecca M. *Cold War Exiles in Mexico: U.S. Dissidents and the Culture of Critical Resistance*. Minneapolis: University of Minnesota Press, 2008.

Schulman, Daniel. "Marion Perkins: A Chicago Sculptor Revisited." In *African Americans in Art: Selections from the Art Institute of Chicago*. Seattle: University of Washington Press, 1999.

Scott, Daryl Michael. "Postwar Pluralism, *Brown v. Board of Education*, and the Origins of Multicultural Education." *Journal of American History* 91:1 (2004): 69–82.

Self, Robert O. *American Babylon: Race and the Struggle for the Postwar Oakland*. Princeton: Princeton University Press, 2003.

Shapiro, Herbert, ed. *African American History and Radical Historiography: Essays in Honor of Herbert Aptheker*. Minneapolis: MEP, 1998.

Simpson, Moira G. *Making Representations: Museums in the Post-Colonial Era*. New York: Routledge, 2001.

Singh, Nikhil Pal. *Black Is a Country: Race and the Unfinished Struggle for Democracy*. Cambridge, MA: Harvard University Press, 2004.

Sklaroff, Lauren R. *Black Culture and the New Deal: The Quest for Civil Rights in the Roosevelt Era*. Chapel Hill: University of North Carolina Press, 2009.

Smethurst, James. *The Black Arts Movement: Literary Nationalism in the 1960s and 1970s*. Chapel Hill: University of North Carolina Press, 2005.

——. "Poetry and Sympathy: New York, the Left, and the Rise of Black Arts." In *Left of the Color Line: Race, Radicalism, and Twentieth-Century Literature of the United States*, edited by James Smethurst and Bill V. Mullen, 259–78. Chapel Hill: University of North Carolina Press, 2003.

——. "Retraining the Heartworks: Women in Atlanta's Black Arts Movement." In *Want to Start a Revolution? Radical Women in the Black Freedom Struggle*, edited by Dayo F. Gore, Jeanne Theoharis, and Komozi Woodard, 205–22. New York: New York University Press, 2009.

———. "SNYC, *Freedomways*, and the Influence of the Popular Front in the South on the Black Arts Movement." *Reconstruction: Studies in Contemporary Culture* 8:1 (2008). http://reconstruction.eserver.org/081/smethurst.shtml/.

Smith, Judith E. *Visions of Belonging: Family Stories, Popular Culture, and Postwar Democracy, 1940–1960*. New York: Columbia University Press, 2004.

Solomon, Mark. *The Cry Was Unity: Communists and African Americans, 1917–1936*. Jackson: University of Mississippi Press, 1998.

Spear, Allan H. *Black Chicago: The Making of a Negro Ghetto, 1890–1920*. Chicago: University of Chicago Press, 1969.

Stanley, Timothy J. *Contesting White Supremacy: School Segregation, and the Making of Chinese Canadians*. Vancouver: University of British Columbia Press, 2011.

Steinberg, Stephen. *Turning Back: The Retreat from Racial Justice in American Thought and Policy*. Boston: Beacon, 2001.

Stepto, Robert. "Washington Park." In *History and Memory in African American Culture*, edited by Genevieve Fabre, 272–83. New York: Oxford University Press, 1994.

Storch, Randi. *Red Chicago: American Communism at Its Grassroots, 1928–35*. Urbana: University of Illinois Press, 2009.

Stratton Morris, Madeline. Papers. Vivian G. Harsh Research Collection of Afro-American History and Literature, Carter G. Woodson Branch, Chicago Public Library, Chicago.

Strong, Carline Evone Williams. "Margaret Taylor Goss Burroughs: Educator, Artist, Author, Founder, and Civic Leader." PhD diss., Loyola University, Chicago, 1994.

Stuckey, Elma. Papers. Chicago History Museum, Chicago.

Stuckey, Sterling. Foreword to *Life with Margaret*, by Margaret T. G. Burroughs, 13–14. Chicago: In-Time, 2003.

Sugrue, Thomas J. *Sweet Land of Liberty: The Forgotten Struggle for Civil Rights in the North*. New York: Random, 2008.

Thompson, Era Bell. *American Daughter*. Chicago: University of Chicago Press, 1946.

Thompson, Heather Ann. *Whose Detroit? Politics, Labor, and Race in a Modern American City*. Ithaca: Cornell University Press, 2001.

Tinson, Christopher M. "'Harlem, New York! Harlem, Detroit! Harlem, Birmingham!' Liberator Magazine and the Chronicling of Translocal Activism." *Black Scholar: Journal of Black Studies and Research* 41:3 (2011): 9–16.

Tracy, Steven C., ed. *Writers of the Black Chicago Renaissance*. Urbana: University of Illinois Press, 2011.

Travis, Dempsey J. *An Autobiography of Black Chicago*. Chicago: Bolden, 2013.

Trotter, Joe William, Jr. *Black Milwaukee: The Making of an Industrial Proletariat, 1915–1945*. Urbana: University of Illinois Press, 2007.

Turner, Lorenzo Dow. Papers. Melville J. Herskovits Library of African Studies, Northwestern University Library, Evanston, Illinois.

Turner, Michael A. *Historical Dictionary of United States Intelligence*. 2nd ed. New York: Rowman and Littlefield, 2014.

Uetricht, Micah. *Strike for America: Chicago Teachers against Austerity*. New York: Verso, 2014.

Van Balgooy, Max. *Interpreting African American History and Culture at Museums and Historical Sites*. Lanham, MD: Rowman and Littlefield, 2014.

Van DeBurg, William L. *New Day in Babylon: The Black Power Movement and American Culture, 1965–1975*. Chicago: University of Chicago Press, 1992.

Von Eschen, Penny. *Race against Empire: Black Americans and Anticolonialism, 1937–1957*. Ithaca: Cornell University Press, 1997.

——. *Satchmo Blows Up the World: Jazz Ambassadors Play the Cold War*. Cambridge, MA: Harvard University Press, 2004.

Wald, Alan M. *Exiles from a Future Time: The Forging of the Mid-Twentieth-Century Literary Left*. Chapel Hill: University of North Carolina Press, 2002.

——. "Narrating Nationalisms: Black Marxism and Jewish Communists Through the Eyes of Harold Cruse." In *Left of the Color Line: Race, Radicalism, and Twentieth-Century Literature of the United States*, edited by James Smethurst and Bill V. Mullen, 141–62. Chapel Hill: University of North Carolina Press, 2003.

Washington, Mary Helen. "Desegregating the 1950s: The Case of Frank London Brown." *Japanese Journal of American Studies* 10 (1999): 15–31.

——. Foreword to *Trumbull Park*, by Frank London Brown, vii–xx. Chicago: Regnery, 1959.

——. *The Other Blacklist: The African American Literary and Cultural Left of the 1950s*. New York: Columbia University Press, 2014.

Waters, Enoch P. *American Diary: A Personal History of the Black Press*. Chicago: Path, 1989.

Weems, Robert, Jr. *Desegregating the Dollar: African American Consumerism in the Twentieth Century*. New York: New York University Press, 1999.

Weinberg, Carl R. "Marching in Marquette Park." *OAH Magazine of History* 26:1 (2012). http://archive.oah.org/magazine-of-history/issues/261/weinberg.html.

Weissman, Dan. "Civic Watcher." *Crain's Chicago Business* 29, September 11, 2006.

Welch, Rebeccah E. "Black Art and Activism in Postwar New York, 1950–1965." PhD diss., New York University, 2002.

Wheeldin, Donald. "The Situation in Watts Today." *Freedomways* 7:1 (1967): 54–59.

Widener, Daniel. *Blacks Arts West: Culture and Struggle in Postwar Los Angeles*. Durham: Duke University Press, 2011.

Wiggins, William H., Jr. *O Freedom! Afro-American Emancipation Celebrations*. Knoxville: University of Tennessee Press, 1987.

Wilkerson, Doxey A. "Negro Culture: Heritage and Weapon." *Masses and Mainstream* 2:8 (1949): 3–24.

Williams, Jakobi. *From the Ballot to the Bullet: The Illinois Chapter of the Black Panther Party and Racial Coalition Politics in Chicago*. Chapel Hill: University of North Carolina Press, 2015.

Wilson, Mabel O. "Making History Visible: World's Fairs, Expositions, and Museums in the Black Metropolis, 1895–1995." PhD diss., New York University, 2007.

———. *Negro Building: Black Americans in the World of Fairs and Museums*. Berkeley: University of California Press, 2012.

Woodard, Komozi. *A Nation within a Nation: Amiri Baraka (LeRoi Jones) and Black Power Politics*. Chapel Hill: University of North Carolina Press, 1999.

Woodward, C. Vann. *Origins of the New South, 1877–1913*. Baton Rouge: Louisiana State University Press, 1951.

Wright, Charles H. Papers. Charles H. Wright Museum of African American History, Detroit, Michigan.

Wright, Richard. *American Hunger*. 1944. New York: Harper, 1977.

Index

IAN ROCKSBOROUGH-SMITH teaches at the University of the Fraser Valley.

THE NEW BLACK STUDIES SERIES

The University of Illinois Press
is a founding member of the
Association of American University Presses.

Composed in 10.25/13 Marat Pro
with Trade Gothic display
by Kirsten Dennison
at the University of Illinois Press
Cover designed by Jennifer S. Fisher
Cover illustrations: Madeline Stratton Morris, 1964
(Madeline Stratton Morris Papers, Vivian G. Harsh Research
Collection, Chicago Public Library); John W. Griffiths home,
later DuSable Museum of African American History
(Inland Architect and News Record, February 1893)

University of Illinois Press
1325 South Oak Street
Champaign, IL 61820-6903
www.press.uillinois.edu